Shanghai Bride

Hong Kong University Press thanks Xu Bing for writing the Press's name in his Square Word Calligraphy for the covers of its books. For further information, see p. ii.

Hong Kong University Press
14/F Hing Wai Centre
7 Tin Wan Praya Road
Aberdeen
Hong Kong

© Hong Kong University Press 2005

ISBN 962 209 714 6

British Library Cataloguing-in-Publication Data

Secure On-line Ordering
http://www.hkupress.org

Printed and bound by Pre-Press Limited, Hong Kong, China.

Hong Kong University Press is honoured that Xu Bing, whose art
explores the complex themes of language across cultures, has
written the Press's name in his Square Word Calligraphy. This
signals our commitment to cross-cultural thinking and the
distinctive nature of our English-language books published in
China.

"At first glance, Square Word Calligraphy appears to be nothing
more unusual than Chinese characters, but in fact it is a new way
of rendering English words in the format of a square so they
resemble Chinese characters. Chinese viewers expect to be able
to read Square Word Calligraphy but cannot. Western viewers,
however are surprised to find they can read it. Delight erupts when
meaning is unexpectedly revealed."

— Britta Erickson, *The Art of Xu Bing*

Shanghai Bride

Her Tumultuous Life's Journey to the West

Christina Ching Tsao

香港大學出版社

HONG KONG UNIVERSITY PRESS

1

Everything begins in the east, you know. Now the Western — American — ways are consuming the world, but the sun will always rise in the east. Though I was willingly seduced by this vibrant Western world at such a very young age, the fact remains that my spirit was born in that place of beginnings.

The blood of emperors and silent women with bound feet runs through my veins as I walk these streets of New York. Ancient men in silk robes — silk robes the colors of night — have profoundly shaped my Western life. And I have learned the truths of women. Truths to be found where the sun both rises and sets. Some of these truths came as gifts of my mother — an honorable First Wife. There were also truths shared by a beautiful courtesan. But I learned so very much in the truths and wisdom and love of Jade Wang, my father's favorite — and wise — concubine.

My defining moments came in the East. Destiny is formed in defining moments — those moments in your life when, through choice or circumstance, you reach your core and accept, or change, that destiny with clear eyes.

It was 1933, in Shanghai, China. I was seventeen. I was not married. I was pregnant. And my eyes were clear.

I had brought shame to our entire family. It was raining that day; one of those heavy, steady rains, completely void of wind — rain that feels like it will stay forever. I was crying; over the previous weeks, I would be certain that my body had no tears left, and then the tears would come again.

My parents were in their bedroom, but their angry voices penetrated the walls and surrounded me as I lay on my bed. My most vivid recollection — as I lay on my bed listening to my parents arguing about my future — was the sound of my mother's raised voice. I remember that I stopped crying when I heard that sweet sound of my mother's anger. It was the only time I heard my mother shout at my father, and she was standing up for me. My father wanted to send me to Nanjing, to my mother's family to be married to a cousin. My mother knew that I would die contained in such unhappiness. She found the courage to raise her voice to my father. It was an unfamiliar sound in China — a woman's angered voice, falling on her husband.

I loved Shanghai and I did not wish to leave my home to live in a rural village, married to a man whom I had never seen. But, as Jade would say, I had found my passion, and my pregnancy was going to cost me that passion. My passion was independence and emergence from this molded life, which had been shaped for me, over thousands of years. My passion was to contribute to the destiny of my future, and to make choices that could not be made in my tradition-saturated East. My passion could only be realized in the West, indeed my passion had become the West — and I had come so close — my future had been so promising.

As I lay on my bed that day, I said goodbye to dreams I had worked for and nurtured for many years. Yes, more than my family's dishonor, more than the fear I felt when I thought of the public humiliation, and more than the frightening prospect of becoming a mother, this goodbye to my dreams — to my way — hurt the most. I remember thinking that it would have been better to have never known my dreams, to have not heard my spirit, to have been complacent and accepting of the role of women in China at that time. Those silent women whom I had rebuked and rejected.

But I have come to learn that those who dream, and those who are seduced by their dreams, really have little choice. It is painful to dream. It is hard work. And there is a price to be paid for dreaming. The passionate ones — those with the courage to find their passion and to inevitably say goodbye to that which is familiar and comfortable, in pursuit of that passion — they experience so much sadness. If that passion, that way, once discovered, is held out of reach, it is like Mozart with no piano, or Matisse with no paints. Yet they cannot choose to let go of that passion. Not really. Some do try and it comes back to haunt them in hollow eyes. My mother had hollow eyes.

Many Chinese follow the teachings of Laozi, the *Dao De Jing*. The *Dao* teaches that peace is found within, in self-knowledge, acceptance and adherence to that knowledge. Jade had taught me to look within to find my destiny, and I had embraced my self-knowledge. It was that loss — the loss of my peace and my inner self — that I grieved most. As I saw, with clear eyes, my life come crashing down around me.

But the *Dao De Jing* also teaches us to embrace our grief. Yes, there would be much to embrace in my life.

The only honorable solution was suicide. I tried to want to be honorable. Suicide would spare my family the disgrace of my pregnancy, and restore some of my honor. If I willed myself to die, I could no doubt complete the task. Mother had always said my will was as unbreakable as the wind. But my spirit did not wish to die, and it did not wish to kill my unborn child.

I suppose that my spirit did not really say goodbye to my passion, although it would be many years before I would be reminded of my way. My Chinese ancestors would say I was weak to choose life that day. And what would they say years later, when I did not make the same choice?

My years in China were exhilarating, turbulent pages of my country's history. Pages of civil wars and Japanese invasions and the victory of the Communists. I was immersed in the politics — the glamour and the turmoil. Oh, the grand parties — the names are all real. Yes, I came of age dancing with the leaders of China. Dancing with a Western spirit and unbound feet.

So much of my story begins that year — when I was seventeen — but, if I am to tell the whole story, I should start with the real beginning. And that would be Shanghai.

———   ———   ———

My Shanghai was known as the Paris of the East. In fact, it was often said that Paris was the Shanghai of the West.

In the early 1900s, most of China conformed to the foreigner's image — sleepy villages with bamboo groves, willow trees, and pagodas. But as a child, I knew nothing of these rural villages. I had never even seen them. To me, China was Shanghai — the most vibrant city in the world, a bustling trading port on the western bank of the great Huangpu River. I was born absorbing the energy of a city filled with world banks, stock and commodities exchanges, international shipping and travel. There was money in Shanghai. Money from all over the world and the city was as beautiful as it was vital.

It is difficult for Western minds to comprehend my Shanghai; it was actually three independent countries operating within the borders of a city. Yes, Shanghai was divided into three distinct areas: the International Settlement, the French Concession, and the ancient Chinese City. The International Settlement had been governed by the British, who operated as the Shanghai Municipal Council, since the Opium War of 1840–42. The French Concession was governed by the French Municipal Council.

And the Chinese City was in constant turmoil as China's warlords struggled to control the most powerful city in China.

My family was among the elite and we had a lovely home in the International Settlement.

It was all before the Japanese and the Communists came. The people of China had finally won an element of freedom. The Revolution of 1911 was over and the Republic of China had been established; my people — led by Dr Sun Yat-sen — had destroyed the Manchu dynasty ending a feudal system that had controlled the lives of citizens for more than two thousand years.

The Republic was, however, an illusion of freedom. An illusion our people desperately wanted to believe and an illusion we fed the rest of the world. The truth was that warlords ruled Shanghai, and the ruler of Shanghai, in practice if not acknowledgement, ruled China. There was constant civil war as each warlord scrambled for more power.

The truth went even deeper. Inevitably, the victorious warlord had the support and backing of the Green Gang — the Shanghai Mafia. The Green Gang controlled the opium trade in Shanghai, which meant they were some of the wealthiest people in a wealthy city. Of course, money always rules politics. The Green Gang rulers were the most feared and respected among the many powerful men in China — yes, of course, they were all men.

The intensity of the politics of those years in my country's history is staggering. To look back and to read the names of those who struggled to define China's political future, and to recall them as people — real people with smiles, and families, and honor. And to recall them as friends. Even some of those so feared were to be my acquaintances, friends, and more.

In those years, my Shanghai, the heart and pulse of my China, while it reveled in the illusion of the Republic, was in fact, being torn apart piecemeal, by its own people — people I knew — and some of whom I loved, and I feared.

But in those early years, my family — like most Chinese families — was consumed with pride in our Republic. We savored the taste of democracy as though we knew it would not last. My brother was born in the year following the Revolution, in 1912, and was named Kaihua, which means "Opening of the Republic of China."

My parents were intensely loyal to this new Republic, and to its leader, Dr Sun Yat-sen. So you can imagine the excitement in our home when my mother went into labor with me on the birthday of Dr Sun Yat-sen — November 12, 1915.

It was a crisp, fall day. My parents had prayed for the birth of another son, both to honor the birth date of their esteemed leader, and to act as a playmate to my brother. And because in China, everyone prays for sons.

As my mother's labor progressed, eggs were ready to be colored red to announce the joyous arrival of a male child. Dishes of soy-cooked pork, chicken and shrimp with green vegetables were prepared as an offering to the Kitchen God and to Kwanyin, the Goddess of Mercy, who delivered sons to expectant families.

When I — a mere baby girl — arrived, my father, in his disappointment, left our home and did not return for several days. My mother asked our housekeeper, Mrs Ding, to find a wet nurse from the countryside to come in to feed me. She would not give her own milk to a daughter. All celebrations were cancelled.

I was given the name, Zhaohua, which means 'China, the Glorious.' And I grew up nurtured by the beautiful, corrupt city of Shanghai. There were others who cared along the way of course. The Shengs — Madame Sheng — had shown me love, and the opium of China. Old Tutor taught me the words of Confucius, which stay with me today. There was also Jade, my friend, my teacher — my father's concubine. Jade taught me so very much.

But Jade came later. After the Shengs had come and gone. After Grandfather. After Old Tutor and the words of Confucius. And the beginning of wisdom.

2

Some of my first happy memories are of Grandfather, and Old Tutor, and I think it is best to begin with happiness. Of course, sadness is always intertwined with happiness, and it will find its own way.

I suppose I was six or seven years old when I met my beautiful grandfather; he had lived in Nanjing and we had not visited when I was young. Grandfather came into our home with those long, flowing sleeves of his dark blue robes. Sleeves full of treats which seemed to appear as though by magic. Grandfather came with smiles and kindness; he seemed to sense my sadness and isolation as a child and became my special friend, even though I had been born a daughter. I remember that I smiled more often than I cried with my grandfather.

In fact, it is because of this gentle soul that I remember some traditions of my China and smile today.

Of the many treats from Grandfather's sleeves, there were often red packets for me, which contained lucky money wrapped in special red paper. Red packets were generally reserved for the New Year celebrations and the Chinese New Year was the most exciting time of the year for children when I was young! There were decorations of festive paper lanterns and special dishes were prepared for the celebrations, which went on for fifteen days. It was customary for adults to give children and servants lucky money as gifts during the festivities.

I remember sitting on the floor, in the year before Grandfather came, in my mother's bedroom counting my New Year's lucky money when Father and my brother, Kaihua, interrupted me.

"Zhaohua, come here dear. How many red packets have you received for the New Year?" It was rare that Father spoke directly to me. As I rose to share my excitement and recount my impressive number of gifts, my brother slipped around me quietly and scooped up a handful of my red packets, slipping them into his pocket.

"Please, Kaihua, give me back my red packets," I pleaded through my tears as my father laughed from the doorway. We were not allowed to speak harshly to my brother.

"Little Crying Bear, can't you find your lucky money?" My father called through his laughter. "Come over here, they're in my pocket."

I ran across the room, and my father stooped down so I could reach into his pocket. Nothing. His pockets were empty. I wiped away tears with the backs of my hands as my father and brother left the room, clapping their hands and laughing at their games.

No, my parents did not recover from their disappointment at having a daughter when I was born. Kaihua, as the only son, was treasured all the more when my younger sister, Wanhua, 'China, the Magnificent,' arrived, two years after me. Wanhua was soft and gentle and endeared herself to the servants.

I was different from the beginning. As a baby, I was plump and dark-skinned, and my features were more boyish than pretty. Mrs Ding, the housekeeper in whose care Wanhua and I were left, always referred to me as the difficult one, always hungry, always clamoring for attention. I suppose she was right. I have always wanted more. It is interesting; I am rarely unhappy now, and yet I have never become complacent.

No one in the house cared how I looked, and I can remember that my hair was always unkempt as a young child, in loose tangled braids. In the winter, I wore bulky, ugly, cotton-padded robes that made me look like a teddy bear. My thick robes and constant tears earned me the nickname of "Little Crying Bear" at home. I can remember that I felt comfort in crying, in the sound of my voice, and I liked the salty taste of my tears.

As is the way in the families of China, Kaihua was the prince of our home. His clothes were of the finest quality — silk wraps in the summer, soft down in the winter. The special bed in which he slept was made of mahogany, and to drive away evil spirits he wore an exquisite, antique jade pendant on a gold chain. His slippers and bonnet, beautifully embroidered, were hand-stitched by Mother. Mother's days were spent caring for my brother, and she took immense pride in the fact that she had breast fed Kaihua throughout her pregnancy with me.

Of course our home had many servants, and Mrs Ding was our primary housekeeper and family cook. A heavy-set, domineering woman, Mrs Ding had come from my mother's family when my parents were married. Wealthy families generally gave a servant as part of the bride's dowry. The bride's family wanted their daughter to be taken care of during and after her marriage by her own personal servants; the learned servant was also expected to advise the young bride on what to do and what not to do. My grandfather was wealthy and generous and kind, and so he sent Mrs Ding — and even Pretty Plum, another young slave girl — as special gifts for my mother. Grandfather had loved his daughter, my mother, so very much.

Mrs Ding was the domineering force in our home as I was growing up. I can still see her in our small kitchen at the back of the house, standing by the old-fashioned Chinese coal burner used for cooking. Over the coal burner was a shelf hung especially to hold a statue of the Kitchen God, who is supposed to protect the family against evil spirits. I used to imagine the Kitchen God making faces behind Mrs Ding's back, as our housekeeper stood there, hands hidden in those folds of hips, yelling at Pretty Plum and me in that high pitched voice. I remember thinking that even the hair on my arms was afraid of Mrs Ding.

"Pretty Plum," Mrs Ding commanded, "go upstairs and get a sweater for Master Kaihua. See that he is warm enough and does not catch cold in a draft. By the way, have you heard the talk this morning, Pretty Plum? Last night, the mistress next door was heard beating her slave girl. This morning she reported her disappearance to the police." Pretty Plum stared at Mrs Ding, unsure whether this was a veiled threat, or truth, before running to retrieve the sweater. Then Mrs Ding would smile as Pretty Plum took her frightened eyes from the room.

Pretty Plum had been sold to my Grandfather when she was five years old, just before my mother was married. Because of poverty, the peasants sold their daughters (never their sons) either to rich families as maids, or to brothels as prostitutes, with the hope they would marry wealthy men as concubines. After the establishment of the Republic of China, slavery was abolished, but in name only. Another illusion.

Pretty Plum had grown up as a slave in our family. She was shy and timid and too eager with her smile and her desire to please. I sometimes wonder what kind of woman Pretty Plum would have become had she not grown up with the endless threats and beatings and malicious smiles of Mrs Ding. The result of such a life was the weakening, or perhaps the invisible strengthening, of so many young girls in China.

Pretty Plum served as my Mother's personal maid until my brother was born; she then became his slave. She was less than ten years older than I was, and I thought of her more as a friend or relative than a servant. I remember Pretty Plum's long braid down her back; whenever she ran, her beautiful braid danced in the air. I asked her once, why her braid was always so beautiful. She said that her mother had taught her, before selling her. Her mother had said it was a gift she could keep forever, and enjoy day after day. Pretty Plum's mother had told her that every morning, when she used her gift and braided her hair, to remember that her mother was thinking of her, and sending her love, and instructing her to be honorable. Tears came to Pretty Plum's eyes when she told me that she would sometimes braid her hair over and over, especially after a beating at the hands of Mrs Ding.

While I felt sorry for Pretty Plum, I also felt somewhat envious when Pretty Plum spoke of her mother, and how her mother had loved her. My mother rarely spoke to me; my only adult conversation in our home came from Mrs Ding. Though she was not allowed to beat me, she tried to make up for that restriction on her power with her words.

"And you," Mrs Ding would snap, pointing at me as I peered from behind the kitchen door. "You should be upstairs in your room." Then came her favorite speech, "What do I keep saying? A daughter is useless; a son continues his father's name and supports his parents in their old age. A daughter marries and goes to serve another family. No value in daughters." For some reason, I was vulnerable to Mrs Ding's words, and her speech did not lose its sting with familiarity.

In the beginning, of course, I had tried to speak to Mother about Mrs Ding.

"You are a girl, Zhaohua. A girl is to learn and practice obedience," Mother would admonish on the few times I spoke to her of my degradations. Of course, this also made me cry, which further distanced me from Mother. She did not respect crying.

In retrospect, I suppose my spirit was strengthened as I spent night after night crying into my pillow at the words of Mrs Ding. Through my tears, I vowed that I would make a liar of her. That I would take on familial responsibilities like a son; I would take care of my parents when they were sick and support them when they were old.

But I was young, and the words of Mother and Mrs Ding would eventually fade as I was shooed from the kitchen. There was no one to watch over me, so I created my own games and played by myself for many hours. My hands were always sticky and dirty as a result of my long hours spent outdoors. Hours spent jumping rope, riding my bicycle around our house, and kicking a feathered shuttlecock — throwing it up into the air and keeping it aloft with my feet. Anything, to stay away from home, until I was called in for my daily lessons with Old Tutor.

I wonder if Old Tutor would be surprised to learn that, now, in my eighties, I finally understand what he was trying to teach me, and what I saw my grandfather live. Yes, Old Tutor, it helped to repeat the words so many times. But the learning was hard.

I can still picture him, Old Tutor, wearing thick, round glasses, and a faded — but dignified — dark blue robe, seated at a square table in our study, between my brother and me. Pretty Plum sat behind Kaihua.

His words were spoken slowly and with precision, "A thorough knowledge of the *Sacred Books* is the beginning of wisdom. The purpose of *The Great Learning* is to teach the highest virtue, to reinvigorate the people so that they will arrive at true excellence. Once the point where one should rest is known, the object of pursuit is determined. After that, calmness may be achieved. To that calmness there may be added a tranquil repose. And in that repose there may reside careful deliberation, followed by the attainment of the desired end."

While he was explaining the abstract ideas, Old Tutor's bliss was so great that he would swing his head from right to left, and left to right in rhythmic circles. Apparently, he himself had achieved the desired end. He would pause but his head would still swing to his internal rhythm, then he would resume, "There are four books altogether: *Da Xue* (The Great Learning), *Zhong Yong* (The Doctrine of the Mean), *Lunyu* (The Analects), and *Mengzi* (The Work of Mencius). *The Great Learning* is a book published by the Confucian School and forms the gate by which students can enter into virtue. You must read the text many, many times until you know it by heart," Old Tutor repeatedly instructed. "After you have memorized the words, *The Great Learning* will follow. You will come to know the words only after they are spoken repeatedly."

Unfortunately, Kaihua, Pretty Plum, and I, did not master *The Great Learning* as we sat hour after hour, with Old Tutor, receiving our lessons. We listened in silence and watched, but we were young and could not share Old Tutor's enthusiasm. After a while, he would become mildly frustrated with us. "Do you understand my words? Say something — yes or no. If you do not understand, we will go over our lesson again."

"Yes," we replied quickly in a single voice. "We understand clearly Old Tutor," knowing, of course, that admitting our ignorance would only prolong the lesson.

"Now, I will read the text one more time; you repeat after me." Following his lulling voice, we repeated those elusive words over and over. I could hardly keep my eyes open. Now and then, Kaihua's head would begin to nod — Pretty Plum would give him a nudge from behind and he would suddenly look alert again.

After Old Tutor left, my vigor and energy spontaneously returned and I rushed back outside to play, eager to escape Old Tutor's voice, Mrs Ding's harsh presence, and Mother's apathy.

So many memories. So many stories. Yes, I suppose dear, patient, Old Tutor cared for me. At least at the time, he seemed kinder than the other adults in my life. Yes, Old Tutor, knowledge of that which is sacred is the beginning of wisdom. But only the beginning. Wisdom does not come in books alone, nor does it come without pain. But, the pain — the real pain — comes later.

As I said, I must speak of the Shengs. I must also speak of Grandfather, whose red packets, and other gifts, helped to heal some of my memories of his China. And, of course, Jade. I'll get to them. Were it not for their glimpses of love and friendship — and the beginning of wisdom — I'm not sure I would have made the same choice, ten years later when I contemplated killing myself and my unborn child.

They all contributed to my wisdom. And my story — my China — cannot be told without them.

3

As a young child, I have few memories of my mother, as her days were spent either caring for my brother, or in her bedroom. Father was rarely home. When he did appear, it was clear that he had come to visit Kaihua. He wanted to be certain that his son knew his father.

Though theirs was an arranged marriage, Mother did, in fact, love my father. But my handsome father lived the traditional life of many Chinese men before him, including Mother's own father. Concubines were a common part of our culture. It was most ordinary to refer to women as 'First Wives,' or 'Second Wives.' My mother held the respectable position of First Wife. In my China, it is often a sad and lonely position. First Wives are chosen for their virtue and social status. The other wives — the concubines — are chosen for love and beauty.

Just before Grandfather came to live with us, I think Mother was struggling to accept the fact that her husband was free to love — and marry — other women, and her heart was broken. Our entire home had assumed the sadness that seemed to drip from her. I could often hear my mother, who had so often admonished my tears, cry at night in her bedroom ...

"What's wrong, Mother?" I entered her room softly one night and felt the chill of the wood floor under my feet.

"It is late, Zhaohua. You should be asleep," she whispered. But my mother, in an unfamiliar gesture, embraced me as I timidly climbed onto her bed. I remember her soft hand stroking my cheek.

"Are you sad because of Father?" I had heard Father shouting earlier, and I was aware of more than my mother knew.

"Your father is an honorable man, Zhaohua. It is not for you to speak disrespectfully of him." She tried to hold back her tears as we spoke.

"Oh Mama, do not be sad. Please. Tell me a story. About the day you married Father, Mama." My mother hesitated for a moment. Then, quietly, she opened the silk quilt, nodding for me to climb in beside her.

"Oh, Zhaohua, my wedding was an experience you could only imagine; it was like a fairytale. We spent so many months preparing. And finally, on my wedding day, I was seated alone in a covered red sedan chair. The chair was carried by four coolies, who held the bars of the chair on their shoulders. I sat alone, inside the curtains surrounding the chair, on a red, floral cushion, especially embroidered for the occasion. It was such a grand affair! Villagers and peasants would stop working and come out of their homes to watch my entourage as we left Nanjing and traveled to Shanghai by train."

"Oh Mama, I can just picture how beautiful you were."

"Yes, I was beautiful, Zhaohua, but my face was covered with a red satin scarf, which could only be lifted by my groom. In those days, it was still the custom that the bride could not be seen by her groom, until after the wedding ceremony. My gown was so lovely, Zhaohua; red satin, stitched with silver and gold threads in elaborate designs of phoenixes. My head-dress was adorned with pearls and rubies; the jewels had been in my family for many generations. And I wore elegant, tiny, embroidered red slippers. My feet had been bound since I was a child, so my slippers were custom made."

"Were you sad Mama, that your feet were bound?"

"Oh, on the contrary, my little daughter. I was proud of my small feet. Women with small feet were considered to have good breeding; the ancient poets had written songs praising the beauty of small feet, the pleasure of caressing them. So, many years ago, it became an act of love for mothers to break the bones in their young daughters' feet. Then they would fold the toes — and the shattered ball of the foot — underneath the arch of the foot. They would bind them very tightly with strips of coarse cloth to prevent the feet from growing.

"Only peasant women did not practice this custom, because they had to labor in the fields. A mother was considered weak if she gave in to her daughter's cries and released the bindings. My mother wanted a good marriage and a good future for me, and she was a strong woman, so she kept my feet tightly bound. It was very painful, Zhaohua, but I did not cry. It was my duty to endure pain in order to make a good marriage. My small feet were a source of great pride for our family."

Mother had stopped crying. She did not speak for several minutes and I was afraid that she would not finish her story. I took advantage of the closeness of the moment, and gently urged her on. "Tell me more about the day, Mama."

Mother continued to lie quite still in the darkness. But I could tell she was not sleeping, and after a while, she resumed her story. "I remember … a small mirror hung from the back of the sedan chair, a charm to drive away evil spirits. Behind me, a procession of ox-carts followed. Each cart carried servants and red lacquered trunks. The trunks contained every kind of object I might need in my new home, from embroidered pillows and sheets to kitchen utensils, and even wooden buckets, painted in red for good luck. Mrs Ding — and Pretty Plum, who was to be my personal slave girl — came as part of my dowry. I was very young, Zhaohua — only sixteen — and I was so sad to leave my home. Even though I was a daughter, I was my father's favorite child, and I had never been outside Nanjing before. I was traveling to Shanghai, a large city, a dangerous place where there were many types of people. I had even heard rumors that foreign devils lived in Shanghai!"

"You must have loved Father very much to be so brave."

"Oh my dear Zhaohua, I had never even met your father. And as for love, dear, well — love begins after marriage."

"Why did you marry a man you had never met, Mother?"

"It is not so simple as that, Zhaohua. It was different, then. People were expected to marry within the same social status. Your father and I had a compatible family background. For centuries, your father's ancestors lived in Wuxi, a famous silk and textile city west of Shanghai. The Ching family came from a long line of scholars, trained as officials in the Confucian tradition. Your paternal grandfather worked on dynastic records in the Qing Historiography office."

"And did you come from a scholarly family, also, Mama?" Though I was young, I knew that to come from a family of learning was the highest prestige, and I was hanging on Mother's every word, and on every moment that I was being held in her arms.

"Oh yes, my dear. My father was the Chancellor of the Hangzhou Military Academy. I was born in Nanjing, the youngest of three children born to my father's First Wife — I was not the daughter of a concubine, Zhaohua. As a young girl, I was considered very beautiful — and virtuous. Virtue was the most highly sought-after attribute for a woman of my generation."

"So, how did you meet Father, Mama?"

"A matchmaker, Mr Zong, brought us together," my mother smiled as she recalled Mr Zong. "He was your father's uncle and also my father's good friend. He showed my father a picture of Ching Tongli in Western suit. Several times Mr Zong traveled from Shanghai to Nanjing to convince my father of Tongli's fine character, schooling, and appearance. He felt that I was the most suitable bride in all of China for his nephew and friend. I would make an attractive and virtuous wife.

"Mr Zong used to often repeat the Chinese saying, 'Heaven makes a good marriage, but it is we earthlings who must carry out heaven's work.'" My mother actually laughed as she recalled these words.

"When it was arranged that your father and I were to be married, I had to perform the traditional rituals. In bidding farewell to my family, I was obliged to kowtow to my elders as a matter of respect. Kneeling in front of the family altar, I touched my head to the floor in their honor. Then I kowtowed to the household gods — the God of Heaven and the Kitchen God, who were the keeper of the family's well-being. I knelt again in deference to my ancestors, whose spirits were believed to dwell in the house still, and to my father. Then I had to bow individually to each of my family members. It was a very solemn occasion. Then it was my duty to cry loudly to show my sorrow upon leaving home. So before I left home, I was already tired, and the journey would last for many days.

"My wedding entourage boarded a train in Nanjing, and when we reached Shanghai, we continued on foot. I remained in the sedan chair for the entire journey. I remember feeling very frightened when we arrived at your father's house. With the red silk scarf covering my head, I could see nothing around me, and Mrs Ding guided my every move. I heard loud drums and trumpets and shrill music announcing my arrival. I smelled joss sticks burning and fragrant candles. And I remember feeling my heart beating to the deafening sound of the drums.

"The marriage ceremony itself was brief compared to the ceremonies of my mother and grandmother. Your father and I bowed to each other instead of performing the kowtow, and then we bowed to the elders in the room. After the ceremony, Mrs Ding led me to a bedroom upstairs and whispered, 'Young Mistress, you are to sit quietly on this bed and wait for your bridegroom to unveil you. Do not be nervous. He is a handsome and gentle scholar. Remember, you must listen to him and obey his commands. I will come to see you tomorrow morning.' Then she turned and left me. Alone.

"The silence in the room seemed to last forever. I was so frightened. Then I heard your father enter the room. I could not see him, but I could hear his movements. Slowly, he lifted my veil. Your father was so very handsome, Zhaohua. He smiled at me. He was pleased with his bride. He held out his hand to me gently, and then …"

Mother reached out and brushed my face gently, "Mrs Ding came in the next morning and congratulated me. She said the ceremonies of the

Duke of Zhou were completed. The marriage had been successfully consummated. And after that day I began to love your father, Zhaohua."

Then I could feel the sadness creep into my mother again. She was sad because she did love my father. Although my mother did not speak of it in front of me, it was common knowledge that my father had taken a concubine, Cloudy Lily.

I had recently heard my Aunt Liming, 'Beauty and Elegance', speak of Cloudy Lily many times. Aunt Liming, my father's younger sister, lived close to our home; Pretty Plum and I visited her cheerful home almost daily. I can still picture my Aunt Liming; she was indeed quite lovely, always wearing brightly colored dresses, and a black shawl draped over her slender shoulders. Everyone knew that Aunt Liming's husband, Uncle Stanley Qian, loved her very much and did not choose to have concubines. But Uncle Stanley had graduated from an American university — Cornell — and did not practice many of our Eastern traditions. During my visit, I remember thinking that Mother could be as lovely as Aunt Liming, if only Father loved Mother, like Uncle Stanley loved my aunt.

As Aunt Liming laughed with Pretty Plum and me, I said that I wished my mother laughed like that. I told my aunt that I did not think my mother knew how to laugh.

"I know that your mother is very sad, little Zhaohua. But, she is aware that your father is following the tradition of his generation. He will continue to support his family, and there is no dishonor in taking a concubine. Cloudy Lily will never hold the status of your mother, Zhaohua. It is the way of successful Chinese men. Your father is a very warm-hearted man, but he is also hot-tempered. I sometimes worry that his temper will get him into trouble. Some of my brother's associates are very dangerous men, Zhaohua. So if Cloudy Lily will keep his heart occupied for a while, perhaps his temper will rest."

Aunt Liming had tried to comfort me, but once again, I could not hold back my tears. The tears of a young child who misses her father, and who listens to her mother cry at night.

Then, on that special night, as I lay curled under the silk quilt with my mother, I thought of my memorable visit with my aunt earlier that week. I hated Cloudy Lily for taking my father from our household and making my mother sad. I did not conceive that a concubine of my father could ever become my friend.

As I lay there with my mother, I remembered how my elegant Aunt Liming had taken my chin in her soft, petite hands and wiped my tears. "You look like your mother, little Zhaohua. You have her large black eyes, her straight nose, and that lovely oval face. One day, you will be as beautiful as your mother."

I had looked into the rich eyes of my aunt. No, she had not spoken her words to simply dry my tears. And my heart smiled each time I remembered her genuine words of praise. No one had called me beautiful before.

Then my thoughts returned again to Mother, whose sadness had returned as we lay together in silent darkness. I wished to say something to make her feel happiness, as Aunt Liming had done for me.

"Thank you, Mama," I whispered in the darkness.

"For what, my Zhaohua?"

"For not binding my feet when I was a child."

My mother's tears did not return that night. As my mother held me, and shared her sadness, I knew, for the first time, that she loved me. It struck me as a discovery, and I thought that perhaps Aunt Liming was right; perhaps I was turning into a beautiful young girl and that was why I was experiencing love. Or perhaps it was her thoughts of Grandfather — and his love for her — which helped my mother show her love for me that night. All I knew for certain was that my mother's love, and her embrace, was a beautiful feeling.

Of course, I remembered that night, and the stories of my mother's grand wedding, the day I was seventeen, and contemplating my own marriage. I had, as my aunt predicted, grown to be a beautiful young woman. Like my mother, my beauty had contributed to my sadness. Mother was a beautiful woman, and her husband had all but deserted her. Her heart was broken. The rest of her life would be spent alone. My father would love many women, but my mother, who would never be legally divorced, was not allowed to consider a relationship with another man.

Yes, love had begun after marriage — and love had ended.

No, my own wedding would certainly not be as traditional as my mother's had been. And my marriage was to have its own sadness.

As I recall these memories again, I see that so much sadness in the women of China — and so little power to do anything about this sadness — helped the Communists to gain control over my country. As Mao Zedong led the Communists to power, the young women of China experienced something their mothers and grandmothers hadn't dared to dream of. The women of China united with the peasants — in spirit — to experience, for the first time in thousands of years, hope. Hope for power over their lives. Hope for freedom and independence.

My sister would embrace the Communist form of hope. My mother, as well. What were her choices? She knew the sadness of Old China. Her beautiful, tiny, bound feet — along with her heart — had lost any hope of happiness.

Ah, but the Communists come later. After Chiang Kai-shek. After the Japanese. No, first, I must continue with some of the happiness. I must speak of Grandfather, and of my year with him. I have not yet spoken of the Shengs, and the opium of China. So much in my China to know. So much to remember.

Thank you Aunt Liming, for making me feel beautiful when it felt good to feel beautiful. You were right, Aunt Liming, about many things. Yes, my father did have some dangerous associates.

Thank you, also, Mother. Thank you for that night in your arms. For showing me Old China so beautifully. And thank you, Mother, for not binding my feet.

But no, Mama, love does not always come after marriage.

4

I have been promising to speak of Grandfather, and it is time. Grandfather's words will help the rest of the words to come.

As I have said, I had not met my Grandfather as a young child. He remained in Nanjing after my mother married and moved to Shanghai. My grandmother had died when my mother, and her two brothers, were quite young. My grandfather had then taken two concubines and had fathered children with these 'wives' as well. So when he wrote that he would be arriving for a visit, along with his wives and children, there was much excitement — and much preparation to be done. I was shooed from the house as Mother, and Mrs Ding, bustled about preparing Grandfather's favorite dishes. Long-distance travel was difficult in those days so we were not certain of his precise time of arrival. There was much anticipation and energy in our home — and it felt nice.

I returned from Aunt Liming's, where I had wandered for the afternoon, to find our spacious sitting-room filled with people.

I think I loved Grandfather immediately. Everyone did. He was like soft thunder.

My eyes were immediately drawn to his. His face looked like the Buddha statues I had always seen, and he was smoking tobacco through a beaten silver water-pipe. Somehow, Grandfather could smile without moving his mouth. Perhaps it was his eyes. I thought immediately of Old Tutor, although Grandfather did not resemble him in the least. Then I realized that this — my Grandfather — was what Old Tutor had been trying to teach me. My Grandfather radiated peace. I knew that he had achieved *The Great Learning*.

Grandfather lay down his pipe and held out his arms to me. "This must be Zhaohua," he said softly. "You are even more beautiful than your mother, my dear, and I can see that you are wise, as well." Mrs Ding had been right, when Grandfather looked into your eyes, you felt as though your soul could keep no secrets from him.

I climbed into Grandfather's lap — into his soft, dark, blue and black silk robes — in the midst of all those strangers, and felt as though I had been there for hundreds of years. In that moment, I felt that I was special. That I was wise. Even though I was a daughter.

Over the next few months, our house was bustling with activity — and people. Both of Grandfather's concubines had come with him, and their three children. Although he loved all of us, he seemed to single me out — or perhaps it was I who sought him. I was so young, and so receptive to his attention and love.

I think my brother, Kaihua, who had always enjoyed the constant doting of Mother, felt displaced by my Grandfather. He resented any loss of my Mother's time and attention, and spent many hours sulking and throwing tantrums. Wanhua had taken her quiet place under the protective arm of Mrs Ding. My Grandfather's other children were loved and cared for by their mothers. Yes, perhaps it was my lack of attachment to anyone else in our home. Or perhaps it was that Grandfather saw so much of my mother and my grandmother in me that a special friendship developed between us almost immediately.

I would wake each morning eager to pay respects to my Grandfather, and would dress carefully, then run downstairs where I would find him in our study. He would be holding onto the edge of the handcarved mahogany desk with his right hand, while swinging his left leg, and then he would reverse his position.

"Always remember, Zhaohua. Balance. Make time for a healthy body. And make time for a healthy mind. One works much better, if it has the other." Then he would smile and pull a treat from those long silk sleeves of his robe. Sometimes red packets. Sometimes something sweet. But always presented with those eyes that smiled at me.

"Two sleeves full of breeze," my mother would say shaking her head. "Your grandfather has held high positions in the Qing government for many years. He has taken in much wealth. And, little by little, it has been handed out of those beautiful sleeves of his to anyone who needed it. He is a man of little material wealth, Zhaohua. And a man of great compassion. As a young girl, I can remember villagers coming to my father when they needed assistance. And he was always generous. He has little left for his family now, and still he gives." Mother would shake her head as though rebuking my Grandfather for his generosity. Yet she could not keep the love from her words as she smiled.

Grandfather helped me to know the China in my bones. He also taught me that it was time to say goodbye to that China. He knew the time was near. Of course, it would be many years before I would understand his lessons.

During our strolls through the streets of Old Shanghai, Grandfather, with his arms folded in his beautiful, night-blue, silk robes, told me story after story of Old China. Grandfather was born in Nanjing, just after the Opium War with the British. The peace treaty had been signed in that same city in 1842, after the British had defeated the Chinese forces in every major port along the coast.

"This was the beginning of the end of my China, Zhaohua," he said. "The British, and their opium, filled the people of China with their Western thoughts. When I was a child in Nanjing, our people pretended to despise the Western ways. We had all lost loved ones in the Opium Wars. We tried to close our ports to the opium and save our honor and our people. But we could not match their force — we were defeated. By the British, and by our own love of the opium. That was when we gave them Hong Kong, and even this International Settlement of Shanghai. But we continued to smoke our opium, and make the British rich as we bought it from their ships. Little by little, Zhaohua, we are embracing the Western spirit. I think the spirits of the women, and the peasants of China, are gaining strength in the Western philosophies. But physically, my dear, the opium, and the conflict, are making us weak."

"But the Republic is good for China, Grandfather," I objected. "Shanghai is beautiful, and the Western schools are the best."

"Yes, child. The Western thought is not all bad. Certainly, my China was not good to everyone. I was fortunate; I was a government official, born to an educated family, so we were not subject to the random violence and cruelty inflicted on so many of our people. You will have opportunities, Zhaohua. Opportunities that would not be possible — if our people had not suffered defeat in those Opium Wars. Yet, I fear that our China, which has existed for so many generations, is coming to a close, little one. That is sad. And that is also good."

"I don't understand, Grandfather."

"Of course not, dear. But you will, someday, you will remember these walks through this bustling city, and you will recall my words, and you will understand everything. The Republic will not last, little Zhaohua. And governments do not fail peacefully. China was ruled by emperors for more than two thousand years, dear. It is what we have known. Now she is starting over, Zhaohua. She will falter. I fear for you, my dear child, as she falters. For you will see China in a new youth. Youth is difficult, my dear."

"But Grandfather, Sun Yat-sen is saving China. He is creating democracy."

"Sun Yat-sen has no power, child. The warlords, the Green Gang. And opium, Zhaohua. They rule China. We are slicing our country, piece by piece. Old China, and her dreams of a new democracy will be handed over, by her own people."

"This sounds so sad, Grandfather."

"My dear child, I also said it was good. Old China was not always beautiful — and not always right, little Zhaohua. Do you know how your grandmother died, Zhaohua?"

"No, Grandfather. Mother does not speak of it."

"Your grandmother, whom I loved with my soul, Zhaohua, died from an infection. An infection which began in that rotting flesh of her tiny bound feet."

"But, Grandfather, bound feet are honorable. My mother's feet were a source of pride for your family."

"Yes, Zhaohua. That is the tradition of Old China. But the tradition has caused her women so much pain. The women had to keep wrapping their feet, every night, year after year. Your mother, like so many others, has not practiced this custom since the Revolution, so you do not know. I saw your grandmother's flesh, one night — near the end. Underneath those bindings, my child — the flesh simply rots away. I can still see the wretched contortion of her feet, Zhaohua. I can still smell the stench of that infected flesh. Yes, it is rare, but occasionally, there will be complications. Bones are not meant to be broken and bound. Your grandmother and I were taught to believe in the beauty and honor of those tiny bound feet. But the flesh underneath those bindings was not beautiful, Zhaohua. It was grotesque and sad and painful. For your grandmother, the dead flesh led to an infection, which spread to her blood and killed the woman I loved. The day your grandmother died, I learned to question tradition, Zhaohua. Many traditions are valuable. Many are good. But many are no longer good. All should be questioned. Not always abandoned. But questioned."

"Is that why Mother did not bind my feet, Grandfather?"

"The Revolution changed many things, Zhaohua, including this practice. Just in time for you, little one. But in my letters to your mother, I asked her to question this, and other traditions, of our beloved China. Your mother is wise, Zhaohua. You have her wisdom. You also have your grandmother's sense of adventure and fun! And that beautiful smile, Zhaohua. I hope there are more smiles than tears in your life, my child. But there is much in store for China. I think she must have tears first. You are part of China. You share her name, and China is in your bones. So when China cries, you will cry."

"Mother does not like for me to cry, Grandfather. She says it is weakness. And not honorable."

"Your mother is a strong woman, Zhaohua. She must be strong to be married to your father. I often fear for my daughter; your father is acquainted with dangerous men, Zhaohua. His associates are the ones who run China now. They will not allow Sun Yat-sen to hold his position for much longer. Your mother must be strong to be the first wife of such a man. She knows that tears are easy, Zhaohua. It is strength and perseverance, when tears are all gone, that are hard. There is honor in these, Zhaohua. If they are used with wisdom."

"But, why will China cry, Grandfather? I do not understand."

"The understanding will come. Too soon, I fear. The Japanese are threatening our borders. The warlords will continue to fight each other for more. More power, more money, more opium, and more territory. They do not hold the hearts of the people, with their acts of corruption and cruelty. We are saying goodbye to our history and we are uncertain as to our future. Yes, Zhaohua. The understanding will come. It may take many years to fully reveal itself; perhaps China will still be struggling when it is your time to say goodbye to her. But if you question, Zhaohua. Question, and balance your wisdom with your heart, you will learn quickly."

"You are making me sad, Grandfather. You are not saying goodbye to China. You are here with our family, and my mother is smiling, and Shanghai is beautiful."

"Yes, Zhaohua. It is a happy day. Shanghai is beautiful and grand. And it is good to smile and enjoy this time. But yes, child, I am saying goodbye to my China. So, perhaps it is time."

One morning, soon after that day, I dressed rapidly, and ran downstairs to pay my morning respects. I found my Grandfather slumped in a chair in our study. He was honorable and peaceful, even in death. He was dressed in his best robe and sat upright. His eyes were closed and his mouth seemed to smile.

Yes, Grandfather. I have shared China's tears. Though so far away, I still share China's tears. I have also had tears of my own. They have dried, and I have tried to use my strength and my perseverance with wisdom. But sometimes, Grandfather, it has been too hard. I sometimes think of you, and your sleeves full of breeze.

You were right, Grandfather. About everything. About your sleeves, about opium, and about China. And about my father's friends.

5

After Grandfather's death, my mother's grief was almost unbearable. That grief, in a heart already broken, forced my mother into a deep depression; she retreated to her bedroom. Of course, Father came to Grandfather's funeral, but he did not come home to share our grief. Our home embraced its familiar, dark sadness.

Grandfather's wives and children now looked to my mother as the head of the family, for she was the child of the First Wife, thus she was the next legitimate relative of my grandfather. But she was of little use to them, in her dark bedroom, and soon they returned to Nanjing to live with Mother's two brothers.

I remembered what Grandfather had said. He knew he was going to die. It was as though he chose the moment, rather than death choosing him. In death, as in life, he was at peace. Yes, I too, grieved deeply, following his death. Some days, I would pass by our study and forget, for a moment, that he was no longer there. Then my grief would catch me by surprise as I looked at the empty chair. The tears, and the sadness would come. But sometimes, it was as though Grandfather would enter the room and hold out his arms. I could almost feel that starry night of his long sleeves come around my shoulders, and I would feel his peace come into me.

Now that I look back on it, I suppose Grandfather's death was also one of my first defining moments. I felt like I grew much older, the day he died. Grandfather had taught me to embrace sad things, and to look through them for peace. I took walks every day, the same route Grandfather and I had taken, and I replayed his conversations, over and over in my mind. I never doubted that he had spoken the truth, although I understood so few of his words. But I knew that the understanding would come with time.

It was during these walks that I began my friendship with Madame Sheng. Sheng Seventh, and his wife, White Peony, lived near our home in the International Settlement. The Shengs embodied the spirit of Shanghai at that time. They were quite young, and extravagantly wealthy. Sheng Seventh was the youngest son of Commissioner Sheng, a very powerful — and therefore very wealthy — official in the Qing government. Commissioner Sheng was a modernist and had started several major industrial and educational projects in Shanghai. As was customary with his position, the Commissioner had many beautiful concubines, and many sons, although Sheng Seventh was known to be his favorite child. Perhaps because his mother, a favored concubine, had died while giving birth to him. Sheng Seventh was quite spoiled, and yet, he seemed to retain his kind heart and gentle nature.

White Peony — Mrs Sheng — was both youthful and refined in her elegance. She was barely eighteen when I met her, and already she had been married to Sheng Seventh for three years. White Peony was born to a very poor family in Suzhou, the beautiful garden city along the Grand Canal. At the age of nine, her family sold her to a courtesan house. Most Westerners know the term Geisha House. Geisha is a Japanese term, which also means courtesan. White Peony's fair skin and lovely cheek-bones saved her from becoming a lower-class prostitute, and she was trained in the graces of a courtesan. She quickly mastered the art of Beijing opera singing, and ink brush painting, but her success was due to her abilities in the most essential element of a courtesan — the fine sense of grace required for dealing with men of influence and education.

For White Peony, grace was intrinsic in her being. The elegance of this young woman was not learned. Her youthful heart and zest came through without compromising that elegance. In fact, her easy, natural laugh, and the way she genuinely embraced life, only enhanced her graceful presence.

Sheng Seventh met White Peony at a dinner given by his father — she was hired as a courtesan to entertain the guests. White Peony was fourteen at the time, and Sheng Seventh was only four years older. Sheng Seventh said he fell in love with White Peony the first time he saw her. Commissioner Sheng had always indulged his young child, so he did not protest when Sheng Seventh proposed to marry — and take as his first wife — this young courtesan. It was quite a scandal for the traditional thinkers of China. To take a courtesan as a first wife was not honorable. But the Commissioner had become more modern and Western in his thought, and wished only for his son to be happy. I thought of Grandfather's words when White Peony relayed this story to me, after we had become so close. Yes, Grandfather, I thought, the Western ways are not all bad. Tradition is to be questioned.

But I am getting ahead of myself. As I said, Madame Sheng and I first became acquainted during my strolls following Grandfather's death. In the beginning, we would politely smile. Then occasionally, she would say hello, and remark that I was a lovely young girl. It was impossible not to be drawn to her charm and her warmth. But our real friendship started one day, as she found me in one of my sad moments, on the bench where Grandfather and I had shared many talks.

"A beautiful face should not hold such sadness." She smelled so fresh as she sat next to me on the bench. "My name is Mrs Sheng, and I have wished to meet you for many weeks now."

"You have wished to meet me?" I could not understand how such a lovely lady would wish to become acquainted with a child.

"You are a charming girl, and you seem to hold so many thoughts. I am intrigued by the way you take your walks and think, young lady."

"My name is Zhaohua. I am the first daughter of Ching Tongli."

"Yes, I have met your father at dinner parties. Well, Zhaohua, it is with pleasure that I make your acquaintance. Do you mind if I sit and talk with you for a while?"

"Of course not, Mrs Sheng." I tried to put away my sadness and be polite with my new friend.

"Tell me, Zhaohua. Why do you look so sad today?" Her voice felt like silk on my skin.

"I was thinking of my grandfather. We used to take our walks around this street, and he used to tell me wonderful stories, and sort of smile. But my Grandfather died, and I miss him very much."

"Of course you miss him, Zhaohua. Forgive me, sometimes it is right for beautiful faces to hold sadness."

"Your face could never be sad, Madame Sheng." I thought Madame Sheng to be the most beautiful woman I had ever met.

"Oh you are wrong, little Zhaohua. My face has known much sadness. I just choose to turn my face to the happiness. There is much happiness, Zhaohua, even in that which makes us sad, we can find happiness. I have an idea. Would you like to ask your mother if you could come to my home for a visit? Mr Sheng would be charmed by your presence, I am certain."

"I would love to come for a visit, Mrs Sheng."

She stood up and offered her hand, and I walked with White Peony Sheng. We stopped by my home, and I told Mrs Ding that I would be spending the afternoon with Madame Sheng, and asked her to convey the message to my mother.

The Sheng mansion was near our home in the International

Settlement. Their connections, both with the 'legitimate' government, and the underworld of the Green Gang and the warlords, were well known. Even as a young girl, I knew the Sheng name was always spoken with an air of respect. And as we entered their home, I was overwhelmed with the obvious wealth. The financial status of the Shengs was not subtle. They personified the decadence of Old Shanghai, the extravagance. It was through the Shengs that I saw the power of opium in China.

"Little Lotus," Young Mrs Sheng addressed the head housekeeper as we entered her home with surprising firmness — she had seemed too young and warm to be the mistress of such a home, "please bring some ice-cream and almond cookies for our guest. And tell Old Wang that we are going to the Grand Theatre tonight — Mei Lanfang is performing — we will need the car by seven. Ask cook to serve dinner at six sharp." The servant bowed and backed quickly out of the room.

"Would you like to attend the opera with us this evening, Zhaohua? Mei Lanfang is China's most celebrated Beijing opera singer. The critics have praised him over and over — they say he can portray a female role better than any woman!" Mrs Sheng's easy laugh returned as she led me to the sitting-room.

"I would need to check at home, but yes, I am certain Mother will not mind, and I would love to accompany you, Mrs Sheng." My eyes widened as we entered the sitting-room. I felt I had stepped back a thousand years, out of my modern Shanghai and into Old China.

The room showed no signs of Western influence with its red satin curtains on the walls, thick rugs with elaborate designs, and handcarved mahogany furniture. The focus of the room was a grand couch with delicately embroidered silk cushions. The couch was divided in the center by a small table. On that table was a small alcohol burner alongside two beautiful pipes, inlaid with pearls, rubies and jade.

"Good afternoon, and who is our guest, my lovely wife?" As Sheng Seventh entered the room, I could see the love between these two young people. The room, the day, these beautiful people — it all seemed to be a dream.

"This is my new friend, and our neighbor, Zhaohua. Zhaohua, I would like to introduce my husband, Sheng Seventh."

"It is a pleasure to share the company of two most elegant ladies for the afternoon." Sheng Seventh actually bowed to me, a child, and his face held a smile more playful than that of his young wife. I could see why White Peony was so in love with him. His youthful charm was an obvious match to hers.

"Please, my Sheng Seventh, lie down on the couch and rest a while before dinner, we have a full evening planned. I have good news; I think our friend will be joining us — I have asked Little Lotus to go to your home for permission, Zhaohua." She gracefully led Sheng Seventh to the ornate sofa; a maid in a starched white blouse and black trousers came in immediately.

The maid, who looked oddly Western in the frame of the Eastern room, used a metal rod and took a small quantity of black colored liquid from a jar. As she held the rod over the flame of the alcohol burner, the liquid began to bubble and turn brown. She then dropped the brown liquid into the beautiful pipe, and handed it to Sheng Seventh.

White Peony smiled pleasantly, as her husband began to swallow the white clouds, blowing out mists in long breaths.

"Come, Zhaohua, let's go up to my rooms and I will choose something to wear for dinner. Sheng Seventh will rest now." I almost tripped over the table in the center of the room, which held a lovely solid gold tea service.

"I take it from your expression, young Zhaohua, that your parents are not opium smokers?"

"No, Mrs Sheng —"

"Please call me Auntie Sheng, we are to be friends, are we not?"

"No, Auntie Sheng, my mother does not smoke opium." I stopped just before I blurted out what Grandfather had said. That opium was destroying China. But Madame Sheng seemed to sense my confusion.

"Yes, dear, there have been efforts to wean China from her love of opium. But it is not all bad. Did you see how peaceful my husband was, little Zhaohua? A man of his wealth — and charm — could have many wives if he desired. Oh yes, he loves me, but a man can love more than one woman. Or, as they used to say in the courtesan house, a man can love the woman he is with — and opium. Opium keeps him from becoming restless, my dear. I can see, Zhaohua, that it will be fun having you as a friend. There is much you do not know, and I shall enjoy teaching you the many truths."

"Old Tutor teaches me *The Great Learning*, and Grandfather taught me so much, about China and about so many things."

"Yes, dear. Those are good things to know. But there are other things, Zhaohua, truths — which can only be taught by a woman who has learned them. All women are not capable of learning them. Men love women who know these truths, Zhaohua; and women — if they are strong — respect the women who have learned them. I have learned well. And I will teach you, if you wish."

"I do not understand, Mrs Sheng — Auntie Sheng."

"Of course not, dear. You are young." Again, Madame Sheng's youthful laugh. "Lesson number one. Do you see my fair skin? Black. Zhaohua. A simple black dress against skin kept fair. So many women go for bright colors; they do not realize that the eyes of men are drawn to the color. And not to the eyes of the woman." White Peony spoke from behind a dressing screen in her bedroom. The entire bedroom seemed to be made of yellow silk. She stepped from behind the screen in a matter of minutes and I was stunned at the vision of elegance.

The dress was cut perfectly for her petite figure. Yet one barely noticed the dress. It was the presence, which was captivating. The fair skin. The black hair, which White Peony Sheng had slicked close to her head, and smoothed behind her ears, seemed to be made of the same silk as the dress. The dress rose smoothly above her breasts but did not seem revealing, although her graceful shoulders were completely bare. It was the lines. The simple lines of the dress, of her slender body, all leading to that lovely face. She was right. All the elaborate designs, the best efforts, of the greatest designers, have never surpassed the elegance achieved by White Peony Sheng, in a simple black dress.

We returned to the sitting-room to find Sheng Seventh lounging lazily on the opium couch. Auntie Sheng joined him in another round of opium, but I noticed, as she winked at me, that she did not inhale as deeply, or as often, as Sheng Seventh.

As opium clouds filled the room, I felt my lungs taking in that sweet scent, and I was lulled into a dreamy sleep. Thus, my education began. I slept, and I dreamt, with the help of the opium. My dreams that day were of Old China, and yellow silk and elegant black dresses.

6

The streets of Shanghai were brimming with energy and activity. There were automobiles, rickshaws, bicycles — everyone seemed to be moving in a different direction at the same time. Shanghai was enamored with bright colors. Anything conveying energy. That which was subtle was so often overlooked, and unfamiliar, in the eyes of Shanghai.

Auntie Sheng and I spent our days making our way through the crowds and the shops, stopping whenever something caught our eye. Madame Sheng had an eye for fashion and beautiful things. She would point out to me, over and over, the beauty in the simplicity of an object. Though everyone found Madame Sheng enchanting, few could pinpoint the reason for her captivating presence. Her eye for lines, for simplicity in her appearance, was her secret.

For all her subtle appearance, however, underneath that graceful exterior lay a vitality that surpassed any energy in Shanghai. Even the opium could not quench her thirst for life. She laughed so easily, with friends, shop-keepers — they all loved to see her coming. I think Madame Sheng was lonely in all her wealth. She had no children of her own and enjoyed indulging a young companion. Before long, the Sheng home became my home; I would dash over every morning before school.

Mother remained in the world behind her bedroom door, and Mrs Ding was, I think, relieved to have me so occupied. Although Father now lived exclusively with Cloudy Lily, he was rising in his political office, and felt that a man of his prestige should have Western educated children. Kaihua attended the most elite school in all of Shanghai; Wanhua and I were enrolled in one of the leading Western girls' schools.

I always awakened early, dressed myself, and dashed over to Auntie Sheng's to enjoy breakfast with her and Sheng Seventh. We would make our plans for the afternoon as we had our morning rolls and green tea, and then she would walk me to school, holding my hand the entire way. She would be there waiting when classes were over, and we would walk back to their home often stopping for ice-cream along the way. Though I did well in school, in those years, I saw it only as a large block of time separating me from Auntie Sheng.

My love of music and verses was born that year. Night after night we spent attending sold-out performances at the Grand Theatre. Of course, they were always preceded by Sheng Seventh's 'rests' on the opium couch. But Auntie Sheng joined him less and less as I spent more time with them.

"Tonight, Zhaohua, we wish to do something special. Your birthday is tomorrow, and we wish to hold our own celebration. We have reservations at the Chez Paris Restaurant on Avenue Joffre in the French Concession. We'll go a little early and pick out a new dress for the occasion." Enthusiasm for my birthday was something I had not experienced before.

I could barely focus on my studies in school that day, and when the dismissal bell rang, I nearly tripped as I ran out the doors. A birthday celebration. For me.

It was a beautiful fall day as Auntie Sheng, Sheng Seventh and I strolled down Avenue Joffre, perhaps the most elegant street in the world at the time. There were Parisian boutiques displaying original designs. French and Russian restaurants and elegant coffee shops. There seemed to be music playing everywhere and as we approached a cross street, we noticed a large red and black horse-drawn carriage parked on the corner. A crowd seemed to be gathering around the carriage. Auntie Sheng seemed to walk more slowly.

"Can we look, Auntie Sheng?" She always consented when I asked to do something, but she hesitated momentarily, and Sheng Seventh seemed nervous and distracted.

"Okay, Zhaohua, if you wish," she answered after an awkward moment.

As we approached, we saw that it was a street performance; the performers were children. I felt White Peony's hold on my hand tighten.

"Street performers." Auntie Sheng's voice seemed flat.

"Auntie Sheng! Look at the colorful costumes — the red satin pants — that young girl doing somersaults!" I stood amazed as the children performed stunt after stunt. They built human pyramids on bicycles, walked tight ropes, and sang folk songs. I clapped my hands in delight, as the adult in charge would announce the new act. I'm not certain how long I was absorbed in the show before I noticed that Auntie Sheng was not sharing my enthusiasm. Sheng Seventh had shifted and held his wife in his arms. His eyes still had their distant, nervous shift, but he was obviously trying to comfort his wife. I did not understand.

"Zhaohua, I think it is time to go to the restaurant," Sheng Seventh did not take his eyes from Auntie Sheng. Of course I did not object; I could sense the turn in the mood of our evening.

The silence between us seemed to drown out all the street noise as we walked down Avenue Joffre, to the Chez Paris. As we took our seats, I reached up and touched Auntie Sheng's hand.

"Didn't you enjoy the street performers, Auntie Sheng?" I did not understand the cloud that had descended onto my party.

Sheng Seventh spoke for his wife. "My wife's family were street performers when she was young. Street performers have no home, Zhaohua. They have very little money, and their lives are very difficult. The smiles on their faces are part of their performance. There are few smiles inside."

"Oh, Auntie Sheng, I am so sorry. I did not know."

"It is okay, Zhaohua. It was a sad time, but there are happy memories, too. My parents did love me. But we were so poor, Zhaohua. So many in our villages are poor. And hungry. My mother thought I would have a better chance in life, if I could be trained as a courtesan. She said I was the most beautiful of her children and that my beauty would help me in Shanghai." Auntie Sheng was distracted for a moment by her husband; he seemed unable to focus and was glancing wildly around the room. She softly caressed his arm before continuing.

"So they sold me, Zhaohua. To a courtesan house. Had I not been beautiful, I would have been a prostitute at the age of nine. That is not right. It is not right that the position of cheekbones, and the straightness of your teeth, and the fairness of your complexion, can mean the difference in your future. Yes, I was fortunate, but most are not, Zhaohua. There were young girls in that house who were not as fortunate. They would tell me stories of men who ... men who you should never know, Zhaohua."

"I did not know." I had never seen Auntie Sheng's face hold such sadness.

"But I remember dancing in the streets when I was young, Zhaohua. With my brothers and sisters, before my parents sold me. We were often hungry. Our bare feet were always caked with dirt. Sometimes, Zhaohua, I will go out into my lovely courtyard, take off my designer shoes, and feel the cool dirt on my bare feet. I dance in our courtyard until dirt is caked thick on my feet. I feel that I am with them again. Though we were hungry, and dirty, I feel strangely happy recalling those times. But, the truth is, my mother was often sad. I suppose she made the right choice. My life is so different now. There is much happiness. But sometimes I wonder. I wonder what became of my family. Where they might be. As we approached the show tonight, I thought for just a moment that it might be them, Zhaohua. Of course, my brothers and sisters would be much older now, but still there was that moment."

"I have an idea. A wish for my birthday." I wanted to make Auntie Sheng happy, but I was momentarily distracted by Sheng Seventh; he was perspiring and seemed to be disoriented. Auntie Sheng was obviously trying to draw attention from him.

"What is your idea, Zhaohua? Yes, it is your birthday celebration. We must not dwell on sadness." Auntie Sheng smiled as though she had just put on a lovely shawl. She was also holding Sheng Seventh's arm and rubbing it as if to calm him.

"Let's have them package our food, and let's order more. We can take it to the family on the corner. Please. It is my birthday wish." My words obviously touched Auntie Sheng, but at that moment, Sheng Seventh fell from his chair, doubled over, holding his stomach. His body was trembling; he was obviously in excruciating pain. Suddenly, he pulled himself up and stood there, looking at us as though we were strangers. He seemed disoriented, with a glaze to his eyes. He intentionally knocked his wine glass to the floor, and glanced wildly around the room.

The maitre d' of the restaurant rushed over, anxious to avoid a scene. Madame Sheng quickly took charge.

"My Sheng. Where are your pills? You did bring the pills?" Madame Sheng was frantically searching Sheng Seventh's pockets of his dinner jacket. Finally she produced a small jade box, trimmed in gold. She opened the box and immediately placed two small gray pills onto Sheng Seventh's tongue. She held his mouth closed for a moment, then forced a drink of water down his throat.

Sheng Seventh calmed in a matter of seconds, and the maitre d' led us to a private dining-room where Sheng Seventh rested on a sofa by the window.

Madame Sheng did not lose her composure and acted as though her husband's reaction to the need for opium was an everyday occurrence. She spoke calmly and with authority to the maitre d'.

"Jacques, I would like to use your telephone, please. We will need the room for about an hour. Also, please package our food, and prepare extra dinners; enough for ten people; we will be taking them with us."

"But Madame Sheng, we do not —"

"Of course, you will." She smiled warmly and that was the end of the discussion. The maitre d' nodded, and showed Auntie Sheng to the telephone in the corner. She spoke softly into the receiver, but with a sense of urgency and command.

"Your friends are bringing opium, my dear. Rest. You will be fine." Madame Sheng stroked her husband's face and as he looked at her, through the haze of his opium pills, his gratitude, and love, filled the room.

Within minutes a man entered the private room. He was carrying a bag from which he produced a simple opium pipe, which he then proceeded to fill and light.

Madame Sheng leaned over the couch and took Sheng Seventh in her arms as the man in the corner stepped back and seemed to blend into the mahogany paneling. "You cannot do it like this, Sheng. You need help to break free from this drug. Get through this night, and we will do this together." Auntie Sheng held Sheng Seventh's head as he vomited on the thick, oriental rug.

Then I watched as Madame Sheng took the pipe, and held the long narrow mouthpiece to Sheng Seventh's lips; she spoke softly to him, as if to a baby, as he inhaled. He choked at first. For a moment, I thought he was going to vomit again. But soon, with the gentle assistance of his wife's graceful hands, he was breathing more peacefully, and began to resemble the man I had seen on their opium couch so many nights ago. His body relaxed completely. Someone produced a porcelain bowl with water and a cloth. Auntie Sheng squeezed the excess water from the cloth and wiped Sheng's face with one hand, holding the pipe to his mouth with the other.

Grandfather's words came back to me as I stood in that elegant private dining-room, and watched White Peony — Madame Sheng — lovingly ease her husband into his familiar serenity. Grandfather said that opium was destroying China. As I watched Sheng Seventh lying there, I saw what Grandfather meant.

Auntie Sheng rose from the sofa looking composed and in charge. She held out her hand to me and spoke to the man in the corner. "Thank you for your assistance. Your kindness will be repaid." The man recognized that he was dismissed, bowed slightly, turned and left the room. The maitre d' entered, as if on cue, awaiting instruction.

"My young friend and I will take the dinners now. Thank you for your kindness. My husband will rest here for a while and we will return for him within the hour." Then Madame Sheng took the maitre d's hand in hers. "Jacques, I thank you from the bottom of my heart. We will be back soon."

This nineteen-year-old, former-street-performer-turned-courtesan, seemed to carry herself as though she were a queen. A most gentle, humble, and completely in control, queen.

"Now, my Zhaohua. We must continue with your celebration. Your wish, my dear." We carried the packaged food back to the corner where the street performers were concluding their acts for the evening. I saw the children with different eyes this time. With those sad eyes I had seen in my Auntie Sheng, as we watched them earlier. I saw their smiles were not the smiles of children. Their smiles were learned and fixed. And I noticed, for the first time, the dirt on their feet. I could not help glancing at Auntie Sheng's elegant shoes. They were spotless.

"My young friend and I find ourselves abandoned by our dinner companions this evening. We have an abundance of food and a long way home to travel. We were wondering if you might do us the favor of helping to lighten our load?" Auntie Sheng bowed and addressed the man who appeared to be the father of the children. She held out the elegant containers of food to him with an air of humility. The woman who had just been issuing commands in the most elegant restaurant in Shanghai was barely recognizable.

As their father accepted the dinners with humble thanks, I saw the poverty of Shanghai. I saw it in the speed with which this hungry family ate their dinner, and the relief in the eyes of the father and the mother, as they watched their children eat to the point of contentment. And in the gratitude with which they looked at my Auntie Sheng.

Years later, I would recall that evening. The elegance of the Chez Paris restaurant, witnessing a kind man suffer from opium addiction, and then dining with the homeless. I realized that I have been given a rare glimpse of Shanghai. The schizophrenia of my Shanghai had come together that evening to give me a whole picture of the forces shaping my life.

Those years with Madame Sheng were among the best of my young childhood. Now, in New York, seventy years later, and thousands of miles from the streets of Shanghai, I catch glimpses of my Auntie Sheng. As I go for my morning swim, I will sometimes pass a mother holding the hand of a young daughter, on the way to school. I can smell Auntie Sheng's elegant perfume and feel her soft hand around mine. I remember my lessons. The truth in that silk voice.

But I must continue with the story.

Eventually, Auntie Sheng asked my mother's permission to adopt me. It was not uncommon, in my country, for families to give up their daughters for a variety of reasons.

My mother emerged from her depression long enough to be angered by the request.

"So, Zhaohua. It is not enough that you spend every night at the opera. Dining in the finest restaurants. It does not even matter to you that I am left here alone, does it?" My mother spoke softly, with quiet rage.

"Oh, Mama. You have Kaihua. And Wanhua. Auntie Sheng has no children." Tears were streaming down my face, as I pleaded for the life I thought I wanted.

"You have tasted the finest luxuries at a young age; I suppose it is natural that you should wish to make this your life. But no, Zhaohua. You are my daughter — my daughter, you will remain."

"Mama, please …"

With this, my mother's eyes turned to fire. "You will not desert this family. You are a daughter, and of little use, but no, Zhaohua — I will not just hand you over." Then my mother's rage fell to the floor and I saw her sadness so vividly. "I can't, Zhaohua. I cannot do it."

I turned and ran up the stairs to my room. As I sobbed into my pillow, I thought of Auntie Sheng. Mother had undoubtedly been angry with her, as well. She had told Auntie Sheng that the adoption was not possible because there was a mutual ancestor in the lines of the Shengs and the Chings. According to Chinese tradition, it is disgraceful to hand over a daughter to a relative. It would not be honorable.

I suppose I should have felt comforted that my mother, on some level, actually wanted to keep me. But all I felt was anger. And immense sadness.

Yes, the relationship between mothers and daughters will always be complicated, regardless of the country in which they are born. But in China, these relationships must endure the belief that daughters are useless. Mothers must fight to subdue the natural love a woman feels for her daughter.

Our mothers were taught not to value us. Yet, in Mother's anger, I had glimpsed her love. At the time, however, my bond with Auntie Sheng was much stronger than the one I shared with Mother, and I knew only that I wished for mother to treat me like the rest of China's unwanted daughters. And the daughters of China shared so many tears. Auntie Sheng had once said that the tears of unwanted daughters in China were the source of the great Huangpu River.

7

Mother's sadness continued to hover in our home like a black velvet cloak. The death of Grandfather, along with my father's continued absence, made her long for the comfort of her family. My own sadness at the loss of Auntie Sheng in my life seemed to fit the mood of our home most comfortably.

The day arrived when Mother emerged from her bedroom and announced that we would be leaving our lovely home in the International Settlement. We would be moving to the Chinese City of Shanghai, to live with my mother's cousins — Aunt Sha and her husband, Uncle Sha, who practiced law in the Chinese City. We were to leave within the week. I turned quietly, following Mother's announcement, and went out into our courtyard to contemplate our move.

The Chinese City was the part of Shanghai left to the Chinese citizens. It did not hold the rich vibrancy of the International Settlement or the French Concession. It was not under foreign governments and warlords still struggled for power in the Chinese City. We had occasionally visited my aunt and uncle there. Crossing the gates leading into the Chinese City, I always felt I had entered a foreign land; there were no traces of my familiar Shanghai behind those gates.

The Shengs had immersed me in the diversity found in large international cities. Mother was right; even at my young age, I had developed an appetite for the energy felt in international Shanghai. Of course, I couldn't articulate these impressions to myself at the time; I was only aware that I felt so very sad at the thought of moving to the Chinese City. I felt as though I were being pushed back into Grandfather's Old China. Even then, I knew it was a China to which I did not belong.

I decided I must tell Auntie Sheng about our move. Without a thought of the consequences of disobeying Mother, I walked directly to the home of Madame Sheng, whom I had not seen in many weeks.

Auntie Sheng opened the door herself. She said that she had sensed I would be coming on that day. She knew immediately that I had bad news.

"Mother says we are moving to the Chinese City. Next week." I did not even enter the house before I spoke.

"Oh, Zhaohua." Auntie Sheng put her hand to her mouth. It was the only time I saw her lose composure. Being White Peony Sheng, however, she quickly recovered and retrieved her warm smile, and held out her hand to me. "Do come in, my Zhaohua."

I felt like I had come home. Yet I knew it would never be my home. I tried to accept this inevitable truth with grace. I had learned that from Auntie Sheng.

"I will speak with your mother, Zhaohua. I will apologize for proposing a dishonorable arrangement with your adoption, and I will get permission to see you. I promise." Auntie Sheng took me in her arms and I felt the familiar warmth. The warmth that every young girl is entitled to feel in her life — the warmth so many young girls in China were denied.

Thus, my family moved to the Chinese City; my family consisting of Mother, Kaihua, Wanhua, Mrs Ding and Pretty Plum. Father stayed in the International Settlement.

I think the first thing I missed was color. The Western influence stopped at the gates of the Chinese City. Perhaps it was the grayness that accompanies manual labor, the fixed expressions. Perhaps it was the absence of multicolored lights and expensively designed buildings. Or perhaps it was the fact that the residents here, all Chinese, had lived through decades of civil wars, as warlords struggled for control of pieces of China. I could feel these wars in their eyes.

Of course, now I can clearly see all these contributions to the mood behind those high walls. I recognize the scars of wars to be seen in eyes. But as a young girl, who was born into the most vital and diverse city of the world at that time, as I crossed the gate, I was aware only of gray.

As the somber fog of the city enveloped me, I watched, amazed, as my mother came back to life. She thrived in the familiarity of the reminders of her childhood. She and Uncle Sha took walks through the city and seemed to develop a special friendship. Mother, and Aunt Sha, and other ladies from the area, played mahjong every evening. The clicking of the ivory tiles accompanied my evening sadness.

I remember one summer night hearing laughter coming from downstairs. It was such an infectious laughter that I was drawn from my room — and I remember being stunned to find that this sound was coming from my mother.

"Hello, Zhaohua. Why don't you come down and watch; you can learn mahjong — I think you are ready." Mother's invitation was light and cheerful. Part of me wanted to join in their game, but I could not. I stood quietly and shook my head, refusing her offer.

"Oh Zhaohua, you must try to adjust. You will make some new friends in school; everything will be better, here, you'll see." My mother and I had reversed roles. I had glimpsed life with Auntie Sheng, but had quickly reverted to the quiet, withdrawn member of the family. My mother, on the other hand, in the midst of the gray surrounding us, flourished.

"I miss our old home, Mother. I miss Auntie Sheng. I miss Father. And I miss my Western school. How can you be so happy here, Mother? Why can't you be happy in our real home?" I thought Mother would be enraged. Not only had I been disrespectful, but my behavior was in the presence of guests. To my surprise, Mother did not react in anger. Mother spoke to me with unfamiliar tenderness, as though we were the only ones in the room.

"You would not understand, my Zhaohua. To me, even though I have never lived in the Chinese City, this is my home. The traditions with which I was raised are still honored here, Zhaohua. I do not feel displaced here. I can walk through the city with my dainty steps, the steps of feet that were once bound, and not feel intimidated by the wide Western strides all around me. I find comfort in the traditional dress. In hearing the Chinese dialects, the tones of the voices. Our home in the International Settlement did not feel like my home, Zhaohua. I was in a foreign land in my own country. And this — this — is your heritage, daughter. It is good that you can know it — experience it — the richness of your ancient culture, here in this City." My mother brushed my hair from my face and looked into my eyes. She had rarely allowed me — or anyone — such a personal glimpse into her thoughts.

"But we will not see Father. He will not come here at all." I knew my words would hurt Mother. I wanted them to hurt. I was still so angry at losing Auntie Sheng.

The realness of my mother's mood evaporated with these words. She assumed the numb strength so common in the women of China. That way of looking into, but somehow past, the eyes of the person with whom they are speaking. It was as though she was trying to recite these familiar, painful, words with conviction. "Your father is a busy man and he is happy with Cloudy Lily. He will continue to support us. We do not have to worry."

"But I miss Auntie Sheng, Mother. I know you do not wish me to speak of her, but, please, Mother, it would mean so much to see her."

"Madame Sheng has spoken with me, Zhaohua, and I have decided to let you visit the Shengs from time to time. She is a very charming and persuasive woman. There is to be no more talk of adoption, however."

Once again, she looked past my eyes; my mother's words were spoken casually, but from that moment on, my life in the Chinese City became more bearable. The mahjong game ended early that night, and my mother and I were more at ease after that evening. In the evenings to follow, I even occasionally joined my mother, Aunt Sha, and their friends.

True to Mother's words, the Shengs arrived that Friday to pick me up for a long weekend. I hardly recognized Sheng Seventh. His complexion was deeper, his energy contagious, and his eyes seemed more alive.

"Auntie Sheng," I whispered as we were driving through the gates of the Chinese City, "Uncle Sheng seems so different. Has it been that long since I have been with him?"

Auntie Sheng laughed at my puzzled response, "My dear, Sheng Seventh is no longer smoking opium. He went through a great deal of pain to free himself from the hold of the drug. He was in a special hospital in the suburbs of Shanghai for many months. Since his return, he is like a child experiencing life for the first time; he feels so alive. I was mistaken, Zhaohua, to encourage him in his smoking. He was dying at the hands of opium. Now, he is openly opposing the acceptance of opium smoking in Shanghai — and he is angering many powerful people. Armies are built and supplied on the dollars made in the trade in opium, Zhaohua. When armies control both money and minds, they are most dangerous. Money can buy freedom, but there is no freedom if someone — or something — controls your mind, Zhaohua. And you, my darling, must always be free. This, I know."

Her words were lost however, as our driver drove us through the streets of the International Settlement, and to the French Concession of my multifaceted Shanghai, I felt what Mother must have felt in the Chinese City. I was home. Amidst the energy and the crowds and the diversity, I was home.

I lived for my weekends with the Shengs. For my trips out of the gray Chinese City, and into the familiar Western pieces of Shanghai. Sheng Seventh continued, during that year, to enjoy life without the aid of his opium. He became more and more opposed to the widespread distribution of the drug, and used his considerable wealth and power to expose the hazards of opium.

It was a Friday in the spring; we had lived in the Chinese City over a year. Auntie Sheng was to pick me up after school; it was not like her to be late. I waited outside my school in the Chinese City until almost dark and then walked home. I was aware that people were speeding about; everyone seemed in a hurry for that time of day. When I arrived, I found my house in a flurry of activity.

"Zhaohua! What are you doing here? You were to have left with the Shengs after school today." My mother, Pretty Plum, and Mrs Ding were rushing around the house, quickly packing luggage and items of sentimental value.

"Auntie Sheng did not come for me. I do not understand what is happening, Mother."

"No time for explanations, Zhaohua. Put your bags in the car out front. Uncle Sha — and Aunt Sha — have gone to stay with friends. Take anything of value. Your father has sent the car and word that we are to leave the Chinese City at once."

Within ten minutes our driver was speeding for the gate of the Chinese City. Kaihua, Wanhua, Pretty Plum, Mrs Ding and I were all crowded into the back seat. We could sense danger and I knew better than to ask questions. As we approached the gates, my mother gasped and covered her mouth as armed guards stopped our car. Our driver immediately took charge, ordering everyone to relax.

"These people are to be guests of Liankui Ching." Our driver spoke with an air of authority and produced a piece of paper, apparently signed by this Liankui Ching. The guard looked at the paper carefully and then motioned for our car to pass through the gate.

I had no idea what was happening; I did not know that with darkness would come civil war as, once again, rule of the Chinese City was being decided. For several years, Zhang Zuolin, Warlord of Manchuria — known as the old Marshal — had governed over this section of Shanghai. Warlord Sun Chuanfang had decided that the time was right to take control; it was his forces invading as we drove out. I could see people running on foot to reach the gates. Some carried children on their backs with luggage in their hands. Others bicycled with a child and a few bundles in a basket. Children were crying. All around there was chaos and confusion. People were crowding around the car, hoping to escape to the International Settlement or the French Concession, which were under the protection of foreign governments and away from the warlords. Victorious warlords were known to brutally torture, before killing, those who had supported the defeated administration.

As we sat in line waiting to pass, I watched men — men of dignity and honor — kneel down before the soldiers and plead for the passage of their families. I watched soldiers as they looked at the young girls; choosing the ones who would remain behind for their pleasure. I watched their mothers cry as they left their daughters behind, carrying their sons and babies through the gate.

As our car crossed the gate and entered the International Settlement, it was as though someone had thrown a switch and transferred us to a different place in history. People were walking along the sidewalks, some in Western dress, as though life were normal. As though people, just a few blocks away, were not begging for their lives and leaving their homes forever. Occasionally I would see a cluster of refugees huddling together, carrying a few belongings, and I would know that they had just come through the gates with us. I could see the fear mixed with relief in their eyes. But they were only surreal glimpses amidst the crowds and the glamour and the bustle of the city, my Shanghai.

The driver took us through the streets without instruction. Eventually, he pulled up to a high, elegant building deep in the city. My mother motioned for us to follow her as we entered the building.

At the age of ten, I met Liankui Ching. The man whose name had saved me from the soldiers at the gate.

Liankui Ching entered the room wearing a dark blue Chinese gown and a pair of black satin shoes. Were it not for his cigarette, and nicotine-stained fingers, he would have resembled Grandfather in his traditional appearance and surroundings. He was a handsome man who walked with his shoulders square, and the air of a scholar.

Liankui Ching bowed deeply to my Mother. His actions signified the deepest of respect and yet his air seemed to indicate indifference to us. His manner implied that we were to handle this matter with utmost expedience. He had used his name to save us, as a favor to my Father, who was a close business associate of his, indeed a distant relative. He had accommodations for us reserved in a hotel near his office. Every detail was arranged. I instantly felt both gratitude and fear of this man. It was a combination of emotions I would feel for many years to come.

My mother thanked Mr Ching for his kindness and we turned to leave. At that moment, to my surprise, Auntie Sheng walked into the office.

"Lawyer Ching?" Auntie Sheng glanced quickly around the room as she bowed before Liankui Ching, and gave me a brief, warning look. I knew instantly not to approach her.

"I am Madame Sheng, the wife of Sheng Seventh. My husband has disappeared. I know that you are a friend of his, Lawyer Ching. And that you, you could speak to Mr Du. Mr Du is very powerful and I believe that he might have information, or might know something regarding my husband's disappearance. Would you, please, help me, Lawyer Ching?" Auntie Sheng was obviously choosing her words carefully, yet she did not seem flustered. On the contrary, anyone in the room could feel her strength as she spoke so politely to Liankui Ching.

Liankui Ching turned to us and bowed deeply once again. "If you will please excuse me, Mrs Ching, I can see that I must deal with this, unpleasant matter. If you need anything once you arrive at the hotel, simply call my office."

It was his eyes. During our brief visit, Liankui Ching's eyes blinked constantly and nervously. Yes, it was his eyes which bothered me most. They knew no peace.

We turned and left Liankui Ching's office without acknowledging that we knew Madame Sheng. I knew as I left, that this man had not helped us out of the Chinese City because of kindness.

8

With the rule of Dr Sun Yat-sen, there had been an uneasy alliance between the forces who aspired to control China. There were so many political players — the rightists, centrists, radicals, as well as the Communist Party. So when Dr Sun died in 1925, China exploded. There were chaos and assassinations; all parties scrambled for power. Yes, the death of Dr Sun had instigated the invasion of the Chinese City, by Warlord Sun Chuanfang, from which I barely escaped. I had escaped because my father was politically connected to Warlord Sun, who easily took control of Shanghai that spring. The transition of power was relatively blood-free.

Other warlords also scrambled to build their own power during this time of political chaos, through conquering incremental pieces of China. Militarist Chiang Kai-shek also emerged, and established control in many parts of China. But they all focused their sights on Shanghai.

Of course, at the age of ten, I was not fully aware of these political maneuvers. Nor was I aware of how these historical struggles so closely touched my life.

Father arranged for us to settle into a lovely home in the French Concession. I was so happy to be away from the Chinese City, and I ran from room to room in sheer delight — in childhood oblivion to the political devastation that had led me home. The house was three stories with servants' quarters separated behind the house. Mother did not share our enthusiasm, however, and I could tell she missed the familiarity and comfort she had found in the Chinese City. I tried to help her decorate her own rooms to bring her comfort. We carefully placed her exquisite antique, mahogany furniture in the feng shui tradition, to keep positive energy and good fortune ruling in our home. But it was as though the very presence of her beautiful furnishings — the pieces given as part of her dowry when she was married — was a painful reminder of her family, and the China in which she no longer lived. Mother hung her thick, red, silk draperies on the long windows, and she rarely bothered to open them.

Father was favored in Warlord Sun's administration and our family was, for the moment, financially secure. Kaihua was enrolled in Nanyang Model School; Wanhua and I boarded as students, through the week, at the Elizabeth School for Girls.

The Elizabeth School was in a Chinese-controlled area located near the northeastern border of the International Settlement, but it was separated from most of that section by a large bridge. The school was operated by American Baptist missionaries; it was a lovely English Colonial building, surrounded by a lush green lawn. Wanhua and I went home every Friday and returned to school on Sunday morning.

At home, we followed our Chinese customs, observing ancestor worship and paying respect to the God of Heaven, the Goddess of Mercy, and the Kitchen God. We kowtowed to our elders during Chinese New Year and their birthdays. But at school, we were subject to the discipline and education of our American Baptist teachers. We were taught to kneel down in church, say prayers to the Christian God, and read aloud from the Bible.

Although it was somewhat confusing, it simply blended with the tapestry of confusion of Shanghai at the time. The entire city was a meeting of the East and the West. Practicing the religions of both cultures did not seem unusual to the generation in which these two cultures met.

I loved the new Western school, and our lovely home in the French Concession, but I was also worried about Auntie Sheng. Sheng Seventh had not returned. Auntie Sheng was devastated. We all felt that she could be in danger as well. I often prayed in the Christian church for their safety.

I still recall, most vividly, Auntie Sheng's goodbye that year. Though still elegant and composed, the stress of the year was showing on her.

"I can only think that my Sheng offended many dangerous people, Zhaohua. He attempted to expose the corrupt use of opium in our country; he spoke openly about the fact that it was our own leaders who were creating the need for opium. He spoke too much, Zhaohua. I think they have taken him away. I think it is not safe for me here, so I am leaving for a while, Zhaohua."

"But, where are you going, Auntie Sheng? I will write to you."

"I do not wish to endanger you, Zhaohua. I will contact you when things are safe." Auntie Sheng held me to her for the longest time. Then she took my face in her hands.

"Such a beautiful face should not hold such sadness, my dear girl." Auntie Sheng tried to smile, but her own beautiful face was also consumed with sadness.

"Auntie Sheng. I cannot imagine life in Shanghai without you." I held back the tears; I knew that to see me cry would bring Auntie Sheng even more sadness.

"Oh, I will be with you, Zhaohua. Just as your grandfather's words come back when you need them. The love, and the truths, and ways, I have attempted to teach you will come to you when you need them. Your grandfather was so right — China is coming apart at the seams. Opium and her own leaders are destroying her. Your grandfather is with you in his words, Zhaohua. And, as you grow further into the beautiful young woman you are becoming, I will be there with you. When you choose your first evening gown, and you go for the simple black one, I will be there. When you experience pain and sadness and fear, and you straighten your shoulders and hold your chin high and face sadness in the eye, I will be with you, Zhaohua."

"Oh Auntie Sheng! Please, stop. You sound as though I will never see you again. I do not want you to be with me in my thoughts, Auntie Sheng. I wish to spend my days with you."

"Oh, I know, Zhaohua. I know, dear." And Auntie Sheng took me in her arms and held me. "And I wish to be with you, Zhaohua. I want to watch you become the strong and beautiful woman I see blossoming before me. I want to see you as you grow so smart, and enter the university. And I want to see you marry, if you should choose to marry, a man who loves you as beautifully as Sheng Seventh has loved me. Oh, I'll be with you, Zhaohua. One way or another, I will be with you during these times in your life, my daughter. I do think of you as my daughter, Zhaohua."

With those words, I pulled away from Auntie Sheng, and I stood in my most graceful, elegant posture. I tilted my chin ever so slightly, extending my neck and emulating the poise of this exquisite woman. I looked Auntie Sheng in the eyes. I gave her one of her own looks. A look of calm acceptance, and peace, and a look of composure, that defied the torturous moment. Just a hint of a smile.

And Auntie Sheng was so moved, she had to catch her breath.

"Yes, Zhaohua. I can see. I will be with you. Thank you, Zhaohua, my brave girl." Then she walked so gracefully out of our lovely new home in the French Concession, her elegance completely intact.

After Auntie Sheng left, our lives settled into the routine of school, and short weekends at home in the French Concession. The political situation in China continued to unfold in all its drama, and my own family's connections to such matters were discussed more openly. Looking back, I suppose it should have seemed more fascinating. Of course, as a child, the extraordinary is rarely seen as such. It is in retrospect that the pieces fall together.

Meanwhile, Chiang Kai-shek was using his army to establish power, province by province. We knew he was coming to Shanghai. It was simply a matter of time. My mother hoarded and rationed food. The Communists dominated the labor unions, and constantly threatened strikes. Of course, these historical details were obscured by those things more important to children.

The Elizabeth School for Girls was just outside the Hongkou area, in a part of the Chinese-controlled section of Shanghai. One day, as our rickshaw approached the border, we saw piles of sandbags lining the road. There was barbed wire on either side of the border and as we turned the corner, we saw hundreds of warlord soldiers along the road. The sight brought back the panic of the day we had narrowly escaped the gates of the Chinese City.

"Please, turn around at once," I instinctively directed our coolie.

"But, Zhaohua, what about school?"

"Something is happening, Wanhua. We must return home and wait for Father."

On arrival, Wanhua and I found Father was addressing the entire family, "Warlord Sun Chuanfang is preparing to defend Shanghai against the invasion of Chiang Kai-shek. He still thinks he can hold Shanghai against Chiang. And yet the Communists have grown steadily in power since he took control." This fact alone told us the seriousness of the matter.

"I do not understand, Father."

"Of course you don't, Zhaohua. It is not a matter to be understood. You must all follow my instructions. Do not leave the courtyard. Do not return to school until you have heard from me that it is safe to do so. We are attempting to reach a peaceful resolution to the situation, but it is not safe. The Green Gang leaders are considering the value of the protection Chiang Kai-shek can offer. His army is experienced and well armed. We are going to need the experience — and the arms — I fear, as the Communists grow in power."

"But the Communists wish to free the people, Father. They will feed the hungry and end the corruption and the fighting of the warlords." I did not realize that the Communists were responsible for much of the information we were receiving in school. Nor did I realize that the rise of the Communists could endanger not only our livelihood, but my father's life as well. My father turned to me, a puzzled expression on his face.

"Zhaohua. What are you saying? We would lose everything if the Communists gained control over China. Everything I have worked so hard to achieve. It would all be gone." My father's voice was more amazed than angry. Then he looked at me as though he was seeing me, his twelve-year-old daughter, for the first time.

"My, my, Zhaohua. You have turned into a remarkably beautiful young lady. When did this happen?" He took my face in his hands. I could not remember Father touching me before that day. I felt elated and embarrassed by his words and simply looked down, away from his eyes.

Mother, Wanhua, and Kaihua were as surprised as I, by Father's attention. He quickly reverted to the subject at hand, however, and resumed our conversation.

"As I was saying, you are not to leave the courtyard surrounding our home until I have heard from Lawyer Ching that it is safe."

We had heard Liankui Ching's name from time to time since he helped to rescue us from the closing gates of the Chinese City. Although I had not actually seen him since that day, he and Father were working more closely together, and were becoming intimate friends. Whenever I heard his name mentioned, I could always vividly picture his nervous eyes.

"I will see that your studies are continued at home. We will arrange for tutoring until things calm down. Then, I think it is time to register you, my Zhaohua, in the McTyeire School. Your teachers at the Elizabeth School say that you are the brightest student. The McTyeire School is the best school in China. One of the best in the world. You will learn the skills that should accompany such intelligence and beauty, my daughter. I will arrange for you to enroll as soon as the political disputes are settled."

"So, Tongli, does this mean that you will be staying at home with us for a while?" My mother did not look at my father as she posed her question.

"No, Chongwen. I will not be returning to your home. It is true that Cloudy Lily has left. You would not consent to a divorce and she did not wish to be a second wife. But I will soon have Miss Jade Wang as my second wife." At my father's words, I was perhaps the only one to notice my mother's eyes sting with tears. She recovered immediately, and Mother's outward reaction did not reveal her sadness. She was fortified with the honor of a strong First Wife of China.

"I think it will be lovely for Zhaohua to begin at the McTyeire School, Tongli. It is an excellent decision." With those words, Mother bowed slightly to Father, turned, and left the room, with her head high. She went in and began instructions for dinner as though her heart had not been broken again.

That was how I first heard of my father's concubine. And I resolved at that moment to hate Jade Wang.

We spent the next two months confined to our home and courtyard. Chiang Kai-shek had the support of the foreign governments, who feared a Communist ideology would interfere with their profits. That spring, he gained the support of the Green Gang.

Although our home was in the French Concession, we could hear the echoes of artillery fire coming from the Chinese territories. Everyone knew that Chiang would not risk alienating his foreign alliances by bombing either the International or French Settlements, yet fear gripped the entire city. There was always the smell of fire in the air. Occasionally, the smell would deepen and take on a harsh, bitter odor. I later recognized the smell; it was the distinctive, and most unforgettable odor of burning flesh. And burning hair. I fell asleep at night to the distant sounds of gunfire. The sounds of war. I smelled the burning hair, and the burning flesh, and I knew it was death. It is interesting. Things of which no one tells you, and yet, even as a child, you know.

I awoke one night — from the sounds of the bombs — to find my mother downstairs with a man whom I did not recognize.

"Zhaohua, this is your Uncle Lin." Mother's voice was anxious.

The striking gentleman smiled and stepped toward me, holding out his arms, "Zhaohua. What an enchanting young lady you are becoming; your mother has told me you are very clever as well. It has been so many years — I am so glad to have this opportunity to see you, Zhaohua." Uncle Lin was tall and slender and looked immaculate in his Western suit. But the most striking feature of this stranger who was my uncle — whom I met in the middle of the night amidst the sound of bombs, and the smells of war — was the calmness with which he greeted me. I had grown so accustomed to the anxious mood of adults around me, that nervousness became routine. I barely noticed it as a child. Until I was in the presence of calm.

I have learned that there are some people, who enter your life only briefly, and yet their impression can be felt greater than that of some people with whom you might spend years. Uncle Lin and I shared that element of intimacy on that war-enchanted evening. We had a long and most lovely chat, Uncle Lin and I. He brought Mother news of her cousin, his wife, who had been like a sister to Mother in Nanjing. He told me stories of their childhood. He casually repeated the phrases of Old Tutor in his stories. He told me of his time in Tokyo and of his friend and idol, the late Dr Sun Yat-sen. My mother smiled during his visit. And late in the night, I fell asleep on the sofa beside him — a peaceful sleep induced by this calm presence and this soft, soothing voice. I remember him gently stroking my hair.

The following morning, my dear Uncle Lin was gone. Mother instructed me to keep absolutely silent about his visit. I did not understand but was beginning to sense the dangerous political circles in which I was living.

Dangerous, indeed. I was to read of my Uncle Lin in the future. As history — the tragic, dramatic, history of China — was recorded, I was to come to know my Uncle Lin more clearly. As China knew him. As it turns out, my Uncle Lin was Lin Zuhan. He traveled under the alias of Lin Boqu, and was a charter member of Dr Sun Yat-sen's secret revolutionary society, the Tung Meng Hui. Years earlier, when Dr Sun had merged his Tung Meng Hui with other revolutionary groups to found the Nationalist Party, Lin became a charter member. He and Sun were personal friends; he was even with Dr Sun when he died. And following Dr Sun's death, Uncle Lin opposed the military rule of Chiang Kai-shek. As I had fallen asleep on that surreal evening, with Uncle Lin stroking my hair, the members of the Green Gang were under instruction to eliminate this man who had given me such a beautiful, peaceful evening.

Years later, in 1949, as Chairman Mao stood proudly at Tiananmen Square, declaring the establishment of the People's Republic of China, and the victory of the Communists, my same Uncle Lin stood next to Chairman Mao atop Tiananmen rostrum.

Uncle Lin had miraculously escaped the arm of the Green Gang. He had remained loyal to his convictions — people should rule their own lives. At that point, my own political views differed from those of my uncle. But I recalled him, as he was on that sleepy evening, amidst the bombs of Shanghai. And I knew he was a kind, decent man. Uncle Lin had given me a calm interlude amid the bombs that year. He believed in the Communist government, and the People's Republic of China. As many did, in the beginning. But once again, the Communists must wait. It is not time for them yet.

No, first there was Chiang Kai-shek. And bombs on Shanghai.

Chiang's forces penetrated all of Shanghai and the atmosphere was so volatile, even the foreigners began to fear for their safety. We saw foreign troops march into the settlements and declare martial law. In retaliation, the Communists organized workers who attacked police stations and army posts all over the city.

As the Green Gang members secretly shifted their support, and joined Chiang's forces, stories were everywhere. It was rumored that Du, as emerging leader of the Green Gang, invited the warlord's commander-in-chief to the most renowned courtesan house in Shanghai, under the pretense of a grand party. The celebration, complete with courtesans and feasts and, of course, opium in massive quantities, went on for many days. The commander was persuaded to join Chiang Kai-shek's forces, bringing his army with him.

That commander was later executed by the warlord whom he had betrayed, but his forces had insured Chiang's victory.

Then Chiang's forces moved in and began slaughtering Communist workers, once again, with the assistance of the Green Gang. Du again intervened; he invited one of the Communist labor leaders, Wang Shouhua, to a private dinner party at his home. Unaware of the Green Gang's secret support for Chiang, Wang was most honored at the invitation. Wang's driver and bodyguard disappeared as they parked the car at Du's house. Wang was tortured and buried alive in a forest close to Fenglin Bridge.

Anarchy soon followed. Banks, government offices, and schools were all closed. Looting was rampant. Random murders were reported in all the districts.

It was my first real taste of war. There would be more. My Christian teachers at the Elizabeth School would say that I was blessed to live in the French Concession that year, somewhat distanced from the cruelties within the Chinese City. In that year, and years to come, I found myself wondering just why I had been so blessed. While others had not.

In that eternal spring, there were constant political discussions. I had so many fragments of information, and so many questions about the war. I kept hearing of Mr Du, and the Green Gang. I did not understand their power.

Time, in its unique ability, would fill in the pieces. Like the mafia in Italy, the Green Gang in China was an integral part of our culture. As is the way with most everything, the reputation of the Green Gang was neither all good, nor all bad — they were both feared and respected.

During the late Qing dynasty (1644–1911), the Green Gang gained control of the transportation workers on the Grand Canal. In Shanghai, they controlled the primary element of transportation — rickshaws. To control transportation is to control what is transported. Opium is transported. Opium was the primary source of capital — in one of the wealthiest cities in the world. The leaders of the Green Gang, by virtue of their wealth, controlled the politics of China.

For more than three centuries, the Green Gang had existed as a secret society. Members had their own secret codes and observed strict rules and regulations. They pledged to die for one another, if necessary. They existed to preserve tradition and to make money. If anyone got in their way, that person was eliminated. The police did not cross them. The government looked for their support. And the citizens feared and respected them.

Everyone knew that leaders of Shanghai in the 1920s were Huang Jinrong (Shining Gold), Zhang Xiaolin (Whistling Forest), and Du Yuesheng (Moonlight Musical Instrument). Huang was the senior leader; he made his fortune in the theater business. His power was known throughout China.

A few years earlier, the French government called on Huang to negotiate the release of some foreign VIPs who were being held hostage on the Jiangsu border. Huang intervened and they were freed within twenty-four hours. Boss Huang's reputation as generous — and powerful — was common knowledge in Shanghai.

Zhang Xiaolin, however, was a different story. He was the less 'refined' of the troika. He wore the expensive clothes of a gentleman, but was notorious for his crude behavior — and cruel temper. A friend of my mother's was at a dinner party with Zhang; one of the guests had the poor taste and misfortune to misunderstand what Zhang had said and asked Zhang to repeat himself. Zhang was immediately enraged and threw a knife at the man across the table. It was a fatal misunderstanding.

Then there was Du. Du was a poor orphan who grew up to be a gambler. His mounting debts led him to join the Green Gang. But Du proved himself loyal and clever. He had helped Huang recover a large shipment of opium that had been stolen; Huang gave him more responsibility, and he quickly worked his way to the top. Du was the brains; he knew every member of the Green Gang. Du was known to be as generous as he was fierce. All members listened to him and respected him.

Whenever someone spoke of the Green Gang, there were inevitably stories of torture and death for anyone who got in their way. Fear is a powerful ruler.

Yes, every child in China eventually learned of the power of the Green Gang. I was to learn more — so very much more — with time.

9

In that spring of 1927, Chiang Kai-shek took control of Shanghai, the financial capital of China — one of the financial capitals of the world. His victory, with the support of the Green Gang, would be short-lived, as the Japanese would soon begin to drain his strength, leaving him vulnerable to the Communist forces. Still, there was a period of tenuous peace. In those few peaceful years, I was to be introduced to my father's concubine, Beautiful Jade Wang.

"Zhaohua, please pack a bag. Your father will be here to pick you up soon. He would like you to visit his home for a few days." Mother's words were flat, as though it was a common occurrence for me to visit my Father's home — the home he shared with his second wife. In fact, I had never been there. Even Kaihua had not been invited.

"Mother, I do not wish to go. I will not go." I assumed a mature, resigned posture as I openly defied my mother. Of course, in my defiance, I was also honoring Mother.

"My daughter, you will not bring dishonor to your family by obeying me. Please pack your bags." Mother touched my shoulder gently. I knew she was saying thank you.

When Father picked me up later that evening, I again assumed my most mature and graceful air. I did not protest, as I silently put my bags into the car and seated myself in the front passenger seat. But Father could read my eyes. Indeed, I intended for him to know that I had no intention of making this a joyful encounter. At the same time, I did not dishonor Mother by being openly disrespectful.

We pulled up in front of his home. And then I met Jade.

I was immediately disarmed by her beauty. Jade, to this day, is the most beautiful woman I have known.

If her beauty was not enough, the grace and intelligence of Jade Wang was felt immediately. She reminded me of Grandfather. This tall, slender, beautiful woman possessed the tranquility and the gentle warmth of my wise, silk-robed Grandfather.

"My name is Wang Meiyu, Beautiful Jade. Please call me Jade. And you must be Zhaohua. I have so wanted to meet the beautiful and intelligent daughter of Tongli." Jade held out her hands and I instinctively placed my hands in hers. It was a sincere greeting.

My eyes could not soak up this beautiful woman fast enough. She looked like a college student. She was in Western dress, a plain white cotton blouse and a long floral skirt. She wore no make-up and her hair was short, accentuating her lovely jaw-line. Her wide, prominent cheekbones gave Jade the elegant bone structure of that rare beauty which does not age. But what one first noticed were Jade's eyes. They were what reminded me of Grandfather. They were at peace. Yes, her eyes were stirring.

I felt young and awkward in the presence of such beauty. I regained my poise however, and straightened my shoulders, attempting to mask my insecurities. Father said he had a meeting and would return in time for dinner. He gave Jade a kiss on the cheek, and I knew as I saw in the way he looked at Jade, that he would never return to Mother. I felt guilty as I thought of Mother.

"Yes, I am Zhaohua. The daughter of Father's First Wife." Immediately, I regretted my cold words. Within moments of meeting my father's concubine, I wished to be her friend. I could not reconcile this desire with the loyalty I felt toward Mother, but I knew that I would not be able to carry out my plan to alienate this woman.

Jade sensed my regret and gave me a smile — she accepted my apology. That marked the beginning of a special relationship in which we would often communicate silently.

Then we entered Father's home. I was immediately struck by the feeling of light in the home. I realized, for the first time, that Mother's houses were always dark. Curtains were drawn, and windows were rarely open. Jade had chosen this house in Rue Vallon, on the east side of the French residential area. The entire street was enchanting, with Victorian lamp-posts dotting the tree-lined avenue. The house was at the end of the street, and the garden in the front courtyard seemed to be the treasure of the avenue. The low brick wall was lined with large, untrimmed camellias. It had been a cool spring, so they were all in full bloom, with varying shades of deep reds and pinks against the lush green foliage. The camellias in Jade's garden made me think of roses; roses who had found a more comfortable place to reside.

The house was full of windows — bare, open windows in every room. The windows, and the rooms, seemed to be inviting the garden inside.

The light graceful scent of Tea Olive shrubs could be detected in every room, obviously a gift of Jade's garden. There was a small terrace at the back, which was shaded and lined by a row of Magnolia trees. Jasmine had overtaken all the iron railings. There was so much green around the cottage that I felt like I had stumbled into a sunny spot in the middle of an enchanted forest.

Everywhere I could sense Jade's touch. I had always wondered what Father's other house was like. I now knew that this was Jade's house. Yes, Father paid for it. But the presence, the comfortable feel of the place, was the result of Jade Wang.

The white walls were filled with unframed watercolors. All sizes of original paintings were hung without attention to symmetry or furnishings. I was immediately drawn to a very large painting in the main room, which was the center of the house.

"Yes, I believe it is my favorite, as well." Jade spoke from behind me. She had given me silent permission to walk through the house, absorbing the light and the garden and the richness surrounding me. "Of course, my most recent painting is always my favorite painting." She laughed easily at herself.

"You did all of these?" I could not mask my surprise.

"Yes, and many more. I'm afraid it's my passion. Well, one of my passions. Tell me, Zhaohua, what is your passion?"

I was taken aback by her question. Her manner was simultaneously casual and intense. "I, I do not know, Jade. I suppose school has been my passion. I've been working on some poetry writing lately, and I do love my studies and am looking forward to beginning classes at McTyeire now that the war has ended."

"Yes, your father says you are an excellent student. Perhaps that is your passion for now. Tell me, do you like music — Zhaohua?"

"Oh yes. Very much. Auntie Sheng used to take me to the Kunqu opera, and the concerts several nights a week."

"Auntie Sheng?"

I told Jade everything about Auntie Sheng. It was the most I had spoken of her with anyone since her departure. She had been gone almost two years now; I had not heard from her. As I talked on and on, pouring out story after story about White Peony Sheng, Jade quietly made me a cup of tea. She added milk without asking if I would like it. Her movements were graceful and she seemed to listen to every word as she served me tea and almond cookies.

"You have been so fortunate to have such a special woman in your life, Zhaohua." Once again, her words were sincere. Jade was an unusual woman in that I never saw evidence of jealousy or competition in her spirit. She had the rare ability to love other women, and appreciate their beauties, and their strengths. Some would say it came from the fact that Jade, herself, was so beautiful, but I have known many elegant women who are not secure enough to appreciate beauty in others. No, Jade's security came from somewhere other than her physical beauty.

Before I realized what I was saying, I found myself telling Jade about the day White Peony Sheng had walked into Liankui Ching's office, asking for his assistance in locating Sheng Seventh. I had instinctively guarded myself around Father. I somehow knew that it would not be good to mention the scene we had witnessed during our first meeting with Liankui Ching. And from the way Mother had reacted that day, and never spoken of the matter since, I was certain that she, too, felt it would not be safe to relay this story to Father. As Father had been absent for so many years, he was not aware of the closeness of my relationship with the Shengs.

Jade sensed my apprehension as I realized what I had told her.

"You know, Zhaohua. I am your father's Second Wife, but I also wish to be your friend. You do not have to worry that I will relay everything you tell me to your father. I know Liankui Ching well. Your Auntie Sheng obviously knew his capabilities. She was very brave to approach him. I hope she, and her husband, are safe."

"Jade, I have a question." I was, within an hour with this woman, completely comfortable.

"Yes, Zhaohua?"

"Why am I here, Jade? I have never visited Father's other homes. I have never met his friends. I do not understand his sudden interest."

"Well, Zhaohua. That is a big question. But I do not wish to begin our relationship with untruths, so I will tell you what I think. I know that when he last met with your mother and family, your father was struck by your beauty. And he does care for you, Zhaohua. In the way many Chinese fathers care for their daughters. Silently. But there is comfort to be found in truth, Zhaohua. Even if the truth is bitter. I'm afraid, Zhaohua, that your father has probably brought you to our home for reasons other than these. He is very busy, and he is afraid that I will become bored and that my interests will wander, Zhaohua. He does not understand that I am an honorable woman. I have accepted our arrangement and would not betray his trust. So you are to be my babysitter, little one. And I think it is going to be a lovely arrangement."

I had never imagined that my father had brought me to his house out of a desire to be with me, so Jade's words did not hurt. On the contrary, they were the basis for my lifelong trust in my father's concubine.

"I also think it is going to be a lovely arrangement, Jade," and I finished my tea in silence with my new friend.

It was a year of learning. Learning from the wise and beautiful Jade Wang. Learning about myself and 'my passions.' And that year Father enrolled me at McTyeire School.

Women have a capacity to bond in a unique way and the friendships of other women in my life have been sources of comfort and learning and strength. In that year, while Jade was sharing her wisdom and her passion with me, I was also learning from my friends at McTyeire.

Oh, how I loved that school! It lived up to its reputation as challenging and special and unique. McTyeire offered me more than my opportunity to reach the West; and so much more than the academic knowledge, which I came to crave. McTyeire School gave me lifelong friends.

The campus itself was one of the loveliest spots in Shanghai. McTyeire took pride in their reputation as the premier Western school in China, and kept their lush, green lawns and grounds manicured in the style of formal English gardens. It was established by American Methodist missionaries during the second half of the nineteenth century to educate upper-class Chinese women in Shanghai. The main building, a four-storied colonial brick structure, full of long, divided windows, and large white columns along the front, was modeled after the Ivy League campuses in England and America. Many days, as I looked out the window of my sparsely furnished room, I would pretend that I was there — in America.

Students boarded at McTyeire, returning home every two weeks. I had made friends at my other schools, but I had never made real friends before. The intense relationships in my life had always been with adults. Then I met my roommates Nancy Wang, and Janet Xie. They were both two years ahead of me, but treated me as an equal immediately. We were soul mates from the beginning, and embarked on friendships of loyalty and closeness — those rare friendships, which do not fade with time or separation. I found it comfortable and refreshing to revel in my youth, and in the company of others my age. I think girlfriends are the same — whether they are in the East or the West. We giggled, we gossiped, and we shared the secrets of our hearts until the wee hours of the morning. We were inseparable during our first year.

Nancy was my best friend, winsomely pretty yet also dignified and mature in manner. I also spent a great deal of time with Janet, who was always full of fun and gossip.

One fine spring evening, Janet and I were walking along Lover's Lane, a part of the campus near the gym. The gentle willow trees swayed toward the tulips, and all the yellow and white daisies. Some shoots were coming from the pink peonies from the ground, and the smell of freshly cut grass was so sweet. At that time President Yang and Miss Olive, a singing teacher, were coming toward us. Janet whispered, "What an odd couple! President Yang is short and plump while Miss Olive tall and heavy."

"By the way, you have to watch out for Miss Wu, the dean. She is an important person here."

"Wby?" I asked. "I met her the other day and she said hello to me."

"She is good-natured," Janet replied. "Still, as dean she is feared by all the students. She works all day long in her office, then at night she tiptoes through the hallways from one dormitory to another when lights are out. Whenever she hears any noise or spots any lights on after 9 p.m., she knocks on the door to warn the students inside. She always marks the number of the room in her notebook."

"What happens then?"

"If a particular room is noted a second time," Janet said, "the names of the students involved are posted on a notice-board, and they are summoned to the dean's office for a 'big feast.' That means a big lecture."

"So her nickname 'Maotouying' (owl) suits her well." I said. "She looks like an owl, too, with her round face and round thick glasses, peering about at night." So, I thought, this is the kind of gossip the girls from wealthy and powerful families indulged in to while away their time there.

After Chiang's successful Northern Expedition against the warlords and the establishment of the National Government in Nanjing, all schools in China had to include the study of Dr Sun Yat-sen's Three Principles of the People. McTyeire was no exception. This class was taught by a cadre sent from the Nationalist Party. Most of the students were completely uninterested in the subject and dozed during his lectures. What they were really interested in were current fashions, popular songs, American jazz music, and the latest dance craze.

My time at McTyeire was a rite of passage in youth. An opportunity for me to bond with others who were experiencing the confusion and exhilaration of adolescence. Adolescence in any country is a time of confusion and exhilaration. China was to give me my share of both.

Fortunately, I had Jade Wang to guide me.

10

$\mathbf{M}$y father's concubine was rumored to be the most beautiful woman in Shanghai. Most people did not know that she was also one of the most intelligent. Jade spoke several languages. She was an intuitive and passionate artist. Jade Wang sprinkled her magic throughout Shanghai. And some of it fell on me.

Of course, every man who met Jade fell in love with her to some degree. I saw, for the first time, how loving a beautiful woman could turn powerful, strong men into a childlike presence of insecurity. Jade was always sincerely cheerful with my father. She was always fresh and energetic when he arrived home. She was spontaneous and considerate. Her actions were those of the perfect, storybook wife. Yet no one in the house imagined, for a moment, that she was in love with him. Well, I suppose my Father imagined it; he had to. But deep down he knew that theirs was an arrangement — that he would never really possess the love of Jade Wang. Still, he did try.

I was boarding at McTyeire, and spending most of my free weekends with Father and Jade. The students were members of the most powerful Shanghai families, and as I became acquainted with them, there were endless parties. Jade was immensely popular in Shanghai, and she and Father were always invited to exclusive events. Thus my life took a turn into the inner social circles of the city. I still remember it — my first grand, Western party.

"You want to take me along? To a party at the Majestic Hotel? Jade, I, of course, I would love to go."

The Majestic Hotel in the International Settlement was the most exquisite hotel in Shanghai. Chiang Kai-shek and Soong Mei-ling had celebrated their wedding there, in December of 1927. The newspapers and magazines were filled with pictures of curving staircases with gold banisters and red carpets, crystal chandeliers, and huge fresh floral arrangements. I could not imagine attending a party there, at the age of fourteen.

"Of course we will take you, Zhaohua. You will be the belle of the ball! Now, what will you wear? Shall we go shopping?" Jade clapped her hands in delight at the prospect of presenting me at the upcoming event.

"A simple, black dress would be lovely, Jade."

"I see White Peony Sheng taught you well. You are young — but, black it is."

So I attended, at the age of fourteen, my first elegant, Western, formal affair. The men all wore perfectly cut tuxedos. Evening gowns and diamonds danced under the sparkling light of the chandeliers. It was a party in honor of Mr O. S. Liu's son, Frank, who had just returned from the University of Pennsylvania, having earned a master's degree in business. Frank's father was one of Shanghai's tycoons; he had made his fortune in textiles and matches.

As we entered the room, Father between Jade and myself, I felt the energy. The energy of the West as it consumed the East. There was a White Russian orchestra in the center of the room, playing modern American jazz. The sounds of Benny Goodman and Duke Ellington drifted through the air. There were French doors open to marble terraces overlooking candle-lit gardens. The terraces seemed to overlook the stars themselves. The room was filled with the scents of fresh flowers. There were champagne fountains and trays of caviar and delicacies. As we walked through the elegant crowd, everyone looked at my father's concubine.

Jade shared White Peony Sheng's taste for understated elegance. Yes, her dress was simple, black silk and beautifully cut. But in a room of diamonds and rubies, Jade had chosen less pretentious pearls. She seemed to wear her jewelry, not so much to catch the eye, as to quietly surprise and caress the eyes of those who lingered on her beautiful presence. And almost everyone lingered on the charming presence of Jade. She wore pearl ear-rings, but no necklace. Her dress, which left her shoulders bare, seemed to be wrapped tightly around her waist, with a simple large pearl as a pin just above her right breast. The skirt of the dress was straight, but smooth, with a slit exposing a graceful glimpse of her ankle and calf. At the top of the slit, another pearl would surprise the eye. Her hair had been pulled into a bun, just above the nape of that beautiful long neck, with a ring of pearls massed around the thick bundle of hair.

Jade did not sit down the entire evening. Everyone wanted to dance with her. My father beamed with pride as he took his turn. Jade danced closely with my father; her eyes told everyone she had come with Tongli Ching. Yes, she was honorable. She lived up to their arrangement.

"Would you care to dance, Miss Ching?" I was caught off guard by the handsome guest of honor, Frank Liu, as he approached me and invited me to dance.

"I am afraid I am not very experienced, Mr Liu."

"Please, call me Frank. Come on, I am a patient teacher." So I took his hand for my first waltz with a man.

"My, my, Miss Ching. You have been hiding your talents! You are quite good at the waltz. Where have you been gaining this experience, lovely lady?"

I smiled at the thought of being considered an experienced dancer. Jade had been patiently trying to teach me over the past few days in preparation for the party.

"Oh, in a lovely setting, Mr Liu. It is a most enchanting place amidst beautiful gardens and lovely paintings." Then I laughed. "Jade has been teaching me at home, Frank. I am quite new to such an affair."

"Well, I have a feeling, Miss Ching, that you will get lots of experience in waltzing over the next few years. And you will be most popular when you go to America."

"What makes you think I will be going to America?"

"Your English is quite good, Zhaohua. You are at the McTyeire School now, are you not? Many of their graduates go on to American universities. I can tell that you are an intelligent young lady. I just assumed that you would plan to go to America as well. I would highly recommend the experience."

I think it was at that moment — as I danced with Frank Liu, I became completely intoxicated with the music and the evening — that I decided I would, indeed, go to America. Actually, it was one of those decisions that is not so much a decision as a realization. My life, my philosophies, my grandfather, Auntie Sheng, and Jade — they had all been preparing me, whether they knew it or not, to leave China. I would work harder at school. I would learn everything I could possibly learn. I would be accepted at an American university. As Jade would say, it was to become my passion.

I danced the evening away; as the evening progressed and I danced with our host, Mr Liu informed me that he had twelve children. "Frank is a bit old for you, Zhaohua, but I have more sons who are studying abroad. I think you could have your pick of them when they return, Miss Ching." He laughed as he led me in a waltz. I glanced at Father and Jade and they smiled with pride. My social debut, at the age of fourteen, was a resounding success.

After the Liu party, Jade and Father invited me to accompany them to most of their engagements. Between boarding at McTyeire, and my social engagements with Father and Jade, I now spent little time at Mother's. When I was there, I tried to subdue my enthusiasm for my life with Father and Jade. I watched Mother accept her lonely sadness, in her dark home with the heavy drapes drawn, and I reaffirmed, over and over, my determination for a Western life.

Jade, though a second wife, set the conditions for the 'arrangement' of her life. She did not let life pass her by outside closed windows. Jade embraced everything life had to offer. She never passed up an opportunity to grow and to enhance her life. And she taught me to do the same.

"I have signed us up for opera lessons, Zhaohua! You and I are going to become amateur performers of Beijing and Kunqu opera; we are to start lessons at the Zhong Club next week. You will be wonderful, Zhaohua. I think you should concentrate on Kunqu; it would be most challenging. Also, opera was originally written in poetic verses, so it will be helpful in your studies as well."

Kunqu required a sound knowledge of Chinese classical epics and lyric poems. Jade said that Chinese lyric verses were like Shakespearean sonnets — with a touch of humor! So I began to study the classics, while also attempting to master the appropriate voice and the ease of a natural actress. Of course, Jade encouraged me in my hard work.

"You are very fortunate, Zhaohua. Every woman should receive training as an actress — trust me, dear. It will be your skill most often employed." Jade laughed knowingly as she relayed her words of wisdom.

"Sometimes I do not understand you at all, Jade."

"Oh you will, Zhaohua. All too soon, my dear, you will understand so many things. And you will laugh when you are old, and remember the words of your father's concubine!"

"Could you explain one thing to me, Jade? I do not wish to pry, but I do not understand why you are with Father. Any man in Shanghai would fall in love with you. Yet, you seem to — to really love no one, Jade."

"That is not true. I love you, Zhaohua, very much."

"I mean a man, Jade. I do not think that you love Father. You never say that you love him."

Jade's eyes became thoughtful. For several moments, I thought she would not respond.

"You are right, Zhaohua. I am not in love with your Father. He is a very kind man. He takes good care of me — and of my mother, as well, Zhaohua."

"Your mother?"

"She lives close by; your Father supports her as well. It is part of our arrangement. My mother and I are very close, Zhaohua. I visit her every day on my morning walks. I have been waiting for the right time to introduce you, Zhaohua."

"You have never spoken of your life before Father, Jade. Did you and your mother always live in Shanghai?"

"Oh, no, Zhaohua. We were peasants. I grew up in a tiny rural village outside Wuxi. We were very poor. My father was killed in one of the raids on our village and Mother could have sold me many times when I was young. But she did not; she left her family and her village and brought me to Shanghai. She thought I could learn more here and have a better life. It took much courage, Zhaohua, for my mother to come to Shanghai — such a large city — knowing no one, and having no money or education. She went to work as a maid for a French doctor and his wife; we lived in a small room behind their kitchen; that is where I learned to speak French."

Jade was so sophisticated, I always assumed that she had grown up in Shanghai. I did not have to ask her to continue; she read my interest in my eyes.

"My mother is so wise, Zhaohua. She knew the only way out of our poverty was for me to learn. To learn everything I could. She arranged for me to study in the afternoon with the doctor's children as they did their school work. She insisted that I read every evening. She told me not to rely only on my beauty. She said there were many beautiful — and hungry — women. That most women who were educated did not starve. I will always be devoted to her, Zhaohua." Jade was obviously moved as she spoke of her mother. I remember feeling envious of their bond.

"So you left the French family to be with Father?"

"Oh no, Zhaohua. The doctor became — he became — well, let's just say we had to leave their home suddenly. I was young and naïve. I married a young and very handsome tramcar driver. I was immature; I did not know that I could not be happy with a complacent spirit. He did not make enough money to support both Mother and me, and he did not work hard. To make extra money, I took a job as a dancehall hostess at the Black Cat Ballroom. I would charm and dance with wealthy men who enjoyed cheerful company in a Western setting. I was not a prostitute, but still, it was not something that my husband wished me to do. He became enraged when he found out, and he left me. By that time, I did not care. I knew I wanted more from my life.

"It was soon after that I met Ching-pie Nien.

"We met at the Welcome Café; I was having tea and he was painting on the open sidewalk. He was using oils in rich, vibrant colors, Zhaohua. Such talent. I sat, sipping my tea, for hours, transfixed by the focused energy he exhibited as he worked on his painting. He did not even notice me and I did not interrupt. Finally, after several hours, he stopped painting and sat back in his chair. He tipped his head backwards and closed his eyes. I spoke softly to him, in French, as his eyes were closed. 'The colors touch in just the right places,' I said to him. Then we had an easy conversation, in both French and Chinese, as he sat there with his eyes closed. I had fallen in love with him as he painted, before I ever heard him speak. And he fell in love with me before he ever saw me, Zhaohua. With his head back and eyes closed, peaceful and exhausted from the painting." Jade walked to the window and did not try to conceal the deep emotion of the memory.

"So why are you not with him, Jade? How can you be so happy here with Father? He is so much older than you."

Jade took a deep breath and paused for a while before continuing. "It is not so simple, Zhaohua. Mr Nien comes from a conservative, scholarly family. I come from country stock. I have been married. His father is the Commissioner of Finance in Suzhou. They would disown him if he were to marry me; it would bring dishonor to his family."

"Where is he now, Jade?" I could not help remembering Mother's words so many years ago. "It is not so simple, Zhaohua," she had said to me. No. Marriage. Love. They are rarely simple.

"He is in Paris, mostly. He is painting there, although I hear that he occasionally visits Shanghai. It is better that we do not communicate or see each other." When Jade said these words, I saw that look. That same look I had so often seen in my mother when she resolved to accept the conditions of her lonely life. She looked into my eyes, but not really.

"So when did you meet Father, Jade?"

"I met him at the Black Cat Ballroom. He used to come to dance with me. He was very kind, both to me, and to my mother. Your father is not complacent. He takes care of us — and I am free to paint. Sometimes when I am painting, Zhaohua, I know Nien is painting, too, and I wonder if our brushes are moving at the same time, if they are dipping into the same colors. We used to paint together for hours, without speaking or looking at one another. He would be on one side of the room, I on the other. Our brushes would dance in rhythm, until evening came. Then we would dance. It is in the peace, Zhaohua, that love resides. So many people think love is to be found in energy, in restlessness. But when you can sit on a busy sidewalk, and you can speak with your eyes closed. Or not speak at all. If you can just sit quietly and feel at peace, then your spirits are compatible."

I was so young, still fourteen, but I knew that Jade should be with Mr Nien. That backgrounds and marriages meant nothing. That she should not be with Father. Yet I could not picture my life without Jade Wang.

"Do you have any of his paintings, Jade?"

"Oh yes, but I keep them at Mother's. It would not feel right to have them here."

"May I see them someday?"

Jade looked at me for a few moments before answering. "Well, my husband's daughter. What are you doing right now? I find that I wish to be with them myself at this moment."

So we walked to the home of Jade's Mother. The remarkable woman who had produced this delicious and intense woman. Who had nurtured her, and educated her, and earned the undying love and loyalty of Jade.

Her mother's house was a few blocks from the house Jade shared with Father. The garden was conspicuously simple, and Eastern, in the middle of the French Concession. The house itself seemed comfortably austere. It was very different from Jade's rambling lush garden, but inviting, nonetheless.

As we entered, Jade put her fingers gently to her lips, and we walked quietly into the center room and sat down on the floor. A woman, whom I knew instantly to be Jade's mother, was sitting across from us with her eyes half closed, and her legs crossed. She was meditating and murmuring to herself, counting a string of Buddhist beads in her hands. She did not acknowledge our arrival, and I had an opportunity to study her as she chanted. She was a peasant woman from her appearance, plump, dark, and solid skinned. Her forehead was creased with lines that climbed down around her eyes, and her hands were rough and callused. She had obviously had a hard life, yet, despite their difference in age and marks of life, I could see where Jade had inherited those exquisite bones. Later, when Mrs Wang opened her eyes, I could see only Jade.

She did not seem at all surprised to see us sitting there, and yet I did not think she heard us come in.

"Mother. I would like for you to meet Tongli's daughter, Zhaohua." Jade's tone of voice carried deep respect. "Zhaohua, this is my mother, Mrs Wang."

I bowed in respect, and Mrs Wang put her hands on my face. "What a beautiful young lady. My Jade tells me you are bright as well." I did not respond, but raised my eyes and returned her penetrating look.

"Oh, yes, Jade. You are right. She is a remarkable young lady." Mrs Wang spoke with Jade's sincerity.

"I will make tea." Jade turned quietly and went into the kitchen, leaving me alone with her mother.

"Your father, Zhaohua, is a fine man. He has been very kind to Jade — and to me." Mrs Wang was not a woman to say words she did not feel, even to the daughter of her benefactor. I found it strange that I had not thought of my father in that way before. Kind.

"Jade has been most kind to me, Mrs Wang. Her friendship has come to mean a great deal to me. Has she told you that we are to take opera lessons together?"

"Oh, yes, she tells me you will be quite good. She thinks you have natural abilities and are a very hard worker. It should please your father very much, Zhaohua, if you do well."

As Mrs Wang looked at me, I knew that she understood my unspoken desire to please Father — to somehow, experience the affection and pride he had always shown Kaihua. Mrs Wang had shown me the way. Yes, it would impress Father if I performed well.

"Would you like to see the paintings now, Zhaohua?" Jade entered the room carrying a handcarved wooden tray holding an earthen handmade teapot and three matching cups. Everything in Mrs Wang's home seemed simple and unencumbered. Even thoughts.

"Yes, Jade."

"Come out here." She motioned me to follow her through a doorway into a room, which seemed to be surrounded by windows. "Would you care to join us, Mother?" she called from the room of light.

"No, Jade. I will have my tea. Thank you, daughter."

As we stepped through the doorway, Jade turned with her back to the windows, facing the wall that separated us from the room where I had met Mrs Wang.

"Here they are, Zhaohua. A few of the many masterpieces of Mr Ching-pie Nien."

The paintings took my breath. Jade was an accomplished artist, and her work was powerful in its softness. But these paintings — they seemed to reach out from the frames and take hold of the viewer. The colors were the richest and deepest I had ever seen. Yes, one first noticed the color. Then the images. Most were still-lifes in Western style. There was only a slight trace of the familiar, sparse Chinese softness in his work. It was powerfully intense and romantic. I felt torn; I wanted to spend all my time on one painting, but could not wait to see the others; and then when my eyes moved to the next one, it was that same feeling of wanting to linger, but anxious to move on.

Then I saw it. It was at the end of the room. The large painting of Jade. Jade was nude with her long, graceful back to the viewer and her head turned over that exquisite shoulder. She was surrounded by every shade of green imaginable. Green silk. I wanted to touch the painting. I was certain it was actually made of silk. The light was so expertly captured. He had captured the grace of her long neck, her jaw-line, those cheekbones, and even her eyes. Caught up in the emotion and power of the painting, I was moved to tears.

"I am sorry, it is just so ..."

"It is so passionate. Yes, I know. That is the element in any real work of art, Zhaohua. Passion. Trained but uncensored, untamed. I have seen this painting so many times. I have spent evenings curled in front of it and mornings welcoming the sun next to it. And still it moves me. Come. Shall we have tea?"

Christina's father, Ching Tongli

Christina's mother, Wu Chongwen

Christina's mother and brother, Kaihua

Christina's maternal grandfather

Christina's paternal grandfather, Qin Dunshi, with his concubine

Christina in her teens

Christina's aunt Liming and her husband, Stanley Qian, with their daughter, circa 1959

Christina in her wedding gown

Liankui Ching, taken in his mid-forties when he was in his prime

Family portrait of Christina, Liankui and their four children

Christina with Anthony, Priscilla and Frank

Christina in front of the Hong Kong Bank
Building, circa 1948

Christina in front of her house in Tawau,
Borneo, circa 1959–60

Christina going to work on bike, in Tawau, Borneo, circa 1959

Christina with Ruby and her husband, Taty Kuo, circa 1962

Christina with members of manufacturers and foreign importers in Hong Kong, circa 1964

Alice, Christina's stepdaughter

Priscilla, Anthony and Alice in New York

Christina with Frank in New York

Christina with her second husband, T.C. Tsao

Christina in her sixties

11

From behind the curtain, I could hear voices and laughter as the guests poured into the grand hall and took their seats around the tables set in fine crystal and silver, on white linen tablecloths. Jade's reputation as a performer had led to an invitation for us to perform at the wedding of the son of the Commissioner of Revenue; my first audience was to be comprised of the wealthiest and most influential leaders in Shanghai. I could feel butterflies in my stomach, and I remember that I imagined them to be in my knees and toes as well. My mind got carried away with the image of the butterflies in my body, and I pictured myself on stage, opening my mouth to sing, and a yellow butterfly escaping.

"Zhaohua. I know you are nervous, but relax. You will be fine. You have done the work. You know your pieces, your movements, the words, so completely. All you need is the last piece. The secret piece. I can tell you, but it will not do any good if you do not hear it. The most important element on stage cannot be seen by the audience. But they will most certainly know if it is missing. It is your mind, Zhaohua. In your mind, you must become the character you are singing. The words, the beautiful graceful movements, they are nothing without the mind, Zhaohua. You must be the maid. Do you understand?" Jade spoke softly, with gentle intensity. It was as though she lay the words on the table and they were mine to either take or leave behind.

"I do not understand, Jade." I searched her eyes for clarification. But Jade only smiled at me.

"Oh, you will, Zhaohua. I can tell. When you step onto that stage, you will not even remember this conversation, which is the whole point!" Jade laughed as though there were not six hundred eyes waiting for me to embarrass my father.

My father. The hours of studying, the relentless rehearsing — they had all been for him. It was not the other guests who were filling my body with butterflies; it was my father's eyes that I both feared and craved.

There was a mix of Chinese gongs, drums and stringed instruments announcing the start of the performance. The Chinese flute, with its lilting, sweet songs, *jie jia che ho,* hushed the audience. Slowly and silently I proceeded to the center of the stage. My embroidered, traditional costume fit tightly and my head-dress was heavy with decoration, and yet I seemed to glide as if I were walking on air. I was conscious of all eyes on me for a brief moment. The eyes were approving and then, they faded. The butterflies were still inside me and all my hours of rehearsing and practicing culminated in a singular moment.

Suddenly, I knew I could do this. The stage was mine; the eyes were mine, and I could fill them, I knew.

I left them all as I entered my role and sang, announcing my part, "Maid Chunxiang, a clever and naughty servant taking care of my noble mistress, Du Liniang." The audience was familiar with the Kunqu opera, "Maid Chunxiang Storms the Class." It was from the well-known story "The Peony Pavilion" written in the sixteenth century by the playwright Tang Xianzu. I suppose this performance would be the equivalent of a Western amateur performance of a Shakespearean play.

The opening scene was inside my young mistress' house, where an old man, her tutor, was seated behind a desk waiting for us. I entered the room first, followed by my mistress who greeted the tutor and sat next to him. My role was the lead, and I took center stage doing all the talking and singing, all along playing silly tricks on the old man to distract him from my mistress' lessons. Although I was completely absorbed in my role, I could feel the vibrations from the audience as they laughed — not polite laughter, but real laugher, like children's laughter; adults sometimes forget how to laugh without inhibition, I think.

I could feel their eyes as they drank in my performance. On some level I was conscious that my voice was touching in all the right places, as Jade would say. Yet I think I was, indeed, completely absorbed in the part. Although I looked into the audience, I could not say where anyone was seated; I did not see tables or faces. I did not even think of Father. Or of Jade. I had become a clever maid, in another century, playing silly tricks on my mistress' tutor.

The curtain came down after the first act with a thunder of applause. My blood was rushing through my veins. Backstage, Jade simply nodded and smiled knowingly at me. Success has no need for praise.

As the curtain was raised for the second act, "Strolling in the Garden," Jade (my mistress) and I entered a beautiful spring garden setting. As we strolled through the staged garden, we sang a duet, praising the arrival of spring and the magic of flowers. As we sang, my mistress confided in me her love for a young scholar. Her confession took the form of a fantasy and ended in my mistress marrying her lover. Needless to say, Jade could play the part to perfection. I was filled with the success of my first performance, and also the joy of performing with one of the most talented individuals I have ever encountered. To say that our performance was a success does not do justice to the energy exchanged on that stage almost seventy years ago.

"Encore! Encore!" The audience was on their feet immediately as the scene ended. Our beaming host invited us down from the stage and into the crowd; the bride and groom were temporarily forgotten as we were surrounded with smiles and words of praise and congratulations.

I followed Jade's lead and responded with humility to the words and applause. We stood still, with our heads slightly bowed and responded with small smiles to the words of praise. But inside I was singing from skyscrapers. And looking for Father.

As the crowds thinned, Father became visible, waiting patiently behind the waves of bodies. He had two dozen long stemmed roses; one dozen for Jade. And the other for me. Like Jade, he did not say anything. He simply smiled and bowed his head to me. I had earned his respect. The adoration of my father. It was as sweet as I had imagined.

I changed that night. My confidence was born. Not in my natural talents; I knew that I had not been endowed with a supernatural gift of song. But I also knew that I could set a goal and, with hard work and a confident spirit, attain that goal. Yes, I would make it to the United States. To the university.

——— —— ———

"Invitations are pouring in, Zhaohua! You and Jade are the talk of Shanghai. Everyone wonders when you are going to turn professional and wants to have you perform at their parties before you are unattainable." Father's pride was evident in his tone as we sat around the dinner table. "Ambassador Ding has requested that you perform 'Maid Chunxiang Storms the Class' at his fiftieth birthday celebration in two weeks. The celebration is to be held at his mansion on Rue Petain."

"Examinations will be held during that week, Father. I would like to decline Ambassador Ding's invitation." As much as I loved performing, I knew that my passion was my studies. I had made a conscious choice to focus most of my energies on school.

"I commend your desire to do well in school, Zhaohua, but you must not ignore the relevance of such invitations. I would suggest you reconsider. You are capable of doing well on your examinations, while also having time to perform." Jade did not often attempt to instruct me. I suppose this made me more receptive to her advice. I also knew it meant a great deal to Father.

"I suppose you are right, Jade. Of course, Father, I would be honored to perform at the Ambassador's celebration. Please tell him I gratefully accept his kind invitation."

My life had taken a new turn. At McTyeire, I was at the head of my class. My life was divided between my mother's dark — traditionally Chinese — life, and a full Western life with Father and Jade. We attended parties and dinners every weekend; they always wanted me along now. I had taken sole responsibility for my studies. Neither Father nor Mother prodded me to study or to keep up with my academic performance. I dreamed and talked endlessly about going to the United States. About becoming as worldly and sophisticated as Jade, yet in my mind, I vowed I would never be as dependent on a man as my father's brilliant concubine. For a girl born to a peasant family in China, Jade had moved mountains with her intellect and charm. Still, she was financially dependent on the generosity of men for her survival.

As I repeated my performance of my Kunqu opera pieces for Ambassador Ding's guests, I did not realize that the esteemed lawyer, Liankui Ching, had also been invited to the Ambassador's celebration. The same Liankui Ching who had used his Green Gang connections to help my family escape from the Chinese City a few years before. The same blinking eyes. Those same nicotine-stained fingers had applauded. He was enchanted with my performance and congratulated me on my success following the show. As he admired my lovely traditional costume, I think he could not see that this young, Eastern girl had embraced the spirit of the Western world.

In the coming weeks, invitations continued to pour in.

"Zhaohua, you are becoming so popular; we shall have to employ a social secretary to keep up with your engagements!" Jade beamed at me. She was obviously proud of my accomplishments on the Shanghai social scene. "But now I have another project in mind for us; I could use your help with something. My mother actually suggested it. Are you interested?"

"Of course, Jade. Anything for you, and your mother. What can I do?"

"My mother has agreed to help a friend of hers, Dr Ding. It seems he has come across a young girl who is in need. Of course, there are many such girls in Shanghai, but according to him this young lady, Sonya, 'tugs at the heart.' He bought her from a brothel and my mother has agreed to let the young lady stay at her house. Sonya has no formal education and is somewhat, well, somewhat slow, I'm afraid. Still, she is most endearing and has a kind heart. My mother and I have decided to try to help her. She has lived a very sad life for a young girl, Zhaohua. Your English is excellent; you are learning so much at McTyeire. Would you tutor her a few days each week? Mother and I have agreed to teach her other things. We thought you might enjoy working with us — and with Sonya. What do you think?"

"Of course, Jade. I would love to help. It will be fun spending more time with you and your mother. When do we start?"

"I thought we'd begin this evening. Very informally, of course. But Sonya and Mother will be having dinner with us and we can all get acquainted."

When Sonya walked in the dining-room later that evening, it was obvious that she embraced the colorful side of Shanghai. My own style had been absorbed from Madame Sheng and Jade; I gravitated toward the simple. Sonya loved color. She loved patterns and designs. She loved jewelry. She loved flamboyance and they loved her. The obvious curves of her young body seemed at home in her low cut, floral blouse and skirt. Of course, the blouse and skirt didn't match, but somehow the bold clash of color, and pattern, seemed to suit Sonya. She was close to my own age, but those large dreamy eyes were both naïve and old.

Over the next few weeks, I attempted to teach Sonya English, some proper Chinese, and mathematics. And Sonya taught me — about men and sex and the other side of Shanghai.

"Oh Zhaohua, there are different types of prostitutes in Shanghai," Sonya admonished my ignorance when I mistakenly referred to her life as a courtesan. "The courtesans are the most expensive and do not sleep with most of their clients. Only the ones who will pay very large sums of money. Or perhaps men with whom they are in love. They are like the geisha in Japan. No, I was not trained as a courtesan. My stepfather sold me to a third-class brothel. We just sold sex. We were not trained to be charming and graceful." Sonya laughed as she relayed her story, as though it was perfectly natural to have sold sex over and over again at the age of fifteen.

"Why didn't you leave, Sonya?"

Sonya laughed her high-pitched laughter, as though I had said something hilariously funny. "How, my naive friend?" Then she fell into a rare, pensive tone of voice, "I was kept in a locked room and the only entrance to the house was guarded day and night. Besides, where would I go, assuming I could escape? Back to my mother's? Where my stepfather got drunk every night, and beat everyone in the family? At least I wasn't always beaten in the brothel. The men did not like girls with bruises. And I had food. Of course, in the beginning I did not understand, and I cried. They put me in a room that first night. Naked. On a bare mattress. There were four men that first night, Zhaohua. I was thirteen years old. Then they told me if I kept crying, they would send me the worst men who came. The ones who were ... the men who were not so pleasant, they said.

"After a few weeks, I just felt like I was watching from somewhere in the corner. Like it wasn't me having sex with those men. Somehow, I could see what my body was doing, but while it was happening, I always closed my eyes. I couldn't bear to see their faces. Their eyes did not look human when they were on me, Zhaohua." Then Sonya laughed that high-pitched, out-of-place laughter — which was distinctly Sonya — before resuming her role as my teacher, "Sex can be as simple as a business transaction, Zhaohua. Like buying vegetables from the market. Or sex can be painful, my friend. Or — if there is love, sex can be wonderful and beautiful." Sonya spoke so casually and laughed at my large eyes as I listened intently to her descriptions. Mother had never told me about sex. I think Madame Sheng would have considered it part of her truth lessons, had she been there. But sex was a taboo subject in my culture and young girls rarely learn about this enticing subject at a young age, many did not learn until their wedding night.

In the beginning, Sonya was a better teacher than student. No, Sonya did not catch on to our lessons easily. At first, I often became frustrated with her. But, as we learned together, our friendship grew, and I developed a new affection for Sonya. An affection combined with sympathy for her ignorance, but also respect for her resilience. Sonya's life had been a nightmare. Still, she laughed. She often laughed too loudly, and inappropriately. But Sonya laughed so she would not hate, I think. There is honor in that. Yes, I learned much from my student, who became my friend.

Eventually, Sonya learned as well. She learned to nod or shake her head instead of always talking loudly. A soft smile replaced her nervous, loud laughter. Simple dresses found their way into her wardrobe.

Father noticed the changes. And he approved.

12

As my young life so beautifully unfolded in grand parties, stage performances, and the building of friendships, the Japanese decided it was time to take Shanghai.

In fact, the Japanese had been rapidly taking parts of China, with no resistance from our leader, Chiang Kai-shek. Chiang had chosen to concentrate China's resources and defenses, which he now controlled, on the enemies within. He saw Communism as the greatest threat to his power and spent his armies and resources driving them further into the impoverished interiors of the vast country, where they simply enlisted the support of the peasants, the millions of peasants, and continued to grow in numbers.

It was a time when China desperately needed to unite. But there were many within Chiang's own Nationalist Party, the Kuomintang, who disagreed with Chiang's policy of retreat and non-resistance with the Japanese. These dissenting factions, who were still officially under the orders of Chiang, were ordered to fight other Chinese — the Communists. Additionally, the warlords still maintained control of certain cities and regions.

So while Chiang focused on the internal chaos of China, the Japanese took advantage of China's inner turmoil and marched in. They marched quickly, and immediately occupied Manchuria, the Northeastern sections of China.

On January 28, 1932, a date engraved on every person in Shanghai at the time, the Japanese seized the opportunity created by the vast division in our country, and they went for the gold — a surprise attack on Shanghai. The Japanese thought they would take Shanghai in a matter of days. They had not anticipated the bravery and heroism of the Chinese 19th Route Army, which had openly opposed Chiang's policy of non-resistance with the Japanese, and which was stationed in Shanghai temporarily.

The battle went on for many weeks. The newspapers hailed the heroes of this valiant army — these soldiers of Shanghai who were defending our city against an enemy whom our leader, Chiang Kai-shek, had chosen to ignore.

During those endless weeks of Japanese attacks, again I heard the bombs. Again, I smelled the acrid smell. And again I was under the protection of the Foreign Settlements.

Though privileged and relatively safe, the students at McTyeire School were most certainly not oblivious to the political climate. So in that spring of 1932, when the Chinese-controlled sections of Shanghai were being bombed by the Japanese, the students of the International Settlement, including some from McTyeire, formed volunteer groups to work in local hospitals, helping to care for the wounded. Janet, Nancy, and I signed up together, along with another close friend, Emily Tan. We were trained by student physicians, from St John's University, in everything from emptying bedpans to giving the wounded soldiers their regular injections of morphine. I walked the halls of the hospital, and I saw war in its most graphic horror — in the maimed and dying young men, who had saved our city from the Japanese.

In that hospital, I saw war for what it is. War is blood. War is severed arms and legs. And war is proud, courageous men — broken and afraid. Afraid of what they would be leaving behind, in their death. There was one soldier in particular, a corporal, who had been severely wounded in one of the bombings. He was paralyzed from the waist down and his right arm had been amputated in a medical unit before he reached the hospital. Though I generally avoided the eyes of the soldiers, in an attempt to give them a degree of privacy in which to experience their pain, this particular soldier reached out and touched my hand as I was about to administer his four-hour dose of morphine.

"Miss, before you give me the morphine, I wonder if I might ask you a favor. I'm afraid it is quite personal and I do not even know your name."

"My name is Zhaohua. I will certainly do what I can, corporal."

"Zhaohua, 'China the Glorious', a beautiful name. I am dying, Zhaohua. Please, do not offer kind words of protests, I know it is near. And I think there would be an element of peace if I could write a letter to my parents before … my mother and father are very old — I am their only child. They will have no one left to support them. Please, before my mind is again dulled by the morphine, would you help me to write a letter to my parents. I have a few silver dollars with me; here, they will need them …"

"Of course, corporal."

The letter itself was brief; it was in fact an apology and instructions on who to contact for the few silver dollars he had left in his possession. As the young corporal dictated his letter to me, I heard the pain in his voice — a pain far deeper than that of his injuries — as he apologized to his parents for being unable to fulfill his filial duty and care for them. He felt guilty that he was dying and leaving them alone. Though he did not say so in his letter, he felt that his death would result in the eventual starvation of his parents, as they had no means with which to support themselves.

After the letter was finished, the young corporal thanked me and eagerly accepted the morphine. As the numbness flooded his body, he smiled at me.

"Thank you, Zhaohua. It is my hope that our country lives up to your name."

The corporal was dead the following morning.

It was, at this point in my life, my most personal experience with extreme poverty — wrapped in the helplessness of death — and it was to have a lasting effect.

We often walked home, late in the evenings, with other volunteers and medical students. Occasionally we shared stories of our day, but mostly our walks were shrouded in silence. Words — then, or now — cannot convey the experience of sitting next to a man who is dying. Though I had never met these soldiers, they were no longer strangers. I revered them and felt an indescribable sense of gratitude, both patriotic and personal, for their sacrifice.

The 19th Route Army, the unit to which the wounded soldiers belonged, kept the Japanese from taking Shanghai that spring. Naturally, they became the heroes of Shanghai and won the support of the citizens. As they were a wing of the Nationalist party who openly opposed Chiang's policies of non-resistance with the Japanese, Chiang's sinking popularity plummeted. When Chiang signed a peace agreement with the Japanese, many in Shanghai were outraged.

Following the signing of the peace agreement with the Japanese, Chiang promptly ordered the 19th Route Army to Fujian — from there they were to travel on to Jiangxi, to eliminate the Communist capital in Yanan. Chiang thought this policy would result in a double victory — one set of his enemies would eliminate another set of his enemies, while his best-equipped armies remained by his side, intact. Apparently, he did not consider the hearts and minds — and tears — of the people witnessing his actions. Nor did Chiang consider the strength and bravery and patriotism of the 19th Route Army.

The 19th Route Army refused to go. They did not want Chinese to kill Chinese. They wanted to kill the invaders — the Japanese.

In response Chiang sent one of his best-equipped armies to Fujian to eliminate the 19th Route Army — the heroes of Shanghai. In Chinese history, this is called the "Fujian Rebellion."

This proved to be yet another grave mistake of Chiang Kai-shek.

I was not alone in my intense mourning for these men. Even as I cried, I was aware that tears, like words, were inadequate in their ability to convey the depth of my anger and grief. I suppose, if I am to be truthful, that Chiang Kai-shek, who would lead China for many more years, lost my support the day I heard the news of his slaughter of the men whom I had embraced as heroes — who had fought the glorious war against the Japanese in 1932.

——— ——— ———

War has a way of uniting people. Soon after the peace agreement had been signed, and our brave soldiers mourned, social activities in Shanghai resumed, though tinged with a somber air. I was entering the political and social scene of Shanghai by virtue of my activities and connections at McTyeire School. Though the social engagements in Shanghai had become completely Western in format, Chinese families held on to the idea that charming and attractive young girls should complement the guest list — and be seated next to guests of honor. It followed the Eastern ideology that the ultimate pleasure of successful men was to be surrounded by charming and talented young women. My stage debuts, along with my standing in my class, resulted in such invitations.

Thus I was invited to a spring dinner party at the home of Tan Haiqiu, whose daughter, Emily, had also attended McTyeire; Emily and I had become quite close during our time spent volunteering in the hospital. Mr Tan was a department store magnate who had seized the opportunities presented by the wave of Western investment flooding Shanghai over the past ten years and he had made quite a fortune. As my driver approached the Tan mansion, I felt I was being carried to Cinderella's castle.

The Tan home was situated in an exclusive suburb of the International Settlement, where the homes had rolling lawns and gardens. A red wrought-iron gate surrounded the property in a futile attempt to contain the gardens from spilling onto the tree-lined sidewalks. The gates opened as we approached, and the winding, unpaved drive led us through this enchanting oasis. As I was driven past the layers of roses, geraniums, and peonies — all seemingly growing wild and in perfect harmony with the shade trees and thick green leaves of towering camellias, I was struck by the magical richness of the setting.

The Tans had aptly named their home "The House of Autumn Garden." As I took a deep breath, although it was spring, the light scents of the garden indeed seemed crisp with the freshness of autumn. Yes, that drive was a pure delight to the senses. And then we reached the home — an elegant white French colonial mansion, fronted by four smooth white columns. Though the house was massive in size, it did not overpower the landscape. Indeed, the ivy climbing the walls and framing the windows of the house gave the impression that the garden was claiming the house as one of its own.

"Zhaohua, we are so pleased that you could accept our invitation; please come in; make yourself at home," Mr Tan greeted me as though our families were old friends.

"I am honored to be invited, Mr Tan. Thank you." I had chosen a simple black, knee-length dress for the occasion. My only jewelry was a pair of pearl earrings; a gift from Jade for my fifteenth birthday.

"I am glad that you could arrive early to spend some time with Emily before the other guests arrive. Shall we show you around? Make yourself at home, Miss Ching."

Mr Tan was the consummate host. He made me feel as though I were the guest of honor as he led me through their exquisite home. The rooms were breathtaking. The sitting-room was elegantly furnished with English antiques. The walls were painted in pale yellow and the room was filled — but not overly so, with clean lined furnishings of rich cherry. The paintings were original oils of English landscapes, and seemed to have been painted specifically for their places on those walls. The upholstered pieces were done in the same creamy linen as the draperies. It was subtle elegance, gently overpowered by the four sets of towering French doors along the outer wall. These doors, whether opened or closed, seemed to extend the room onto the marble terrace and into the garden. And the garden — if possible, was even more lovely than the drive. Sprays of butterfly bushes and lantana, in full bloom and in varying shades of yellow, had been planted around the terrace — or rather, the terrace seemed to have been built next to the plants — and the butterflies seemed only slightly annoyed that we should intrude on their terrace. When I noted as much to Mr Tan, he laughed and agreed.

The rest of the house was an extension of the elegance. One room done in French — every furnishing and texture, imported from Paris. One in traditional Chinese. One in Spanish. Every detail was brought superbly to that point of quiet extravagance, without being overdone. Of course, there was a guestroom done in contemporary American.

"You will be seated next to T. V. Soong, China's Minister of Finance, this evening. I hope you will find the evening most pleasurable, Miss Ching." Mr Tan smiled warmly. His wife had joined us as we returned to the dining-room to greet arriving guests. She stood quietly by her husband's side, and was a most gracious hostess.

The guests began to arrive as the cacophony of honking cars filled the air. I was standing near Mr and Mrs Tan, absorbing everything — my eyes wide open.

A pleasurable evening indeed. Dr Sun Fo, the only son of the late Dr Sun Yat-sen, was one of the guests of honor. Dr Sun Fo was well respected by all Nationalist officials, and was one of the most sought-after dinner guests in all Shanghai. As Dr Sun entered, and we were introduced, I held my breath. The son of the Father of the Republic of China. I braced myself to meet a man of power. Yet, Dr Sun was not much taller than me, and with his round face and thick-rimmed glasses, seemed positively jolly as he greeted me.

Right behind Dr Sun was a stocky man of medium height, in a well-tailored dark suit, also wearing a pair of round spectacles. This was T. V. Soong, a noted financier, and China's Minister of Finance who had managed to turn around China's chaotic economy. He was one of the best educated and most efficient officials in the Nationalist government. He was also the brother-in-law of both Chiang Kai-shek and the late Dr Sun Yat-sen. These gentlemen had each married one of Soong's sisters. In fact, that period in China's political history is sometimes referred to as the Soong Dynasty.

Of course, there were many other guests as well. Two large tables were elegantly set for the evening; I took my place next to Minister Soong, the guest of honor at the second table, and tried to conceal my awe. I felt comfortable and confident as a young woman appearing at that dinner party. Conversation and laughter filled the house. Glasses in hand, everyone was in high spirits as uniformed waiters presented dish after dish of delicious food.

Minister Soong broke the ice, "Miss Ching, my three sisters were all McTyeire graduates before going to college in the United States, how do you like the school?"

"I like it very much, Minister Soong. I find McTyeire to be liberal and open-minded, compared to what I know of other schools for girls, while not abandoning instruction in etiquette, which I think is important for young girls, trying to get along in modern society. I also think McTyeire does a fine job of preparing young ladies to pursue a university education. The curriculum is most challenging. And the emphasis they place on creativity and self-expression is invaluable."

"Thank you for this information, Miss Ching," said Minister Soong, smiling, "that must be why McTyeire girls are so unique in China. I can tell already that you are a remarkable young lady. A toast, shall we? To McTyeire!" And Minister Soong's glass was met by everyone at our table.

Soon toasts were flying around the room and champagne was flowing freely. Of course the younger guests ordered only soda, but the festive spirit was contagious. The party was becoming quite lively when two White Russian musicians started playing dance music.

"May I have the first dance with you, Miss Ching?" The Minister bowed slightly and offered his hand.

"Minister Soong, I am honored. But I'm afraid my experience is limited."

"Then you are about to gain more experience, Miss Ching!" And Minister Soong led me to the dance floor. He was experienced at dancing; at leading young ladies through uncertain territories, quite obviously. I was able to follow his lead quite naturally and thought I must remember to tell Jade that Minister Soong is a much better leader on the dance floor than she!

I was sixteen years old, and dancing the night away with the Minister of Finance of China. Of course, I was caught up in the magnitude of the evening. And when Minister Soong said goodbye to Mr Tan, with me standing by his side, it did not feel appropriate to object more than once when he told our host that his driver would drop me at home.

"Tell me about your school, Zhaohua," the Minister seemed genuinely interested as we sat in the back of his bulletproof limousine, driven by the chauffeur, and accompanied by his security guard. So I told him stories of my life at McTyeire. We spoke of my friends, and studies, and future plans.

"You are a good student, aren't you, Zhaohua?"

"I work very hard. I plan to attend university in the United States. My teachers say that I have a mind for numbers and business. I think I could do well in America." I was aware that my tone was confident and hoped I did not lose all humility.

"I'm certain you could do well wherever you end up, Zhaohua."

"Minister Soong, I am going to America."

"I have no doubt, Zhaohua." Minister Soong smiled and I had the distinct feeling that we had become friends. "So what do McTyeire girls think of China's current political challenges; I suspect that you are informed on such matters."

"Oh yes, we have many political discussions. I hear much of your reputation, Minister Soong. The people say that you are an excellent Minister of Finance — a real genius at figures and management. People have confidence in the economy as long as you are at the helm."

"And what else do the people say, Miss Ching?" Minister Soong was obviously enjoying this glimpse of himself, as seen by young citizens.

I felt completely comfortable and somewhat emboldened by this level of comfort. "Well, they talk about your first love in China, Minister Soong. Susanne Zhang. They say she was very beautiful; the third daughter of Zhang Jing-jiang, the close friend of Dr Sun Yat-sen, who helped initiate and finance the revolution. They say you loved her completely and were to marry her. But then she left suddenly and married a young actor. They say you were heartbroken and married your current wife, Laura Zhang, because she had the same surname as Susanne. Is that true, Minister?"

"I suppose it is partly true, Zhaohua. But marriage is never quite that simple. You will learn that in time." The Minister put his raincoat around my shoulders as I shivered inside the car. He told me how he had been wearing that same raincoat a few months back when there had been an assassination attempt on his life. His secretary had been killed in the attempt. And as he spoke, the driver took us through the loveliest streets of Shanghai. The moon was full and the sky was clear, and the roads of Shanghai were ribbons of light.

As we neared my mother's neighborhood, I reluctantly called out my address to the driver.

"Zhaohua, I have never met such a charming young lady. I would like to see you again when I am in Shanghai. It seems we have become friends in this brief evening together. May I call you when I return, Miss Ching?"

"It would be my pleasure; thank you, Minister Soong." I tried to hide my awed confusion.

"Good night, Miss Ching." He bowed his head as the driver opened my door.

"Good night, Minister," I said, as I walked from the limousine and up my mother's front steps. I decided to simply relish the evening. I did not dream there would be more such evenings. And other heroes.

No, Minister Soong, marriage is never simple, and I suppose I did not have a good impression of marriage at this point in my life. Although I knew that our goals were different, I was surprised — and saddened — when my friend Nancy told me that she would be leaving McTyeire. I knew the reason without asking.

"You're going to be married, aren't you, Nancy?" Nancy had that quiet, dignified beauty. She was naturally mature and seemed to have an intrinsic composure and grace. The boys, both young and old, had found her most alluring and her social calendar was always full. I knew that she had strong feelings for one in particular, George, but I had seen George with other girls as well.

"Yes, Zhaohua. I love McTyeire, you and Janet, but I am not like you. You will go on — you will graduate. You will make it to your Western university. But that is not my dream. I am a daughter of Old China, and I wish to remain here. It is my dream — a wonderful opportunity to have a family and care for them — and George."

"Are you certain, Nancy, that George is right for you?" I tried to keep my tone cheerful, but my friend knew me too well.

"Yes, you do not approve?" My friend looked into my eyes and I tried to conjure enthusiasm. But I was so saddened that she would be leaving us, and I suppose we always think that our own life choices would be the best choice for everyone. And I felt my friend was passing up on so many opportunities, at such a young age. And no, I did not approve.

"George, well, he seems much older than you, Nancy. And he is always flirting. What makes you think he will change?" My words were colored by Aunt Liming's characterization of my father, of whom George reminded me so much. I did not wish to see my friend end up as unhappily as my mother. I was also selfish — I did not want Nancy to leave McTyeire.

Nancy averted her eyes and I could see the muscles of her jaw tense as she tried to hold in the tears. I immediately wished to retrieve my words.

"Oh Nancy. I am sorry …"

"What do you know? You are still young, Zhaohua. George is charming and he makes me laugh, and he is a good son. He is so handsome; I would be a fool to pass up his proposal!"

Nancy and I had never argued, and her anger cut me very deeply. I knew I had overstepped that fine boundary of friendship. The line at which you care and you love, but you let your friend lead her own life.

"Oh, Nancy. You are absolutely right. I do not know — I am so sorry.

Yes, of course, I am happy for you. Of course, you and George will find much happiness. I was selfish — I did not want you to leave."

I held my breath as Nancy continued to keep her eyes on the ground. I was not sure that she would forgive me.

"I have one question for you, Zhaohua." Nancy still did not look at me and I was certain that my callous words had cost me my best friend. "Would you, would you serve as my maid of honor, Zhaohua?"

I caught my breath and tears came to my eyes. "Of course, Nancy. Of course." We embraced as friends embrace — friends who know the value of friendship.

Nancy's summer wedding was grand. It was a Western — Christian — wedding, as had become the way for McTyeire girls at the time. As I walked slowly down the aisle at the Community Church on Rue Petain in the French Concession, the sun seemed to enchant that crisp summer day, just for the beautiful bride.

Nancy was a vision of elegance as she entered on the arm of her uncle, T. K. Tseng. He was the Deputy Minister of Railways and the Special Envoy to the United Kingdom at the time, so the cathedral was filled with Shanghai's most distinguished dignitaries. Yes, it was exhilarating to be part of such a grand affair — and I, like any young girl, was caught up in the lace and the flowers and the sunlight on the flowing gowns. Yet, I knew, even then, that such a wedding was not for me. That my life would be different. It was my destiny. I was also happy for my friend, who was living her dream.

I had finished school that spring with the ambition of a young girl who is driven. I no longer resembled the unwanted child of the past. I had taken the lead in my family. My grades were stronger than both Wanhua's and Kaihua's. My debut in the social circles of Shanghai had been a mounting success. I had proven myself and knew that nothing was out of reach.

I also continued to spend several afternoons a week with Sonya; she relied on me heavily both as a tutor and a friend.

To my surprise, Minister Soong did indeed call. During the summer when he returned to Shanghai, his aide invited me to dinner with the Minister. As I hung up the telephone, panic struck. I could not have dinner with the Minister unchaperoned, and yet I could not refuse. My mind raced; and then Sonya called. I was most impressed with myself — and a little worried — as I asked Sonya if she had plans for the evening … .

"You are to have dinner with whom?" Sonya gasped when I relayed the invitation.

"Yes, Minister Soong — and it is a perfect opportunity for you to use all your newly acquired skills, Sonya! Put on your plain, blue silk dress and be here in an hour. His driver is to pick us up at six."

I dressed quickly in a black lace dress with matching shoes and handbag — a pair of pearl earrings and necklace. When Sonya arrived, we rehearsed everything, from appropriate tones of voice, to small smiles, and salad forks. I hardly recognized her as she nodded to the limousine driver and sat so calmly — and quietly — on our way to dinner at the home of Minister Soong's personal friend — Mr Tang Hai-an.

"Zhaohua. You are even lovelier than I recall. You have been in my thoughts. I have inquired, and learned that you did quite well in your classes this year. Congratulations." Minister Soong smiled with the ease of old friends. I immediately sensed that his intentions were possibly more than friendship, as we greeted one another in Mr Tang's sitting-room. When Sonya appeared behind me, Minister Soong's surprise was barely noticeable.

"Yes, Minister. The semester was challenging, but I finished in good standing." I returned his smile, but tried to lessen the intimate feeling of the evening. "By the way, I wish to introduce my friend and student, Sonya. Of course I knew you would not expect me to come to dinner without a chaperone. My mother would never have allowed it." Sonya smiled and nodded as she bowed her head slightly in a gesture of greeting. I was so proud of her.

"Of course not. Welcome, Sonya. Please, ladies, sit down; make yourselves comfortable," the host said.

Mr Tang's staff served a lovely Western dinner. Sonya continued with her recently acquired social graces and the dinner was a great success. Afterward, Mr Tang invited Sonya to go for a drive — it was a lovely evening. Sonya looked to me and I nodded hesitantly. She was obviously anxious to go; the stress and confinement of the dinner had left her restless.

As they left, Minister Soong noted my hesitation.

"You are not concerned about being left alone, are you, Zhaohua?"

"Of course not, Minister," it was obviously a lie, but Minister Soong was adept at charm.

"Relax, Zhaohua. I think of you as a daughter. An intelligent daughter. In fact, I would be honored to have you as a member of my family, Zhaohua." He was obviously trying to lighten the mood, and ease my discomfort.

"But I am told you have three daughters already, Minister Soong. You don't need another." I, too was trying to lighten the tension, while not offending my host.

"Ahh, but a father may kiss a daughter. Do you mind?" As he stepped closer to me, I could feel his breath on my neck. It was exhilarating, to be wanted by such a famous man. But I knew, in that moment, that I did not wish to start a romance with Minister Soong.

"Ahhh, Minister Soong. You forget. I come from a very conservative family. My father has never kissed me, and I'm afraid I would find it most uncomfortable if he were to start now!" I laughed, and took a step back from the Minister, continuing the charade of a light mood in the room. And I waited, nervously, for Soong's reaction.

To my relief, he simply stepped back and smiled at me. He smiled for a long time before he spoke.

"Oh, Zhaohua. I did not underestimate you. You are wise. You will not be the second wife of any man in China, will you? No. You will attain your dreams. Very well then. I shall be your friend. And when you are successful in the United States, we can have dinner there, and laugh — and talk — like father and daughter, and perhaps old friends, how is that, dear?"

"Thank you, Minister Soong. You are indeed an honorable man. Can you tell me about the West, Minister?"

Minister Soong described his years at Harvard, where he had earned his master's degree in finance. He spoke of how much he loved the intellectual freedom in the West. "They are not bound by traditions, Zhaohua. Some of the students grumbled that their fathers expected them to follow in their professions, but it is not like China. Young people are free there, Zhaohua. It is both a liberating feeling and also a feeling of sadness. They do not have the respect that we have for our ancestors. In the end, I was drawn back to my China, but with new eyes. Many of our traditions have come to an end, Zhaohua. But many will continue — some are good. But I will encourage my daughters to study in the United States. And you should go too, my young friend. There are more opportunities for young women in their country. Their women find the restrictions placed on the women of China fascinating. I will help you when you are ready to apply to the universities, Zhaohua. I have many connections in the United States and would be honored to write you a letter of recommendation." And Minister Soong smiled kindly at me. The tension was gone. The friendship remained.

———   ———   ———

It was that same, magical summer, that I returned home to Mother's one evening to find a message from Father. When I telephoned him, he informed me that he had accepted an invitation on my behalf. Liankui Ching had chosen me to be the maid of honor at his daughter's wedding. The wedding was to take place in August, just after classes resumed. It would involve a three-week trip to Hangzhou. Accommodations would be first-class, and the weeks would be filled with celebrations. I was also to perform my Kunqu opera pieces at the celebrations. Father and Jade would be going as well. My heart sank, and my determination rose.

I informed Father that I would fall behind if I missed that much school. I apologized, but must regretfully decline Lawyer Ching's gracious invitation.

Father said that was not possible. He would lose face. The arrangements were made. There would be no further discussion. He would expect me to go shopping with Jade in the upcoming weeks to prepare for the trip. The matter was settled.

As I hung up the phone, I thought of all the women in my life: Mother, Madame Sheng, Jade. They were all dependent on men. McTyeire was expensive. It was also my ticket to an American university — my ticket to independence. I could not, even if I had the strength, defy him. Not in China. Not in 1932. I walked to my bedroom with a stronger resolve than ever to succeed in my studies, while also beginning to rehearse for my performance at the wedding of Liankui Ching's daughter.

So glad that I was the maid of honor. And not the bride.

13

The following week, I returned to Father's house. I began preparations to perform at the wedding of Liankui Ching's oldest daughter. Perform my Kunqu opera piece — and perform as maid of honor to a young bride, whom I had never met.

"I know you are upset about missing school, Zhaohua. Don't worry, you will be able to catch up on the work. I will help in any way I can." Jade was the only one who understood my distress over my studies. She tried to console me as we assembled our new wardrobe for the trip.

"This is my most difficult year, Jade. Many girls are dismissed during this year from McTyeire. The curriculum is difficult; there are many books to prepare. Missing three weeks will be hard to overcome."

"I know, Zhaohua. I am sorry. But your father is adamant that you accept the invitation. He is proud of the young woman you've become, Zhaohua."

"He is proud of the performer. And the beautiful daughter. He does not even know the young woman I've become, Jade. He has no idea how important my university plans are to me. He is only concerned with impressing his friend, Liankui Ching."

"You can do it, Zhaohua. You can catch up in school. You can keep your standing in the class." Jade held my chin in her hands and looked into my eyes and smiled. My fears evaporated. She was right. It would take many hours of hard work, but I could do it.

"Thank you, Jade. Thank you so much."

It was with real sadness that I said goodbye to Sonya, when we left for Hangzhou. Of course, she would not be accompanying us. She would stay with Mrs Wang. When we returned from the Ching wedding, I would be immersed in school. My own studies would leave little time for tutoring Sonya once I was back at McTyeire. It's interesting, how we plan our tomorrows, and think they will actually happen according to the plans.

There is a Chinese proverb: 'Above there is Heaven, below there are Suzhou and Hangzhou.' As our train stopped in the city of Hangzhou, my anger at missing school was temporarily forgotten. I was certain that I had entered the most enchanting place in the world.

Spring in Hangzhou is often compared to summers in Switzerland. The city is surrounded by lush, rich mountains and low, moist valleys. The mountains seem to be guarding the secret crown of the valley, West Lake. Spanning West Lake are a pair of graceful stone bridges. The bridges carry the names of two of China's most celebrated poets, Bai Juyi, of the Tang dynasty, and Su Dongbo, of the Song dynasty. Narrow gardens line the sides of these bridges of the poets. From these gardens, and seemingly suspended over the lake, grow willows and peach trees. I thought, as I was driven across this enchanting lake, that the poets had indeed left some of their magic there. Or perhaps they had just found the magic in this special place, and transformed it into their beautiful verses.

We were among the first — of the hundreds of guests — to arrive for the wedding, and Liankui Ching received us as though we were his closest friends. There were so many celebrations. Because of the large number of guests, the celebrations were divided into smaller intimate parties, with the bride, the groom, and their families, alternating appearances at the different parties. But we were always with the bride's family. Liankui Ching had arranged every detail.

West Lake seemed to extend, and disappear, into secret crevices between the mountains surrounding it. 'Uncle Liankui,' as he insisted I call him, heard me wondering aloud about the rest of the lake, so he hired a boat to take us on a tour. Father, Jade, Uncle Liankui, and I spent an enchanting day exploring the ancient Buddhist temples hidden from view on the main part of the lake. There were secluded summer homes where China's wealthiest families spent their vacations. Our guide told us of the ancient legends. As we entered one cove, the water turned exceptionally black and dark. I felt a chill and noticed that the temperature seemed to drop a few degrees. And hidden in a thick grove of trees was an old pagoda.

"This is the Pagoda of Thunderous Mountain," our guide's voice took on an edge as we urged him to go further into the cove. "This cove was the home of two female snakes. They guarded the cove, and the families who lived here, from outsiders for thousands of years. Then a young scholar moved into the valley. The snakes were so drawn to his knowledge that they magically transformed themselves into two women — an enchantingly beautiful lady and her maid. The beautiful lady seduced the handsome scholar and they were soon married. But their marriage brought on a great flood, which destroyed the entire valley. The only survivors were rescued from the flood by a monk, who lived in a monastery on the other side of the mountain. It is said that he recognized the two women as evil the minute he saw them. His goodness subdued the women and transformed them back into snakes. He then buried the snakes and built this pagoda on top of their graves to guard the valley from them."

Jade and I were intrigued. We wanted to explore the pagoda and the hill behind it. The hill was alive with unusual flowers. But Father and Liankui thought it best that we return to the hotel. Of course, we did.

The wedding was beautiful. The event of a lifetime. I decided that if I ever did choose to marry, I would like to be married in Hangzhou, and while I was there I would explore the Pagoda of Thunderous Mountain.

When the celebrations were over I felt that I had hardly gotten to know the bride, Jiaxiu, for whom I had served as maid of honor. But I had made real friends in Liankui's two younger daughters, Margaret and Alice.

Margaret, at fourteen, was just a little younger than me, and with her large eyes and fair skin, was a most enchanting girl. Father said she looked exactly like Liankui's wife who had died when the youngest child was born. Alice, on the other hand, was so like her father. Elegant and eloquent, even as a young child. At the age of nine, however, she had also inherited her father's habit of blinking nervously.

Jiaxiu, Margaret, Alice, and the three boys, were all so different in personality and temperament, and yet they all shared that striking bone structure, that same aristocratic look which they had inherited from their father. They were a handsome family, indeed.

As we were boarding the train to return to Shanghai, I felt a new bond with this family. The Chings were very distant relatives, it was true, but I somehow felt that the past three weeks had bridged the space of the generations. When Liankui Ching suggested to my father that I come to his home on a weekly basis to tutor his daughter Margaret in English, I did not feel the danger in those words.

"I would be honored, Uncle Liankui. Of course, it would be wonderful to spend some time with Margaret. But it will take me a few weeks to catch up on the work that I have missed. Perhaps after the Christmas holiday, we could begin?" I covered my mouth as that nagging cough returned. It had been growing gradually worse over the past couple of days in Hangzhou.

"I am reluctant to put off the lessons for that long, Zhaohua. Margaret knows so little English; she could benefit so much from your help. I believe that you will catch up on your work quickly. We will work on the arrangements when we are home and settled, okay?" Liankui dismissed me and turned to my father as I boarded the train where I ordered some tea with lemon for my cough.

By the time we arrived in Shanghai, my temperature had risen to 104 degrees. Jade tried her best to make me comfortable. She kept me at their home as the influenza, and then the pneumonia consumed my body. For three weeks, I slipped in and out of feverish consciousness. I ate nothing except occasional bowls of white rice soup and cups of broth. Jade fed me and wiped my face with cool cloths and changed my bed linens. Sonya brought me flowers.

In my feverish sleep, I dreamt over and over that I visited the Pagoda of Thunderous Mountain — it was so beautiful inside. I could not stay away. And while there I sometimes had tea with Grandfather and Auntie Sheng. They said that they were peaceful and that, of course, the snakes had fallen in love with the knowledgeable scholar. And that knowledge is rarely an easy thing. But neither is it evil.

When we are weak — and in need — that is when we see clearly those who care. Bonds are formed — or not — in the midst of weakness.

Jade stayed by my side throughout the illness. Janet, Nancy and Emily, phoned daily, and sent notes and cards. A few of the young men I had met at dinner parties phoned. One in particular, Yung Silang, who had attended some of the parties at Emily's house, sent some wonderful books to help me pass the time during my recuperation. It was touching; I barely remembered meeting Yung, and yet the books he chose were some of my favorites — Pride and Prejudice and David Copperfield. It is most interesting. These were friends with whom I had laughed and somewhat taken for granted in my carefree days at McTyeire. Their compassion during my illness helped to seal lifelong friendships.

Of course, Uncle Liankui telephoned and sent flowers regularly.

Despite the doctor's predictions, I survived the pneumonia. I had known that I would. Grandfather had told me so. In the dreams. But, as the fevers subsided, I was faced with the fact that I had missed almost two months of classes. It would be impossible for me to catch up now.

My days at McTyeire were over, and I grieved the loss of those days.

With Jade's help, I said goodbye to my days at McTyeire, and faced my only option. Shanghai had many universities which 'sold' degrees; if you paid the tuition and showed up, you could walk away with a diploma. It would not be as challenging or as prestigious as a degree from McTyeire, but I reasoned that once I applied to transfer to an American university, with the recommendations of Minister Soong and perhaps others, and my previous record at McTyeire, I could still make it.

But the other universities were expensive. Father had already paid my tuition at McTyeire, and he was certain that I had reached a position from which I could marry well. In his opinion, there was really no need to pursue more studies. I was angered and certain that Father was not capable of understanding how important my degree was to me. During my illness, I had not seen how troubled he had been. Jade tried to soften my anger toward my Father, but she did not tell me of his looming financial problems. Jade was noble.

It was Liankui Ching who helped me then.

"I insist, Zhaohua. Had you not come to Hangzhou, you would not have become ill. You would be at McTyeire right now. Besides, if you are going to tutor Margaret in English, you must continue learning yourself. I will be most offended if you do not allow me to take care of the expenses of your new school," Uncle Liankui began writing the check before I spoke.

"But, Uncle Liankui, it does not feel appropriate for you to pay my tuition. I could not … "

"Zhaohua," there was polite force in his voice, "there is nothing more to discuss. I will inform your father that you must continue your education if you are to help Margaret. I will pay you for your tutoring services. There is nothing inappropriate. Please register tomorrow." He handed me the check and turned to leave Jade's sitting-room. He had come specifically to discuss the tutoring plans for Margaret when he heard that I was recovering. He stopped at the front door and smiled, "Please begin Margaret's lessons on Saturday. Saturday morning. Perhaps we could have tea and discuss your university arrangements as well?" Uncle Liankui smiled and bowed and left.

I was young and ambitious. And I would have seized any opportunity to continue with my plans. The next day, I enrolled in classes at Zhengfeng College. They did not offer advanced English courses, so I also contacted a friend of a McTyeire teacher — Mrs Helen Lin. Mrs Lin had married Dr T. G. Lin, a renowned scientist in China and had moved to Shanghai. She was a charming and exuberant woman and she cheerfully agreed to be my English teacher. I reasoned that I would pay her with the money I received for tutoring Margaret. And when I established myself in America, I would reimburse Uncle Liankui for my university expenses. Yes, my plans to enter an American university with a McTyeire degree had changed. But I had pulled myself together and gotten back on track. Jade was most impressed when I told her of the arrangements I had made, although she pondered the motives of Liankui Ching in paying my tuition. It was one of the few times I did not heed Jade's soft and subtle guidance. I was stubbornly committed to completing my education and saw the check from Liankui Ching as my only way to do so.

Jade smiled and said that money always comes with tiny little strings. Like marionettes. Sometimes we have to look closely to see them. But the strings are always there. She said she admired the courtesans and the concubines and the geisha because they acknowledged, openly, this reality of life. And I said that Uncle Liankui was family and my plans were made.

Of course, falling in love that fall was not part of my plans.

14

It was another party at the Tan's.

The house had been enchanting in the spring, but in the fall, the 'House of Autumn Garden' embraced its name. The hardwoods srrounding the home were vibrant in their fall color. There was a slight crispness in the air. An energy.

I saw him the minute he entered the room. We were in the English room — with fine lines and creamy linen fabric. I was speaking with Emily and Janet. And Colonel Zhang, Commander of the Chinese Air Force, arrived.

It seemed as though everyone had been awaiting his arrival. All heads turned toward this handsome, soft man. Everything about him seemed gentle: his walk, the way he moved his hands, even his voice. It did not seem possible that this soft man was indeed a war hero of the Guangdong wing of the Nationalist party — the wing opposed to Chiang Kai-shek.

The room was full of Guangdong Nationalists. The guest of honor was Chen Mingqu, the Communications Minister. There was also General Zhang Fakui, the 'Iron General.' He had been the instrumental general in Chiang Kai-shek's Northern Expedition victory. Admiral Chen Ce, head of the Navy, was also there.

The political picture was staggering; bodyguards were everywhere. The beautiful garden was filled with armed lookouts. They looked oddly out of place in the tranquil setting. I should have been overwhelmed by the historical and political relevance of the evening. But all I saw was Colonel Zhang.

I assumed a graceful posture, and waited. I smiled as I was introduced to Minister Chen, a serious, reserved man. I laughed at Admiral Chen's wit and humor. As I was introduced to him — to Colonel Zhang, the band slid into *Nevertheless*.

"Fortune is mine. I am introduced to the most beautiful lady — in this enchanting setting — just as the band begins my favorite song."

Colonel Zhang made a slight bow as he held out his hand to me. "May I have this dance, Miss Ching?"

As I started to accept, Admiral Chen interrupted with his humorous air, "Colonel, this is no mere Miss Ching; her surname carries the same character as the First Emperor Ching. The same Emporer Ching who built the Great Wall. Colonel, you have just asked an Empress to dance. 'Empress Ching'." They both laughed as my colonel deepened his bow.

"Ahem. Excuse me. Empress Ching, would you do me the great honor of dancing with me, to my favorite song?" Colonel Zhang's eyes met mine.

I played into the humor, and assumed the air of an empress, as I nodded and accepted. When Colonel Zhang held me in his arms, I felt my own blood under my skin where he touched me. I could feel that same blood as it traveled throughout my body.

We ate. We danced. We talked. And we danced again. He requested the band play *Nevertheless* again. Then again. I was under the spell of the music, this man, and the autumn air. Each contained an element of magic. When he suggested that we leave for a cold drink somewhere, I readily agreed. I said goodbye to the Tans, and left with Colonel Zhang.

The Chocolate Shop on Nanjing Road was full of people enjoying late-night snacks and drinks. Colonel Zhang and I were seated at a corner table. We chatted comfortably. Then we were silent comfortably. A quiet understanding grew.

My colonel took a deep breath and said, "I'm thirty-three years old. And married. My wife is visiting our two children who are in school in the United States." We both knew what he had really said. There would not be a life for us. It was our hello and the beginning of our goodbye. "Tell me about you, Zhaohua."

"Well, I'm sixteen; I went to McTyeire with Mr Tan's daughters. My father is a businessman. He lives with his concubine, Jade Wang; I am sometimes with them, though lately, I have been spending most of my time with my mother and younger sister." It felt like such a hollow sketch of my life.

"I see," that was all he said. Yet I felt that he did see. He saw everything about me.

"Shall we go for a drive before I take you home?" We both knew I would say yes.

As we drove, Shanghai was magical, and we did not need to speak. This was not the flattery I had felt at being pursued by Minister Soong. It was not the giddy feeling I had felt when Yung Silang, and other young boys, smiled shyly at me. This was my first taste of mature love. As Colonel

Zhang pulled up and parked in front of my mother's house, he held me in his arms for several minutes. "Zhaohua, I have never felt so comfortable with a woman before, so completely — and passionately — at ease."

After that evening, I did not see my colonel for two weeks. Then one day, I emerged from Mrs Lin's home following my English lesson, and he was there, waiting, on the sidewalk.

"Empress Ching," he affected an air of great humility as he bowed before me, "I have thought of you so often. I must see you again. Will you do me the honor of dining with me this evening? Shall I pick you up at six?"

"I shall do you the honor." I smiled as I assumed my own air of mock benevolence, as though I was indeed an empress. And I completely forgot that I was scheduled to tutor Margaret later that day.

We dined in a fashionable restaurant on Avenue Joffre, where White Russian waitresses wore their red and black national costumes with matching hats. The glow of the candlelight, the aroma of the fresh flowers, and the soft music combined to create an appropriately enchanting mood. Again, there was no tension. No need for idle talk. We were friends, and more.

After dinner, we went for a drive. *Nevertheless* was on the radio. It was a magnificent, clear evening. Aimlessly, we drove on until he asked my permission to park in a quiet street, near the end of Great Western Road. Of course, I said yes.

Without the towering buildings of the city, the countryside offered a clear view of the stars, which seemed to be gently floating on the soft breeze. Colonel Zhang took me gently in his arms and gave me a pleasant lesson in astronomy. I became absorbed in the names of the stars, asking question after question. And when Colonel Zhang interrupted our lesson and gently kissed me, I did not object. My first kiss. It was the kiss of a gentle, charismatic man. And it was most beautiful.

"It's late for you little girl," Zhang whispered. "I will drive you home."

I often think that perhaps my life might have been simpler and easier, had I not tasted that passion with my colonel. Perhaps I would not have expected so much.

Yet, I think there are those who could not live without an element of passion in their lives. I was meant for intensity. I had always been drawn to it. Jade, without her Nien, found passion in her art. Mother had no passion, and withered away before my eyes. But it takes great courage to seize the zest in life. To this day, I do not know if my mother was noble in her life, or a coward.

Yes, I know. We are neither always noble, nor always cowards.

——— —— ——

"Where were you yesterday?" It was Margaret's voice on the phone. I had slept late that morning, dozing and waking to dreamily relive the magic of the previous evening with my colonel.

"Oh, Margaret, good morning. I am sorry. I was not feeling well. I apologize; I should have called," I felt intuitively that it would be best to keep my romance a secret from Margaret.

"Father is very upset. He says you must come today."

"But, I cannot. It is Sunday and I have made plans. Mother is not feeling well ..." This much was true. Mother had been to the doctor and seemed most distraught. I had suggested that we go out to lunch in an effort to cheer her.

"He says you must come tomorrow then. Absolutely."

"Of course, Margaret. Please offer my apologies to your father." As I hung up the phone, my body shuddered. I could see Uncle Liankui standing beside Margaret, blinking nervously and smoking as he paced. And I was afraid.

The following day, I showed up early for my lesson with Margaret.

"I must speak with you, Zhaohua," Uncle Liankui interrupted our lesson just as we were beginning. Margaret got up from the table and left without a word.

"I was very disappointed when you did not show up on Saturday."

"My apologies, Uncle Liankui. I explained to Margaret that I was not well. And I had plans with Mother yesterday."

"Yes. That is what you said," Liankui's eyes seemed to be blinking wildly as he stood over me at the table.

"Perhaps Margaret could learn more from Mrs Lin, Uncle Liankui. She is an excellent teacher and I am becoming very busy with my school work, and my mother is not well, and ..."

"Enough. No. We have an agreement. Margaret is learning very much from your lessons. And I wish to monitor your education. Your father is troubled lately. He is neglecting you. You have been very busy. Your social life, I think, is interfering with your studies." He was obviously trying to control his voice.

"My friends from McTyeire have stayed in touch, and still invite me to their parties. Yes, I have been busy, but my grades are fine. Zhengfeng is much easier than McTyeire. I will have my degree soon. And I will apply to a school in the United States. Perhaps get a scholarship," I was aware that I was speaking as though I was afraid of Uncle Liankui, and I could not reconcile that with the many kindnesses he had shown me.

"Then we must increase Margaret's lessons. Please come four times a week. She will need to learn much before you get your degree. And I think you should choose your company more carefully, Zhaohua. The Nationalist officials are simply new warlords, in disguise. Shanghai bows to them as heroes; they have no power. They do not understand. It is my duty to protect you." Uncle Liankui bowed to me and walked briskly out the room.

I was too stunned to speak. How did he know? I had felt that someone was watching me on my encounters with Colonel Zhang, but had dismissed it as nerves. My skin tingled as Liankui Ching left the room.

I suggested that Margaret and I meet at the library; they had books and newspapers in English, which would be helpful in our lessons. When Uncle Liankui heard the suggestion, he ordered English books and newspapers to be delivered to his home; he said that his resources were more current than those of the library. He said that he wished to work on his English as well, and would be sitting in on our lessons on occasion.

As Liankui Ching sensed my growing apprehension, he tightened his strings.

"Margaret, I wish to have a private lesson with Zhaohua today. I have some letters from some associates in England. Zhaohua could help me to translate." Margaret left before I could speak.

"Perhaps this would be a good exercise for Margaret to test her abilities — translating your letters. Don't you agree, Uncle Liankui?"

Liankui looked at me, but did not speak for a while. I heard the front door close as Margaret left.

Liankui Ching chose his words carefully as he placed a Chinese book printed on thin rice paper and bound in thread on the table between us, "This is our Ching family genealogy, Zhaohua. It contains more than twenty-five generations starting with Ching Guan. Ching Guan was a poet and an official in the Song dynasty; your father and I are thirteen generations apart from the common ancestor. Though we bear the same family name, we don't actually have any blood relationship. Had our ancestors followed all maternal names instead of paternal ones, your father and I would not even be able to trace our relationship to one another. We would have just been strangers. Or friends. And you would not know me as Uncle Liankui, Zhaohua. You would know me differently." He moved closer to me and I felt it again. The instinct.

"That would be so sad, Uncle Liankui. My father thinks of you as family. And I have come to think of you as a dear uncle, indeed." My words agitated him. I had known they would. Still, he continued with his story.

"Zhaohua, Ching Guan was numbered seven of all his first cousins. I am number seven in my family — I am the reincarnation of Ching Guan. Do you understand what I am saying, Zhaohua?"

"I do not know the story of Ching Guan, Uncle Liankui." But I did. I knew the story so well, and I knew what Liankui Ching was about to say.

"Another Ching, Ching Kui, betrayed Emporer Song. Remember in Hangzhou? When I took you to the statue of Ching Kui? The statues of Ching Kui and his wife were caged and kneeling outside Yue Fei's tomb. Ching Guan had a beautiful concubine. The most beautiful woman in China, they say. She loved Ching Guan and wept for years when he was exiled. I have always sworn that when I found the reincarnation of my ancestor's concubine, I would make her mine. When I saw you on the stage three years ago, my lovely Zhaohua, I knew that I had found her."

"But Uncle Liankui I, I could never be a concubine." I clasped my hands in my lap, wishing to hide the tremors that were beginning to overtake my body.

"No, Zhaohua. Of course you could not. But I am free to marry you, Zhaohua, as a first wife." Liankui blinked wildly as he took my shoulders in his hands. His grip was so tight that my shoulders began to ache, yet I could tell that he was unaware that he was hurting me.

"Father would never approve, Uncle Liankui. We are, in the eyes of China, related. It would be disgraceful."

"I will speak to your father, Zhaohua. But I will marry you. It is our destiny." And suddenly Liankui released me and turned and left the room. I left without saying goodbye to Margaret.

Over the next two weeks, I phoned Margaret and said that I was sick and would not be able to keep our appointments. Colonel Zhang continued to call and take me for drives and dinners and moonlit evenings ending in passionate kisses. Mother grew worse in her illness and did not keep up with my outings. Father and Jade were traveling.

Liankui Ching was waiting. And I knew it.

During the following weeks, as I avoided calls from Margaret and Liankui, Mother continued to decline in spirit and health. Her doctor had told her that her heart was enlarging, and that her heart problems were affecting her kidneys. But Mother did not seem to care about anything. The very air around Mother felt heavy and weighted.

I arrived home one afternoon to hear her crying in her bedroom.

"Mother? Mother, what is it? Did you get more news from the doctor?" Of course, I was concerned for her, but I was also aware that I somehow found her display of weakness distasteful. It is endlessly fascinating; how much of our mothers are in us. Sometimes, especially, those pieces of our mothers we like least.

"No, Zhaohua. It is not my health. Please. Could you ... could you come in for a moment," Mother stared straight ahead; the tears streaming down her cheeks seemed to be separate from her being as though her eyes were crying, but she was not.

"Of course, Mother. What is it?"

"Zhaohua, I have disgraced our family."

"You are an honorable woman, Mother. I do not understand."

"You will, dear. Sit down, Zhaohua," and Mother took a deep breath. The tears quivered and clung to her chin before they dropped to her green silk robe. "I have been trying to run our household with little help from your father — he has lost his position and cannot continue to give me money on a monthly basis. He thought I could live on the money he had given me to put aside for Kaihua's education. He did not know that I had invested it — over the past few years, I have watched as many of my friends have made money in gold speculation."

"Gold speculation? Mother, why would you?"

"Please, let me finish, Zhaohua. I studied the market with a guru and learned much. I decided that I could do it. I thought I would make enough money to continue our household and have an extra profit besides. When Wall Street crashed in 1929, it led to the collapse in the price of gold. I thought I could wait it out — but no more. I have lost it. Everything. Over fifty thousand dollars, Zhaohua."

"Fifty thousand dollars, Mother? How could you have — "

"Wait, Zhaohua, there is more. Some of the money was not mine. In addition to the money your father had given me for Kaihua's educational expenses, your Aunt Liming had entrusted me with two thousand dollars. I had invested that as well. And now Aunt Liming is moving and has asked for her money." Mother's eyes did not continue to cry; she sat there looking straight ahead as though I were not even in the room. It was more disturbing than her tears.

"I, I do not know what to say, Mother."

"Just say that you will help me, Zhaohua. Please." Again, Mother did not meet my eyes as she spoke.

"Of course, Mother. As soon as I get to America, and get a job, I will send you money — of course."

"No, Zhaohua. I cannot wait that long …"

"I do not understand Mother, I am barely seventeen — what can I do to help now?"

"You have many wealthy friends, Zhaohua. I need two thousand silver dollars — immediately — to repay Aunt Liming. Surely there must be someone you could ask. It is matter of life or death."

"Two thousand silver dollars! Mother, I could not possibly ask for that much money. Who would possibly loan it to me?"

Mother just sat in her chair, looking old and tired and far away. And I could not bear it. I went to her and held her in my arms. It felt as though I was the mother, and she the child.

"Try not to worry, Mother. We will come up with a solution. I promise."

My mind raced through my options. I had not realized the depth of Father's financial problems. It explained his rages and withdrawal recently. No. Father could not help. And Jade had no money of her own. I kept going through my list of friends. They were all so wealthy. But of course, I could not ask them. My family would lose face. I tried to think of anyone — anyone, except him. The obvious person, Liankui Ching.

I lay awake all night. My mother's sadness seemed to close in around me. She was desperate and I could feel it. By dawn, I knew I had no choice. I left a note for Mother and told her that I would return with two thousand dollars.

"Margaret, may I speak with your father?" I had not even called before appearing at Liankui Ching's home.

"He will be most happy to see you, Zhaohua. He has asked about you every day." Margaret sensed my serious mood and went to tell her father that I had arrived. He appeared almost immediately.

"Zhaohua, I hope you are well." Liankui's words were cold, but polite. He was obviously annoyed that I had avoided him since our conversation about our ancestor, Ching Guan, and his concubine.

"Yes. Thank you, Uncle Liankui. I am feeling … my health is much improved. But …"

"What is it, Zhaohua? Something is wrong."

As I told him Mother's story, I tried to hold in my tears as I asked for his help. Tears for my mother. And tears for myself.

"Of course I will help you, Zhaohua. Do not worry. Your mother will be fine. I am honored that you came to me." Uncle Liankui made out a check to my mother in the amount of two thousand dollars. I thanked him graciously and assured him that I would pay him back, in full and with interest, when I got to America and established myself. Lawyer Ching just smiled and nodded as I made my promises. It all appeared to be so simple.

Mother was overjoyed when I handed her the check. She came back to life for a while.

Later in the week, when a package arrived for me from Liankui Ching, Mother did not seem at all concerned as she handed it to me and left my bedroom.

My fingers trembled as I opened the small, plainly wrapped package. I did not even gasp in surprise when I saw it. I had known it would be an exquisite ring. Four carats. Marquis.

It seemed to fit my finger perfectly.

15

Colonel Zhang spoke in his soft way as we drove our familiar roads. But his soft tone could not disguise the unfamiliar tension inside the car that day.

"I am concerned for you, Zhaohua. I think it is not safe to see you for a while. Someone has been following me. Chiang Kai-shek is very suspicious; it could be one of his men. Things are happening within the Nationalist party, Zhaohua. We are on the verge of, well, I should not speak of more. But I will have to be away for a while. In Guangzhou. I don't know how long I'll be. I know only that I shall miss you terribly. Zhaohua? What is it, Zhaohua?"

"Uncle Liankui has asked me to marry him." I had not meant to be so abrupt, but I found that I could not hold the words in any longer. My colonel swallowed audibly and stared straight ahead. I saw his knuckles go white as he gripped the steering wheel. He did not respond for several moments.

"And what did you say, my Empress Ching?"

"I have avoided him since I received his ring. I am — my family is in debt to him. He has helped me very much. He is a very powerful man. I think perhaps that he is the one who has had people following us," I tried to speak without emotion.

"Oh, Zhaohua. Liankui Ching is powerful, indeed. I will speak to my wife … this cannot be. Of course, you cannot marry that man."

"We have both known the situation. You are not free to … there is nothing you can do."

We sat in silence for the rest of the drive. For the first time, I could not read my colonel. I could not tell if he was angry, or hurt, or simply sad. I remember that I wished with all my heart that he would just keep driving.

I received a message the next day saying that Colonel Zhang had left for Guangzhou, for an indefinite period of time. I vacillated between hurt and anger at my colonel's desertion. In the end, I knew he had done the only thing he could do.

Margaret phoned that same week, pleading with me to visit her father, "Zhaohua, Father is very ill. He is in bed, and says he must speak with you."

"He needs a doctor, Margaret; there is nothing I can do for him."

"He says it is urgent. He must speak with you. Please, Zhaohua. Please come."

"Oh, Margaret, I will come this afternoon." As I hung up, I thought of Jade's words. The strings. You were so wise, my dear Jade.

The house was quiet when I entered. Margaret said that Uncle Liankui had left instructions for me to come to his room when I arrived, and she left for the library to pick up some books for her father.

"Zhaohua, I am so glad you have come. Please sit here." Uncle Liankui motioned to a chair by the bed. The room was elaborate — fifteen-feet ceilings — lined on the west with French windows that reached nearly to the ceiling. The blue walls were bordered by wide ivory molding; frames and sconces of gold seemed to be at home in their grand setting. Uncle Liankui could have been an emperor of China, sitting under his ivory silk comforter, looking most distinguished in his black silk pajamas; he was indeed a handsome man. But I was struck by his image as I entered; amidst the pale blues, and the ivories, and the golds, he looked like a spider sitting there, so conspicuously black in the airy room.

"I am so sorry you are ill, Uncle Liankui. What does the doctor say?"

"The doctor knows nothing. I am ill because you have not been here, Zhaohua. The reincarnation of my beloved concubine. Only you can make me well." Liankui Ching's words were so sincere, and as I sat by his bed, I thought how much this man had helped my family over the years, I wondered if perhaps it was all true. Perhaps Liankui was the reincarnation of Ching Guan, and perhaps I was the reincarnation of Ching Guan's beloved concubine.

I realized in that moment that I had always been drawn to Liankui Ching. Always with caution, but drawn. From the first time I had heard his name, as my family had escaped the civil war of the Chinese City, it had resonated in my ears. Over the years, I have come to learn that sometimes, when we first meet people, we are aware — immediately — that they will play a dramatic role in our lives. Of course, now, I have had years to hone this intuition — and to practice the art of listening to that intuition — but as I look back on the years preceding that day, I realize that there had always been a feeling of an inevitable entangling with Liankui Ching.

And on that day, at the age of seventeen, and in that moment, beside this sick man, I made an emotional connection with Liankui Ching. As I pondered the possibility of his words, I wondered if perhaps he spoke the truth; perhaps we were the reincarnation of Ching Guan and his concubine, and it was our fate to be together. These thoughts turned over in my mind, and I was swept back in time; I imagined our souls, existing together, in the bodies of our ancestors. I saw us there, in a village — it was a picture of a place I had never been — but in that moment, I saw every detail. I felt the sandy earth under my feet, and was aware of the air feeling dryer — less weighted with the moisture of the ocean, in my lungs. I saw a canal, lined with homes made of dried sandy soil and clay tiles as roofs. I saw words, engraved in the side of a low mountain.

Suddenly, I was back. In Liankui Ching's bedroom.

I was Zhaohua Ching, and I was only seventeen years old. I was aware that this man had become an integral part of my life, and that his words were sincere, and that he had been very kind to my family. I felt that my imagination had been playing tricks on me, and that I was caught up in the fantasies of Liankui Ching. I realized that when I thought of him — Uncle Liankui — my feelings did not even resemble the feelings I held toward Colonel Zhang.

Liankui Ching was now holding my hand, and the confusion of my emotions became overwhelming. The room felt like it was closing in on me. I knew I had to leave, immediately.

"Uncle Liankui, I cannot … I do not … ," I tried to find the courage to say that I could not accept his ring. That I did not love him. That I would not be his wife.

"No, Zhaohua. It is our destiny." Uncle Liankui's voice was so calm as he reached out with his other hand and gently clasped my own. And I could feel it. I knew what was about to happen. I tried to pull away. I repeated the word no, over and over, and started to pull away. His grip tightened.

He pulled me to him. Time seemed to stand still and simultaneously explode. It was as though this were happening to me under water, in painfully slow motion. When I opened my mouth, I could feel myself drowning and suffocating on my own air. Liankui had pulled me onto his beautiful silk bed. I watched, bewildered, as he meticulously unfastened each button on my white silk blouse. I tried to move, but he was too strong. I kept thinking it was a dream and wishing I could pinch myself and wake up. I had done it during nightmares before. This was a nightmare, a bad dream. It was not happening. Uncle Liankui and I were under the ocean. His bedroom was blue and I tried to tell myself it was a dream and the walls were the water and he was not unbuttoning my blouse and I was not lying on his silk sheets, which felt like cold water.

It was the only time Liankui's eyes did not blink. He stared at me and yet seemed not to be present. My mind was frantic and random and wild. Yet, my body was still being ravished in this endless, liquid moment.

When he untied my skirt, and removed his black silk pajama trousers, I told my mind to go and wait in that corner. That simple corner where the two blue walls met the ivory molding. To go there and not look.

Then the water cleared, and I smelled him. I wished my nausea would grow worse, but it was as though my lungs were filled with water. It was raining against the long, French windows of the bedroom, and then I saw the rain as it beaded on the glass, hovering and defying gravity, turning the window into a kaleidoscope of crystal. Or Spanish glass. And just as this man intruded into my young body, I saw it. One drop on the window could no longer hold. It slowly slid down the glass pane. I watched it trickle all the way down the window; those windows are eight-feet tall, and the pace was consistent and slow and purposeful.

"Across the fence, the wind tossed the moon into my chamber.
In the silent night, the magpies are quiet.
On my pillow, I find my weaving girl.
With great joy, we are transported to heaven."

"Do you know those words, Zhaohua? They are the words of my ancestor, Ching Guan, the one whose soul I now carry. This famous poem was written in celebration of the day that he took his beloved concubine. I knew you had not given yourself to anyone else. I will speak to your father. We will be married. It is not disgraceful, Zhaohua; it is our destiny. Oh, my beautiful concubine; you will now take your place as the First Wife," Liankui Ching stroked my hair so tenderly as I lay there curled in a tiny, shivering ball. The covers had fallen from the bed. I had nothing with which to hide my shame. I could hear that it was still raining outside but I could not raise my head to look out the window. I just lay there; I don't know how long it was. Minutes? Hours? Time folded into that blue and ivory corner, and was lost. I just held my body, like a shivering cocoon, afraid to move.

Somehow — I do not remember — I had the courage to gather my things and cleaned myself as best as I could. Liankui Ching called his chauffeur, and asked him to drive me home. As I walked from his house to the car, I pretended the raindrops were my tears and I was aware that they did not taste salty. I remembered that I used to cry when I was young, I liked the salty taste.

I arrived at Mother's house and went to my room unnoticed. I went straight to my bathroom and ran a steaming hot bath, though I did not even feel the heat of the water, as I sat in the tub. There I cried. My own tears; I tasted them to be certain. They were quiet at first, and then my grief took on a low, primal moan. Sounds I had never made before emanated from somewhere in my bones, as I washed my disgraced body.

Margaret phoned the next day to say that her father was asking about me. He was feeling much better.

I said that I was ill. And I put the phone off the hook.

I spent many blurry days lying in my bedroom. I could not tell Mother. Sex before marriage was a disgrace. Even seduction was not an acceptable excuse in Shanghai at the time. I could not face Jade. She would know immediately when she saw me. There would be no possibility of lying to Jade, and I would feel so weak in front of her. Jade had helped me grow so strong; in my shame, I could not conceive that she would ever have allowed something like this to happen. No, it would be humiliating to face her.

I now know that Jade would have understood. She could have helped me, offered choices, taught me more that it was not a matter of my strength. That it was not my fault.

I did not go to Jade; I didn't go to anyone. I feigned a relapse of my flu as I refused invitations and missed classes. I did not return phone calls. I was so glad that my colonel had left for Guangdong. He took his place as a young girl's fantasy.

Eventually, I could not even cry.

Liankui Ching had copies of our ancestral records and stories delivered to me, and when I read them, I could not believe my eyes. The concubine with whom Ching Guan had been so in love — her name was Zhaohua.

Yes, I knew before the nausea started, before I missed my period, that I was carrying the child of Liankui Ching.

16

To obey your father at home. To obey your husband in marriage. And to obey your son after the death of your husband. These were the three Confucian teachings of obedience for women. From the day we were born, the daughters of China were instructed to live obediently. To seek the four virtues of women: Fidelity, Physical Charm, Propriety in Speech, and Efficiency in Needlework.

Yes, I told Liankui Ching that I was carrying his child. He was elated as though he did not even see what the conception of that child had done to my life.

After hearing the news, Liankui Ching arranged to take me to visit a Shanghai physician, Dr Ge. My spine stiffened and I lowered my eyes as Dr Ge addressed me as Mrs Ching, and confirmed my pregnancy to my 'husband.'

On the way home from the doctor, Liankui told me to wait outside while he went in to consult his fortune-teller, Little Voodoo. I felt so lifeless that day, as Liankui so happily held my hand, and walked me through Shanghai. Liankui, on the other hand, could hardly contain his energy, when he emerged from his fortune-teller.

"Little Voodoo asked me what questions I had, and I told him I had questions about my marriage. At random, I selected a card with the *de* (virtue) character. Little Voodoo smiled, and said that the character signified an excellent marriage; my wife would have the three obediences and the four virtues. You see, Zhaohua, it is our destiny. Your father will understand; he cannot stand in the way of destiny."

I wondered what Little Voodoo would say about our marriage and my obedience, if he knew that I would be defying my Father when I took my vows.

Yes, Liankui went to Father to explain the situation and to formally ask permission to marry me. But no, Father did not understand. He was enraged. He would never consent to the marriage. It was that same evening that I heard my parents arguing; Liankui had just left Father, and Father had charged into our home consumed with anger. He looked at me for just a moment in the hallway before he went into Mother's room; I can still see his eyes — they were filled with disgust. Then he turned his head from me as though I did not exist. I ran to my bedroom and Father slammed the door as he entered Mother's room. Soon after, the shouting ensued.

"Zhaohua must be dealt with immediately. You will send her to Nanjing to marry one of your nephews. Liankui Ching cannot find her there, and perhaps I will not lose face in Shanghai."

And that was when I heard the courage of my mother.

"I cannot do this to our daughter, Tongli. She is only seventeen — to leave her home, to be abandoned by her parents, it would be too painful. She is a child — it was you who encouraged her to spend time at the Ching home. You who introduced her to this man. He is supposed to be your friend — it is Liankui Ching who has behaved dishonorably."

"You will do as I say — you will not defy your husband, Chongwen — you will not. Make the arrangements. Zhaohua must be sent to Nanjing." Father slammed the doors in fury as he left my Mother's house.

But Mother did not make the arrangements; and although Mother had stood up for me, she did not speak to me after Father left. Over the next few days, it was as though I were invisible in my own home. Kaihua and Wanhua were away at school. I tried to avoid Mrs Ding, who only smiled, as if enjoying my shame and misery.

Slowly, and painfully, I realized that my only option was to defy my father, and to marry Liankui Ching. This man who was forty-five years old, and who ignited my fear and my disgust, and yet oddly, had helped me so much in my life. But I had no illusions that Liankui Ching would ever see me for who I was.

At the end of the day, however, all of those thoughts did not matter. The overriding truth boiled down to the fact that this was the man who would legitimize the child inside me.

Liankui, with the help of his sister, hastily made arrangements for a wedding trip. We would be married in Hangzhou where I had served as maid of honor to his oldest daughter, just over a year ago.

Finally, on the morning that I was preparing to leave, Mother came into my room. She sat down softly on the edge of my bed. There were few words.

"Mother, take care of yourself. It is my fate and I must accept it. As the wife of Liankui Ching, I will have a good life. I will see you when I can …"

My Mother smiled at me as she handed me a gift. My fingers were shaking as I opened the paper to see a beautiful hairpin, exquisitely set with jade and diamonds.

"I wore this hairpin on my wedding day; it was a gift from my father, and I know he would want, and I wish, for my beautiful daughter to wear it on hers." Mother held my hands for a moment, before she turned and left the room.

I did not see anyone else as I left my mother's house and climbed into the limousine Liankui had sent.

——— ——— ———

I trembled in fear as I walked down the aisle. I clutched my bouquet of white roses and carnations and focused on my tiny steps. Tiny, sure steps. The room was sparsely decorated and I wondered how many such hasty affairs this room had seen. Liankui had ordered a lovely wedding gown for me — white georgette, with a veil of white and silver hand-made lace. It, like the extravagant, four-carat diamond on my finger, appeared to fit perfectly.

Liankui had miraculously assembled most of his family for the occasion. I think it was all meant as a gesture of kindness for me; to help ease the absence of my own family. Father had forbidden anyone to attend. But I found no comfort that day. And as I walked down the aisle alone, I tried not to remember my previous trip to Hangzhou. The dreaming, defiant girl I had been then.

I simply repeated over and over to myself, in rhythm with my tiny steps, that now my baby would not bear the shame of being an illegitimate child.

Everyone was in Western dress, with the only sign of tradition being a long table covered by a red silk cloth, embroidered with butterflies and Mandarin ducks — symbols of marital bliss and eternal devotion. I recalled the story of my mother's wedding, and thought how much had changed in one generation. And I realized how much had not changed. I reached up to touch my lovely hairpin, and wondered if my mother had made the same gesture as she trembled on her wedding day.

Two attorneys witnessed the signing of the marriage certificates; there was no religious official at our wedding, and we had neither sermons nor blessings.

During our two days in Hangzhou, I did not even ask my husband if we could explore Thunderous Mountain.

The newspapers in Hangzhou and Shanghai all carried the story of the wedding. Of course, Liankui had planned a lovely honeymoon trip — three weeks in Beijing, and I was given a short reprieve from the public humiliation awaiting me in Shanghai.

We stayed at the grand Beijing Hotel on the Boulevard of Eternal Peace, near Tiananmen Square, and I must admit that I found Beijing immensely soothing. I allowed myself to be engrossed in the gigantic old cypress trees, the ancient walls, and the historical monuments. It was nice to be engrossed. The past several weeks had been so draining. It was soothing to turn my attention from my own life and to find beauty in something again.

Liankui was so attentive; often we had a morning stroll in Tiananmen Square, which was dominated by the Gate of Heavenly Peace. Behind the Gate lay the Forbidden City, where the Ming and Qing emperors had lived for five centuries behind high vermilion walls. The intensity of the place — the tradition — could be felt in my being. In my bones, as Grandfather would say. There were actually moments when I thought it might be an acceptable life to be the wife of Liankui Ching. Every afternoon we enjoyed tea at Central Park or Bei Hai (North Sea) Park; Liankui often met friends there and he was very proud of his new, young bride. After our first such encounter, however, Liankui was certain to instruct me to smile at his friends, but not to speak.

And every night I went to bed with my husband.

After three weeks of strolls and rest, my husband and I returned to Shanghai to face the public consequences, and our private lives.

———   ———   ———

"Uncle Married Seventeen-year-old Niece" ...
"Lawyer Ching Eloped with His Teenage Niece" ...
"Ching Marries Ching: Against Chinese Moral Tradition" ...

These headlines had dominated the Shanghai tabloids and gossip columns while we were away. And they were fueled by my father's announcement, which appeared in the papers on the day we returned to Shanghai — Father had purchased a large space for his words:

Announcement by Ching Tongli

Following the command of my father,
Due to the disobedience of my daughter,

Ching Zhaohua,
I hereby declare that
I disown my daughter
For now and forever.

I was devastated.

Of course, I could not contact Mother or Jade; Father would have forbidden it and it would put them in a terrible position. I knew that everyone had read of my disgrace, and I thought that perhaps my ancestors were right; it would have been better to have committed suicide.

My husband did show me tenderness during those weeks. He tried to dry my tears and console me. He reminded me over and over that he would take care of me now; that I no longer had to worry about my family's financial problems. He assured me that the gossip would die down, and Shanghai would embrace us again.

Some of his clients threatened to find other representation because of the disgrace, but in the end they stayed. There were even those who came to visit and offer congratulations — among them, Zhang Jingjiang, one of the founders of the Nationalist Party and his wife, who indicated their acceptance of our marriage with a formal visit and gift — a lovely crystal bowl. And Du Yuesheng, my husband's client and friend, and yes, the leader of the Shanghai Green Gang, called to offer congratulations.

At seventeen, I had taken a step into the inner circle of Shanghai politics — and the doors closed behind me.

Liankui was right; after a few weeks, the gossip died down. The nausea of my pregnancy subsided and I slowly emerged from my depression, and realized that my only real option was to make a conscious effort to accept my role as mistress of this grand house, and stepmother to Liankui's six grown children. I resolved to learn to like my new home — it was quite magnificent. Yes, it was a lovely cage.

Our home was situated on Avenue Foch in the French Concession. Actually, it was two grand homes, with a connecting door. Liankui's offices occupied the ground floor of one of the houses, his older children occupied the rooms above his office. Liankui's sons, who were closer to my age than their father, were instructed not to visit me. The other house was our home. The downstairs was our sitting-room and dining-room, all with modern furnishings. I had two maids; one who prepared meals and one to care for Liankui and me. Upstairs I had two large bedrooms, also newly furnished. There were long yellow silk curtains on the windows, and I smiled sadly the day I realized that I rarely opened them. Liankui kept his own room, the room in which my life had been irrevocably changed, but visited my room every night. I thought of Sonya and wondered if she had spoken the truth; if it were actually possible for sex to be a pleasant, enjoyable, experience.

Liankui systematically cut me off from the outside world. I did not protest. I could have anything I wanted, but he would purchase it for me. As I was forbidden to visit Mother and Jade, there was no need for me to leave the house — servants did the shopping. It was all shrouded in love and a desire to protect me — until the letter came.

Liankui had opened it and read it of course. And it sealed my fate. It was a gesture of friendship, from Yung Silang, the young man who had brought books for me during my illness, and I barely remembered him. He seemed to be a blurry picture from another life.

> Dear Zhaohua,
>
> It was a shock to me when I heard that you got married. I understand your problems, and am ready to help you any time.
>
> Please let me know if you need me.
>
> Yung Silang

Liankui threw the letter at me and stormed out without a word. I just sat in my room and continued to read my newspaper. There was nothing to be done.

Liankui did not speak for several days, as though the letter were my fault. His daughters were instructed to spend most of their time with me — they were to be my babysitters. I thought of Jade, and her graceful acceptance of me in a similar role, and I tried to emulate her friendship and acceptance. But I longed for a piece of my former life. Finally, I mustered the courage, and seized a rare opportunity, to call my old friend, Nancy.

"Hello, Nancy. It is Zhaohua."

"Oh, Zhaohua. How wonderful to hear from you — I have tried to contact you, but am always told you are not in. How are you, Zhaohua? What happened?"

"It is a long story, my friend," I proceeded to tell Nancy of the drastic turns my life had taken. Could it have been less than a year since I had served as her maid of honor? It felt like centuries. I told her of the letter I had received form Yung Silang, and my husband's fury.

"Yung is a good friend of my husband's, Zhaohua. I know that he has admired you for years; I'm certain he did not mean to cause trouble for you. Have you heard, Zhaohua? Janet is getting married next month? Her fiance is James Woo; he was educated in America — a master's degree in Finance from the University of Pennsylvania. Oh, Zhaohua, you must come to the wedding; all of our classmates from McTyeire will be there; it will be so grand!"

"Of course, I will speak to my husband about it. Goodbye, Nancy."

"I'm sorry, Zhaohua. The date is booked; I have to be in Suzhou for an important case before the Supreme Court; of course I expect you to accompany me." Liankui blinked rapidly as he silently dismissed me.

I did not attend Janet's wedding. Nor did I call Nancy back — I found it humiliating and painful. My husband resumed his old schedule, busy days in his office; evenings spent socially, playing mahjong and cards. He rarely asked me to accompany him, and when he did, the instructions were always the same, "It would not be appropriate for you to speak, Zhaohua. Just smile." Eventually, he did not have to repeat his instruction. I smiled, and remained silent, without being told.

That fall, my first child was born — a daughter. No, I had not prayed for a son. Liankui called her Chiayi, but I suppose I did not completely abandon my Western ways, and I called her Judie from the beginning. My Judie was born prematurely, with the umbilical cord wound tightly around her neck. Dr Ge said that the baby must have been sent by Buddha because she has made it despite the odds. I was trembling as they handed her to me, my body shaking — consumed with fear and with love.

That winter, I held my young daughter — my daughter who was sent by Buddha, who would continue to defy odds — as I watched Liankui's family perform their traditional Chinese New Year celebrations.

In the dining-room, a picture of the God of Heaven and several ancestral portraits were hung on the walls. On the table, which was covered with a piece of red satin, was a Chinese feast — large pots of cooked pork, ham, chicken and duck; fresh fruits; cooked rice; and some small cups of rice wine. A live carp was placed in the middle of the table. After the ceremony, the fish was to be put back alive into the river to bring good luck to the family.

In front of the table stood two large red candles, and between them a bronze holder containing burning incense. Chairs with red embroidered covers were placed alongside the table for the deity and the ancestors.

Tradition dictated that each family member, beginning with the males, had to kowtow to the ancestors. Following this show of respect, we would all proceed to the courtyard where Liankui would burn bags of silver and gold paper money in an iron dish; each bag was marked with the name of an ancestor and the money was to be for their use in the afterworld.

I held my daughter, as I heard Liankui's daughter, Margaret, my former student — and now my stepdaughter — insist that she should go after her father, as she was older than her brothers. I watched silently, and held my daughter, as Margaret was subdued by tradition, and followed her younger brothers in the procession.

I thought of my own daughter. And of the other child, growing inside me — I was already pregnant again. Would this child be a son? Would the daughter in my arms someday follow behind her brother?

I decided, as I watched the paper money burn and float into the night, that my children would be educated in the West. They would question. Not necessarily abandon, but question.

17

War was a constant fact of life in China. Indeed, since 1929 there had not been a year when Chiang Kai-shek was not engaged in civil war.

Chiang remained adamant that the country's resources be focused on fighting the Communists. His own party — the Nationalist party — remained divided as a result, and the Communists multiplied.

The anti-Chiang Kai-shek sentiment led to the formation of another party that struggled to control China. This third party was led by Soong Ching-ling, the widow of Dr Sun Yat-sen. Yes, she was the second sister of Madame Chiang Kai-shek. So Chiang was openly opposed by his own sister-in-law! But as many of Soong Ching-ling's supporters were mysteriously assassinated, including Yang Heifu, a renowned scientist, and Se Liang-za, the owner of the *Shanghai Times* — these assassinations, along with Chiang Kai-shek's earlier attack on the 19th Route Army, induced Soong Ching-ling's supporters to become Communist sympathizers.

Many Nationalists — supporters of the original Republic — had no choice under the military dictatorship of Chiang Kai-shek but to become Communist sympathizers. Soong Ching-ling's supporters comprised intellectuals and university students, and they greatly strengthened and advanced the Communist movement.

Du Yuesheng, now the leader of the Green Gang, was my husband's primary client. Du's power was directly linked to the success of Chiang Kai-shek, whom Du had supported both financially and with manpower. So my husband observed the political maneuverings of China with diligence and insight.

Chiang Kai-shek had enough troubles when, in January of 1934, the United States devalued the dollar. The price of silver soared. Chinese currency was based on silver so this demand resulted in record inflation — the drain on China's silver reserves amounted to several hundred million dollars during that year.

This drain was a financial paradox for my husband and his practice. While Du was his most influential and primary client, and threatened by the progressive weakening of Chiang Kai-shek, my husband was also the attorney for many of the principal banks in Shanghai. Of course, the banks had to declare bankruptcy, and that required the services of their attorney. And while I never considered Liankui to be an ideal husband, or a model father, it was widely known that he was a brilliant attorney.

Even my own father continued to consult Liankui for legal advice. I found Liankui's professional relationship with my father to be a personal betrayal to our marriage. But Liankui insisted that it would be disrespectful and dishonorable for him to deny free services to my father, since my father was in fact his father-in-law. He said that he, in advising my father, was showing respect and thanks to my father for raising me to be an honorable wife. He reasoned that by showing respect to my father, he was also showing love to me — his wife. And as Liankui so eloquently defended his relationship with my father, I saw why his services as an attorney were in such demand.

As I conceded my lack of ability to argue with Liankui's reasoning, and marveled at my husband's eloquence, I realized how very much I was learning from this articulate man. About politics, about the world economy, and about men and women.

I absorbed this worldly knowledge from my husband, and thought of the wise teachers who had come before him in my life. Though I realized that none of them had contributed to my growth, as much as my own child had. There is nothing like motherhood to pull you from the fields of childhood, and to teach you so much more than can ever be articulated. At the age of eighteen, I had entered that sacred circle of motherhood, that circle so rich and universal and silently understood that it defies, and simultaneously unites, age and history and countries and words.

Absorbed in new motherhood, and pregnant with my second child, I often thought of mothers before me. And I finally — fully — accepted the fact that I had embraced this knowledge of motherhood. My own dreams were over. It was their lives, which must come first now. I resolved that I would teach them everything I could.

Of course, in order to teach them — I must continue to learn. As I turned my energies away from my own personal unhappiness and toward what I could offer my children, I decided to appreciate the fact that my husband was immensely wealthy. Excellent educations — Western educations, would be expensive. But we would be able to provide that.

Thus, I consciously began to focus my attention toward the financial concerns and plans for my family. It was then, that I began to notice how much my husband loved to gamble.

Liankui Ching loved mahjong, roulette, dice and fantan. Fantan is a Chinese game in which players bet on the number of chips that are left in a pile in a bowl, after they have been counted off in fours. He had also taken a fancy to *jai alai,* a competitive sport popular in Spain and Latin America. Using a curved basket fastened to the arm, each player catches and hurls the ball against the wall to score. Bets were taken on who the winner would be.

There was a period of months when Liankui spent every night at the *jai alai* stadium. I accompanied him on rare occasions and tried to contain my shock as I watched my husband lose hundreds, often thousands of dollars in one evening.

As my concerns for my family mounted, I did not remain silent in my observations. I can still remember the first night I confronted him about his gambling habits. It was just before my second child was born; Liankui had been away, gambling for two days, and I was furious.

This time, I did not swallow my rage and transform it to tears. As he came to my room, as though he had not been gone for days, throwing away our family's security, I started timidly. Then I could not stop my words.

"That stadium is using you as an advertisement, Liankui! You must stop losing so much money there. You have more children to think of — and a wife! This gambling must stop! China's economy is in shambles; you have said so yourself, and war is imminent, we have to save as much as we can." It was as though my mother's silence, and then my own, had built up in me, and came spilling out, without restraint. I had tolerated the humiliation of my husband continuing to show respect to my father, who still did not acknowledge me or his grandchildren, and I had killed my dreams. But I refused to let my children's future be ruined by this man. I would not be silenced.

Liankui Ching turned to leave my room, as though my outburst had not even happened. I felt the humiliation — and then the rage — of a woman ignored by her husband. That's when I made, or rather articulated, my decision. I think it had in fact always been there, just waiting to be acknowledged.

"I am going to return to school, Liankui. If the need arises, I wish to be financially independent. I wish to be prepared." My words sounded rehearsed, as though they had been patiently waiting for an opportunity to escape. In fact, they were not planned or rehearsed, but they were most real. And Liankui knew it.

"You think I am going to die at any moment and leave you penniless. Is that it? No, Zhaohua. You will not return to school. I will care for my family. I will provide for my children — as well as for my wife. If you insist on furthering your studies, you can ask Mrs Lin, your former English teacher, to come here, into my home, to be your tutor. No, you will not return to school, Mrs Ching." Liankui walked away as though he had won.

I opened the yellow silk draperies in my bedroom to expose the beautiful full moon — it seemed to be a crown on the many lights of Shanghai, and I smiled as I thought of Mrs Lin's impending company — and all that I would learn from her.

That same night I gave birth to our second child, Anthony, whom Liankui called Chia-shi. I was less afraid with Anthony's birth and allowed myself to be consumed in that euphoria of fresh motherhood.

Afterward, I looked at both of them, my young Judie who defied odds, and my son who had come on the night I was no longer silent, and my resolve was strengthened. Within two weeks, I made arrangements for Mrs Lin to resume my English lessons, typing, and even American history!

When we open ourselves to our way, the way comes to us. That night, when I found my voice, and opened those draperies, my world started coming back to me piece by piece. No, it would never be as I had planned, Liankui still held a firm grip, but — little by little — I was finding my way and some peace.

A few months later, as I was bathing Anthony — he always loved his baths and I would let him play and splash in the water until it became too cold — my maid knocked on the door and said that I had a visitor, Miss Jade Wang.

I had not seen Jade since I was married, and I felt as giddy as a child as I wrapped Anthony in a towel and handed him to the maid, and ran downstairs to embrace my dear friend.

We did not speak at first; we simply held each other for the longest time. Finally, Jade laughed, and stepped back to look at me, "Zhaohua — you are a woman now. And a wet one! What have you been doing my young friend?"

I laughed so easily with Jade. It was as though we had never been apart, and yet, there was an air of equality between us now. She no longer felt so much older than I was.

"Oh, Jade — I have been bathing my son — you will have to meet him when he is dressed. And I have a daughter, Judie — you must meet her as well. Can you stay for tea? Does Father know you have come? Oh, Jade, thank you so much for coming. I have thought of you so often and wished to see you — I knew it would enrage Father if I phoned, and create problems for you."

"Yes, I know, Zhaohua. I knew that was why you had not called. I knew that you would understand why I did not come. I thought of you so often; I know how eccentric Liankui Ching can be. It must be so difficult for you, Zhaohua — he is so much older than you. I wanted to be here for you, Zhaohua, but I have my mother to think of. Your father would not have been understanding, and Mother is getting older ..."

"I understand, Jade. Do not apologize. We do what we have to do. I have children of my own now, and I understand so much more. I have come to know what a special woman your mother is, Jade. So tell me everything — my days are spent in this house, caring for my children, and I know nothing of what is happening outside these walls. Sometimes, I miss my old life — the parties and the people — so very much, but I have accepted it. This is my life now, and I must do what is best for my children from this point — like you, my life is also not my own."

"Oh Zhaohua. You have grown so much in such a few short years. When I spoke of you to Mother, she would just smile, and say that she was certain you would be fine."

"How is your mother, Jade? Please give her my love."

"She is getting older; her health is not good, but still she laughs, she meditates and she laughs. She says laughter is a free gift of the gods, but even if it costs millions, she had gotten her money's worth! Yes, I will send your love. She will be so happy to hear news of you."

"How is Father, Jade?" I had not seen Father since that day in the hallway in our home. Not in person, anyway. I often saw his eyes in my mind.

"Your father, your father loves women, Zhaohua. I'm afraid we are — our relationship will soon be over. That is one reason I finally came to see you. I no longer care what your father says; it is rumored that Wang Xiaolai desires to have me as one of his wives — Wang is a member of the Green Gang so your father is afraid of him. I can use that to be free of your father."

"I know Wang Xiaolai through my husband, Jade; he has six wives already! How could you consider marrying such a man?"

Jade laughed, "Oh, Zhaohua, you know me better than that! Of course I will not marry Wang. I'm simply using him — and your father's fear of him — to gain my freedom. Still, I have shared much with your father —

and he has been kind to me and to Mother — and I do not enjoy seeing him so troubled. His financial situation is becoming quite serious, Zhaohua. I don't quite know what he will do."

Jade did not expect kind words from me; she knew that I had not forgiven my father for publicly humiliating me, and for never acknowledging his grandchildren.

"And Sonya ... tell me news of Sonya, Jade?"

"Sonya, our former student, has become a companion to your father, Zhaohua. His Third Wife. We taught her well, my friend. I look back and think how ironic it is that I actually trained my successor! Your father likes her so much — her presence will keep your father satisfied, and make it easier for me to gain my freedom, as well!" Again, Jade laughed — there was not a trace of animosity toward Sonya. Indeed, I think Jade was actually grateful to Sonya.

"But I have other interesting news, Zhaohua. It is rumor, but my sources are most excellent — your Madame Sheng, Zhaohua. I think she will be returning to Shanghai."

My china teacup clanked in my hands at the mention of Madame Sheng. Although I thought of her often, I had unconsciously given up hope of ever seeing her again.

"Please, Jade, tell me everything."

"Well, as you know, Sheng Seventh is one of the godsons of Madame H. H. Kung. Madame Kung is Soong Ai-ling — the sister-in-law of Chiang Kai-shek. This sister-in-law did not oppose her brother-in-law general, so the Kungs are quite favored by Chiang now! And Madame Kung has arranged for Sheng Seventh, and your dear Auntie Sheng, to return safely to Shanghai. In fact, Sheng Seventh is to hold an official position in Chiang's government — as Commissioner of Liquor and Tobacco! The Soong Dynasty still reigns over Shanghai, Zhaohua! It is said that the three Soong sisters and their brother, Minister Soong, are more powerful than any man in China. Your Sheng Seventh had the good timing to be the godson of Mrs Kung!"

"It would be wonderful to see her, but I worry, Jade; if Sheng Seventh is to join the government of Chaing Kai-shek, I do not have faith in the leadership of Chiang Kai-shek. He has the force, but not the heart of the people. People will only be ruled by force for so long, Jade. Chinese don't want to kill Chinese, while the Japanese are trying to take over all of China. The civil wars have got to end. If people continue to lose their jobs and their family members, they will revolt; Grandfather was so right. Change is never easy."

"Ahh, but neither is it avoidable, my friend."

We continued to laugh, and chat, and Jade met my children and fawned over them lavishly, as though she was a doting grandmother — the youngest and most beautiful grandmother in China, of course.

I told Jade of my resumed studies with Mrs Lin, and Jade was truly pleased for me. And Jade was the first person I told that I was pregnant again, with my third child. I had not even told Liankui. Jade said that my children were so fortunate — to have a mother who was wise and who had passion.

I still savor the memory of that visit with my Jade. She did not tell me what she planned to do with her freedom, and I had the instinct not to ask — still, I had somehow known as she left, that it would be one of my last visits with the beautiful, and oh so wise, Jade Wang.

I waved goodbye to her, with tears in my eyes and said a silent thank-you. I think she heard it, because she turned and blew me a kiss as she walked away.

My third pregnancy seemed to go quickly. I was busy with my studies — I practiced typing for many hours each day. Caring for Judie and Anthony was rewarding but exhausting work. I was not yet twenty, overseeing a household, caring for my own two babies and trying to tiptoe through my role as stepmother.

Liankui's daughters, Margaret and Alice, and I continued to grow as friends. The girls had never really known their mother — she had died when they were quite young — and the girls' personalities were so different that they often quarreled. Eventually, their incompatibility became unbearable — both for them and everyone else in the house. The girls shared a room, and there came a point when constant shouting, the slamming of doors, and tears were a daily occurrence. As mistress of the house, it was understood that peace in the home was my responsibility. I pondered, and prayed, and meditated on how to restore peace in our home without alienating my stepdaughters. In the end it was simple.

"Alice, please pack your things." I struggled to maintain composure as I spoke calmly to my stepdaughter.

"Excuse me, Zhaohua?"

"Pack everything in your room. It is obvious that you and Margaret cannot continue to live together so closely. There is no peace for anyone. I will not tolerate this behavior any longer. It is affecting everyone in our home."

"But where, Zhaohua, we are sorry ... we will not ..." Both girls were near tears.

"You will be moving, Alice." I could not keep it up any longer, and I laughed at their eyes as I continued, "Into my other bedroom. I will tell your father that I am lonely, and that you will help with Judie and Anthony. I do not need two bedrooms. It will be better for everyone this way!" The girls laughed and actually got along quite well as they worked together to pack Alice's things and move them next door. It is remarkable, how such a simple gesture restored peace to our home, and initiated what would be lifelong friendships with my stepdaughters.

My husband and I took a small step toward a higher level of mutual understanding that year. Or perhaps, I simply reached a new level within myself. I no longer behaved like a frightened child, and he no longer treated me like one. Of course, there would always be limits with Liankui Ching, and ours would never be a relationship of full equality and mutual respect; still, as my confidence and determination increased, so did my influence with my husband. It was a year of small steps, but they were steps, nonetheless.

Liankui and I often discussed politics and world economics, and I could see my husband's respect for me grow, as I contributed insightful comments into the conversation. Our home was running smoothly, and I was managing some of our household accounts. Still, I had no control over his gambling habits. As I dove deeper into our financial situation, my worst fears were confirmed. Liankui Ching had no money. Yes, hundreds of thousands of dollars (silver dollars) came in his doors — legal fees and retainers, and occasional wins at the *jai alai* stadium or mahjong table — but it all went right back out, either for more gambling or to pay off debts. The banks had given him extensive lines of credit.

I tried skimming money from our household budget and saving it for my children's education, but with the level of runaway inflation in China — indeed the world — it soon became worthless.

Eventually I realized, most completely, that I could not rely on Liankui Ching to insure the security of my children. And I craved that security. I further realized that I would either have to accept our financial instability, or take matters into my own hands. I looked into myself and knew that I could never accept it. My only option was to study harder, and be prepared to care for my children. The truth was that my husband was in his late forties, and broke — in an economy that was coming apart at the seams. Further, my father had disowned me. I was just over twenty — and any day now, I would have three children. Three children whom I vowed would have the means to pursue their dreams.

I decided that after I had recovered from the birth of my third child,

I would defy my husband, and pursue a diploma — something I would not get in my studies with Mrs Lin.

And Tommy, Chia-xiang, was born so peacefully. He was a serene child from the beginning. Mothers are so often accused of favoring the youngest child — the baby of the family. Mothers know that they do not love one child more than the other. They simply love their children differently. I do not love trees more than I love flowers, but I appreciate them for different reasons. It is the way with children, although I think that mothers are more relaxed with subsequent children. When Judie was born, I was so afraid of hurting my tiny baby when I held her or bathed her, or of feeding her incorrectly. By the time Tommy arrived, I was experienced in the way and feel of infants, and relaxed as I held my son. When I looked into his eyes, I knew that I had made the right decisions regarding my education. In those primal moments of new motherhood, my resolve to protect my children was strengthened.

I thought I knew how much I loved them. Until they became ill, that winter — 1936.

For two days, I did not sleep as first Judie, and then Anthony, started coughing. I walked the floors with one, and then the other — sometimes both. Tommy's bed was moved to my room, and I checked on him every few hours, but wanted to keep him safe from the germs, so Margaret and Alice were staying with him. Judie and Anthony needed me more — they would be almost asleep, and as soon as I would lie them down on their pillows, they would hold their little ears in pain, the coughs would begin again, and they would wake, exhausted and miserable. The coughs grew deep in their chest. I kept thinking it was a simple cold, they would be well soon. Then, on the third night, the fevers set in. Their bodies were burning hot to the touch and I tried to lower the fevers with cool baths and towels. Liankui called Dr Ge, who came over and prescribed medication for the fevers. I melted, exhausted with relief as the fevers subsided within a couple of hours. I lay between their beds — I was almost asleep when I heard it — my Anthony starting to wheeze and gasp for breath — Dr Ge was summoned again and came immediately.

"It is chronic bronchitis; possibly an asthma attack — I have given him a shot of adrenaline, which has relaxed his air passages for now, but you will have to watch him closely." I held Anthony for several hours — too afraid to fall asleep. To watch your child gasp for air, and to feel helpless — I was sure there could be no greater pain for a mother.

When I was certain that Anthony was breathing peacefully, I went to check on Tommy; I peeked in the doorway — he was sleeping, Margaret asleep on the bed beside him. I was aware that I had not bathed or changed my clothes for three days — I smelled of vomit and old diapers and sick children, so I changed into some clean pajamas and washed my face and hands. I combed my hair back from my face and hardly recognized myself in the mirror. My face was exhausted and drawn, and my eyes were unfamiliar. But my children were well. And resting peacefully.

I heard Tommy wake and cry softly, and I went to pick up my young baby, and almost dropped him — he was so hot — burning with fever. I screamed for Liankui.

"It is pneumonia, Zhaohua. It must be viral — what Judie and Anthony have been fighting — it set in so fast; he was fine when I checked him this morning," Dr Ge had rushed back when she heard the panic in my voice. "I will call some other physicians — and see — see if anyone — I'll read my latest journals tonight, and return in the morning. I have given him something for the fever, but his little lungs are filled with fluid, Zhaohua. He is so young ... . There is no known cure for chronic pneumonia, Zhaohua. And he is too young; his little immune system is not strong. It will depend on ... I will be back as soon as I can ... stay with him ..." Dr Ge could not look at me as she left.

I held my baby to me and I prayed to the Christian God, and I prayed to Buddha, and I prayed to my ancestors, all of them, any of them. Please help my baby! For the next eight hours, or a lifetime, I watched — helpless — as his face became the color of dried ashes. His breathing became shallow, but faster. I counted his breaths, I timed them, and every hour, there were more, tiny shallow gasps for air.

And when Tommy died, a piece of my soul died with him.

18

I went into shock when Tommy died. They said that Dr Ge had to pry my arms from my dead baby.

I could not speak or eat or function.

Liankui hired nurses to stay with me. I don't remember those weeks. They are a blur of sheets and bodies, friends trying to be comforting — all I wanted to do was sleep.

The only clear memory came weeks later. It is a memory of hearing Judie and Anthony crying one day — the servants and Margaret and Alice were evidently busy — I heard them both crying from their bedroom. I was too tired to help them, but they kept crying. Eventually, I pulled my leaden body from my bed, and walked to my children's room. When I had last been there, Tommy had been alive. When my children saw me, they forgot their tears and ran to me.

I sat down on the floor of their room, and then I was the one to cry. At last, I cried.

Now I have another bond — a bond with those who have lost a child. Sometimes I can tell, from the eyes of strangers, that we share that bond. And we know — we know never to speak of 'recovering' from such a loss. One does not recover from the loss of a child. One learns to live with that dead place inside them. One hopefully learns to go on and to find some happiness. But nothing is ever quite the same.

After that day, I knew that I had to go on, in part, for them — for Judie and for Anthony. I could not hide in my bedroom indefinitely. I would try to be there for them. But the truth is, I pretended to be alive — but I felt nothing — for so long. I braided Judie's hair, and I changed Anthony's diapers, and I was as hollow as a log in the forest. I went through motions. I remembered my mother crying behind her bedroom door and I remembered feeling so alone as a child, And I was determined that my children would know that I was there. I tried so hard to feel — anything — for my other two children. But though I loved them enough to get out of my bed, and to bathe them, and to keep them clean, And to feed and care for them, I could not — for so very long — actually feel anything, I could not bring my dead soul back to life.

Mother and Wanhua came to offer condolences.

Mother met her two grandchildren. Wanhua met her niece and her nephew, and they grieved never having held Tommy. Of course, I was comforted by their presence, as much as one can be comforted when one is numb and hollow. We had tea and we chatted, and they caught me up on the world. The world that was continuing without my Tommy, and seemingly, without me.

I think that when we love another person, we glimpse the face of God. And I think the teachings of Laozi are right when they say that the way — the Dao — is both dark and light. Both painful and beautiful. I saw the face of God in my grief for Tommy, and I saw the face of God in my love for my other children.

I think Mrs Wang, Jade's mother, was also right; laughter is a gift of the gods. Or God. Or Buddha. Or whomever it is you see when you glimpse that face. Laughter is the great healer. People who laugh often do live longer, you know; it is proven.

While my tears, also a healing gift of the gods, were the beginning of my journey back to life after Tommy, the journey would not have progressed without my laughter.

Of course, healing came slowly at first. I would smile at Judie as she furrowed her brow and was so serious as she struggled to read books well beyond her years, at such an early age. Or at Anthony, who enjoyed nothing better than teasing his serious sister with childhood pranks. Then, one day — I still remember it — the first time I really laughed after Tommy … .

Mother and Wanhua were visiting again. Apparently, it was understood that Father did not mind, since I had lost a child. Of course, Father did not come or write himself, and we did not speak of him. They brought pictures of Kaihua and his family; he had married Zhihua — I vaguely remembered her from the Elizabeth school. Of course, Father had forbidden my being invited to the wedding.

Mother's affection for my brother had extended, indeed deepened, toward my brother's children. She chatted endlessly about her grandchildren, going on and on, showing pictures and smiling, and I sat there and nodded and smiled with my hollow eyes, and then I began to hear her words.

"Oh, wait until you see it, Zhaohua. It is lovely. Your father has moved us all into a large house in Rue Retard. Kaihua and his family — Wanhua will be there when she is not in school — still I do so miss Mrs Ding, my home has not felt the same since her death; and now even Pretty Plum has married. Still, there is plenty of room for Sonya and —"

"Excuse me, Mother. Did you say Sonya? Do you actually mean to say that Sonya — and you — will be living under the same roof?" I could not believe my ears. Or my eyes. My sad, silent mother was sitting here babbling on about the happy home she would be sharing with my father and his new concubine.

"Oh, Zhaohua! Don't be so surprised! You know — better than I — that your father will always be a womanizer. Besides, I am an old woman, now; it will be nice to have another woman around. Sonya can be quite lively, you know." My mother actually laughed as she so lightly told me of her plans. I recalled all the years my mother had spent with her broken heart, and then I looked at her, sitting in my own sad home, so accepting — utterly embracing — the very situation which had caused her so much heartache. Then as I pictured my silent, sad mother and Sonya — yes, lively, colorful, Sonya — living together in the same house; the very picture of them all struck me as hilariously funny.

I laughed at — and with — my mother. And the laughter felt so good. No, I had not really laughed since before Tommy died; and Mother and Wanhua and I laughed until tears rolled down our cheeks.

Though a piece of my sadness at losing my Tommy has never left me, I have learned, perhaps because of my grief over Tommy, the value of laughter. Laughter heals. I have come to know that the essence of a person can be found in their laughter or their tears.

That year also marked a turn in my relationship with my sister. It was the first time I had ever looked at Wanhua as more than a little sister. She was no longer the quiet one. My timid sister had taken up the politics sweeping through China, and had become somewhat of a radical. I saw her, as though for the first time, as she spoke of joining student protests. She had joined other students in lying down on the railway tracks leading from Shanghai to Nanjing, forming a human blockade and demanding the release of the 'Seven Gentlemen.'

Of course, I was familiar with the cause — the 'Seven Gentlemen,' who, in fact included a female lawyer, were a group of intellectuals and professionals jailed by Chiang Kai-shek for criticizing government policies. They had become a cause celebre. News of their imprisonment had filled the newspapers over the past few weeks.

But when Wanhua said to extend her congratulations to Liankui for representing the leader of this group, I realized, fully, how deeply I had been engrossed in my fog. Of course, I had heard him speak of the case, but it had gone past me in my daze. Seeing my sister so committed to their cause, and realizing the fervor that was sweeping through Shanghai, I felt like I was suddenly plunged into a cold pool of water and transported back among the living. The intensity of what was going on around me was staggering.

I looked at my sister, the one who had stayed at home, while I was dancing at elegant dinner parties with the political giants of Shanghai, and I saw her with new eyes. Wanhua was simply dressed, and she wore no make-up; she spoke confidently and at length about the political situation in Shanghai. And she was so passionate in her political idealism — she openly opposed Chiang Kai-shek's policy of non-resistance with the Japanese, and was certain that the Japanese were going to annex China province by province if the people did not unite against Chiang Kai-shek.

Then I imagined how my sister — my political activist, university student, dear baby sister — must see her older sibling. I looked so pale and thin and weak. Since Tommy died, I had not taken pride in my appearance. I had not continued my classes with Mrs Lin, and I sat back timidly as my toddlers ruled our home. I knew it was time — time to heal.

I called Mrs Lin that afternoon — that same afternoon I had laughed — after Mother and Wanhua left, and arranged to resume my studies. I showered and dressed carefully and met my husband with living eyes that evening for dinner.

As I resumed my life as the wife of Liankui Ching, my first social engagement was to be the event of a lifetime — the birthday party of Du Yuesheng, now the principal leader of Shanghai's Green Gang.

———   ———   ———

I recognized the familiar sweet smell of opium as I entered the grand foyer of Du's home — a traditional Chinese-style, three-storied, red brick building on Wagner Street in the French Concession.

In fact, the entrance to the room was a virtual feast for all the senses. As the foyer opened to the grand center hall of the house, my ears were deafened by the Chinese music — *huqin* (Chinese violin), flute, drum, and trumpet, all being played loudly, and mingling with room after room, filled with voices and laughter. There were several large gas chandeliers hanging from the high ceilings, and as my eyes adjusted to the bright light, I saw beautiful original Chinese watercolors on the walls. I was familiar with the artists — they were some of the most highly regarded and treasured in China.

A large painting of the God of Longevity was hung prominently over a large mahogany table, flanked by two large red candles. Of course, we followed tradition, as did all the guests, and bowed to the God of Longevity as we entered, signifying our respect for the spirits. Elaborately prepared dishes of delicacies and fresh fruits were arranged on the table. Every chair in the house was wrapped with red embroidered covers, symbolizing good fortune and happiness.

The picture of the room could have been taken one hundred years earlier; the men wearing the traditional attire of a Chinese scholar: dark blue silk robes, and black satin jackets. Many were lounging lazily on the opium couches furnished in each room. Most of the women wore traditional embroidered red jackets over skirts; although a few were dressed in modern silk *qipaos*, the fitted dresses with high collars. The men were loud and vulgar, and the women — in the presence of the men — were silent.

Of course, Liankui had given me specific instructions to simply smile.

I watched as my husband greeted everyone as old friends, and I realized how deeply he was immersed with these notorious men. I held my breath as we approached Zhang Xiaoling, Du's partner in leading the Green Gang. Zhang indeed created an elegant appearance — his tall frame draped in a dark blue silk robe and black satin jacket. But his love for extravagance was obvious in his silver water-pipe — inlaid with layers of pearl and jade — and the seven-carat diamond ring on his middle finger of a hand that always seemed to be in motion. No, Zhang was not subtle; and Zhang had never sought the reputation of a gentleman. Liankui had warned me to expect a crude comment upon being introduced — Zhang was known to humiliate and embarrass women. Much to my relief, he simply nodded when my husband introduced me — a polite dismissal. As the evening progressed, and I observed some of the humiliating comments he made to the other women, I realized that his silence with me was a show of respect to my husband.

I was prepared to believe every evil and cruel story I had ever heard of the Green Gang, and to label them all as barbaric and crude, when my husband introduced me to the man of whom I had heard so much, Du Yuesheng. And Du was a vivid contrast to his partner, Mr Zhang.

"Du, may I present my wife, Ching Zhaohua," Liankui's comfort with Du was obvious as he introduced me.

"Happy birthday, Mr Du," I smiled and bowed politely as I met Mr Du, and tried to hide my interest in this mysterious and powerful man.

Du Yuesheng looked into my eyes, most inquisitively, for several seconds, as though he was truly trying to know me, and then a warm smile slowly crept onto his face. His words sounded most genuine — not a trace of stiff cordiality — when he greeted me.

"Thank you, Mrs Ching. It is indeed a pleasure to meet you. And thank you so very much for coming." I think it was his air of humility that impressed me most. In a room full of loud voices and music and extravagance, Mr Du seemed subdued and reserved, yet not aloof.

Over the years, I would come to like Du even more and realize how much he had in common with those individuals in my life, to whom I have afforded great respect. Du Yuesheng was always striving to learn more. Although he was not formally educated, he worked diligently to read the classics of Chinese literature. He practiced the art of calligraphy until he mastered it, and was elected to seats on the Municipal Council of the French Concession, the Stock Exchange, as well as the boards of various financial, educational, and charitable institutions. No, I would never reconcile my fondness for this man with the stories I had heard of his ruthless dealings with his enemies.

After a period of mingling at Du's party — silent mingling on my part — a servant appeared and bowed to me, and asked me to follow him. Liankui nodded his permission and I was led up the winding staircase.

There were three rooms, each with double doors opening into the other, giving the feel of one magnificent, chambered, unfolding room. Each room was set with five mahjong tables and around each table sat four ladies who were enjoying themselves immensely, and were laughing and gossiping — ladies who were most definitely not silent.

As I walked quietly through the room, taking in the energy and the sights of the women of the inner circle, I caught pieces of the conversations at each table, all punctuated by the whacking sounds of the mahjong tiles being shuffled, and the loud exclamations of the game.

"Little Wang was caught naked in bed with Lotus!"

"Old Fong, the old tortoise, shot Small Snake to death when Fong caught him hidden in the bedroom closet at night!" (This remark was met with roaring laughter by the other ladies at the table.)

"Chow, Pung, Kong!" (This meant a full set was on the table.)

"Wu!" (Someone had a complete hand to win the game.)

"Kill you thousands of times little devil!"

"Damn you tortoise eggs!"

I soaked in the unrestrained decadence as I walked through the room; most of these women wore flamboyant dresses with dazzling jewelry. All the diamonds and rubies and jade jewels seemed perfectly at home on these loud, colorful, cheerful women. Most were smoking as they played, and, just as downstairs, there were many opium couches. Only these couches were filled with women. The women were dreamily lounging, in their jewels and colorful dresses, and they seemed to be a natural element in the room.

I was not certain if Liankui's instructions about being silent extended to the presence of these women or not, but I decided that I really didn't care. I smiled as I took a seat on a sofa by the window, and decided to just relax and take it in — every detail of this dream-like place. What a story this would make for my children someday!

I sat there absorbed in my silence, and contemplation, of everything around me. I did not even notice as she approached me, the wife — the Fourth Wife — of Du Yuesheng.

"Hello, Mrs Ching, I am the wife of Du Yuesheng," and then she laughed as she continued, "everyone calls me Mrs Eighteenth Floor because my home is a suite on the eighteenth floor of the building." (The Cathay Building was one of the most glamorous buildings in the French Concession.) "I have heard much about you from your husband; he tells me that you studied at McTyeire. I wonder, did you know a Mrs Han? She is teaching me English now, I should say she is attempting to teach me English — I dare say I am not her most accomplished student!" 'Mrs Eighteenth Floor' smiled warmly as she addressed me. She hardly appeared to be the hostess of such a lavish party, dressed simply in a dark blue, silk dress, and wearing little make-up and jewelry.

Of course, I knew much about Mrs Eighteenth Floor, and had even seen her perform a few years earlier — she had been a famous Beijing opera singer in Shanghai for many years, always playing a male role. Although she would not have been considered a classic beauty — her figure was full, and her features were not particularly striking — I could sense immediately how she and Du would have been drawn to one another. Du admired her immensely. He respected her talent, as well as her intellect and open-mindedness; his other three wives were very quietly traditional. But I think it was her genuine, and down-to-earth warmth which drew Du — and others — to this lovely woman. I felt most honored by Mrs Eighteenth Floor's interest in me, and her obvious appreciation for my previous school.

"Yes, I studied under Mrs Han for two years. I found her to be an excellent teacher — please give her my regards when you see her for your next lesson." Mrs Eighteenth Floor and I sat quietly, and had a most lovely conversation amidst the whacking of the mahjong tiles and the loud laughter and the gossip and the opium.

I left that day having made a new friend, and marveling at how our perceptions of people — people of whom we read and hear, and think we know — have no validity whatsoever. We think we know people through newspapers and stories and public perception. But it is not true. There is always a real person under that perception.

As our driver drove us home, well past midnight that evening, I chatted happily to Liankui about my new friendship — Mrs Eighteenth Floor and I had planned to meet for lunch in the coming week — when I realized that my husband was deep in thought, obviously concerned about something.

"What is it, Liankui? Did I say something to upset you?" I had thought he would be pleased that I had made a good impression on our hostess.

"It will be made public tomorrow, Zhaohua — it is reported that Chiang Kai-shek is being held hostage by the Young Marshal." The Young Marshal, Zhang Xueliang — son of the old Marshal, Zhang Zuolin — and his large Northeastern Army, had been sent to Xian to fight the Communists. But the Young Marshal and his troops were reluctant to open fire on their fellow Chinese citizens. They met secretly with Zhou Enlai, Communist leader, and forged an alliance, in an attempt to organize a united front against the Japanese. It was an open betrayal of Chiang. Upon hearing of the negotiations, Chiang had immediately flown to Xian to meet with the Young Marshal, who tried to persuade Chiang to unite with the Communists, and to help them oppose the Japanese.

Chiang was not receptive to negotiations and it was rumored that the Young Marshal and Zhou Enlai had ordered Chiang to be held in Xian.

"If the Young Marshal and Zhou Enlai executed Chiang Kai-shek, it would be disastrous for China, Zhaohua. The Japanese hate the Communists as much as Chiang does. They would charge China without restraint if they thought the Communists were actually gaining control. Everything is heating up, Zhaohua — something will have to break soon. And I fear it will be China."

19

The impending threat of war could be felt in the air that winter. The Japanese were coming, and we all knew it. To make matters worse, our leader, Chiang Kai-shek — unpopular though he was — was being held hostage by a faction of his own army. The Young Marshal, along with Communist leader, Zhou Enlai, were holding Chiang Kai-shek in an attempt to negotiate an alliance between Chiang and the Communists. Their 'demands' were that Chiang Kai-shek join forces with the Communists and actively resist the Japanese. Additionally, Zhang demanded the release of the Seven Gentlemen, who were still being held.

Yes, the Young Marshal and Zhou Enlai represented the hearts of the people in their attempts.

For ten days, just before Christmas, my husband would wake early, dash for the newspapers and then call his friend, Du. Or sometimes he would go directly to Du's house.

At last, on Christmas Day, the papers reported that Chiang was to be released.

"I don't understand. Chiang must have relented — the Young Marshal would never have released him if there had not been a deal. But there are no clear reports coming from Xian. It is not clear if Chiang's forces have intimidated the Young Marshal, or vice versa. I guess we will know when Chiang returns. I agree with Du — Chiang would never truly join the Communists — and yet — share the Communist's concerns over the progress of the Japanese. We will know soon enough — Chiang is to return to Nanjing today." Liankui saw politics from the inside — there was always so much more happening than what was reported in the papers.

It was announced that an agreement had been reached. The civil war came to an abrupt end. The Communists would be recognized as legitimate in the North, within the loose framework of the Central Government, and they would give up their program of revolution in the countryside. Dr Sun Yat-sen's program as set forth in Three Principles of the People —

Nationalism, Democracy, and the Livelihood of the People — was to be the code of the land.

Additionally, Chiang was to end his policy of non-resistance against the Japanese. It was a step towards the unification of China.

The Young Marshal accompanied Chiang to Nanjing — as a show of good faith. And Chiang promptly placed the Young Marshal under arrest. He was tried by a military court, convicted and sentenced to ten years in prison. Four days later, the Young Marshal was given amnesty, but placed under house arrest and remained under house arrest for the rest of Chiang's life.

The Young Marshal's experience did much to discourage other Nationalist generals who might have been tempted to defy Chiang Kai-shek.

"I am both relieved and worried. Public outrage over the Seven Gentlemen is heating up. The people want their release; I think I have found a way to buy them some time — still, Chiang will lose face if the charges are dismissed. But he will lose support if they are not." Liankui practiced law with great integrity. Although he served as Du's primary counsel and, indeed, dear friend, when the leader of the Seven Gentlemen requested his legal services, my husband saw the merits of their case, and had taken it despite Du's connections with Chiang.

Finally, in June, my husband — leading the strongest team of lawyers in the history of China — argued successfully for a postponement of the trial of the Seven Gentlemen. The prosecutors had attempted to link the crimes of the Seven Gentlemen to those of the Young Marshal; calling them conspirators. My husband demanded that the Young Marshal be called as a witness to substantiate that claim. If the Young Marshal could not be summoned, the prosecution must at least produce records to confirm such accusations. The first judges rejected Liankui's demands.

So my husband promptly filed a motion requesting disqualification of the judges, based on their lack of impartiality. The judges disqualified themselves. New judges were appointed. Again my husband argued that if the Seven Gentlemen were going to be charged with conspiring with the Young Marshal, either the Young Marshal, or condemning records, must be introduced. The newspapers were filled with accounts of the argument — my husband had argued passionately and eloquently. Finally, the court agreed.

The Seven Gentlemen were released 'on bail' until Zhang — or records — could be brought before the court.

The case would not come back into the courtroom.

On July 7, 1937, less than a month after the headline case, the Japanese began their invasion of Beijing by attacking the Marco Polo Bridge. The Seven Gentlemen, and their followers, had been right — Japan was a dire threat to China. It would be over a year before the case was formally dropped, but Chiang Kai-shek could not possibly push for prosecution of those who had spoken out against the Japanese, as the Japanese soldiers were raping and plundering Chinese village after village; it would be political suicide.

No, Chiang Kai-shek had bigger problems on his hands.

"The Japanese will come to Shanghai soon; they're worried about Chiang's reported alliance with the Communists — an allied China would crush Japan — they'll move quickly, Zhaohua. Many people are leaving even within the International Settlement. I have a client, Zhang Tanru, who has rented two apartments in Hong Kong, and has offered to take us all there. I've been giving Tanru free legal advice for years and I've always known him to be a good man, but I had no idea he'd be so generous. But we must decide — and quickly — if we don't want the apartment, others will."

"I think we should go, Liankui. Hong Kong is a British colony; I don't think Japan will attack the British, not yet anyway. And you're right; the Japanese will come for Shanghai soon."

Over the next few weeks, tensions mounted. We were busy making arrangements to leave. It is a most remarkable feeling, to pack your home in preparation for war. To think that anything left behind could be bombed or pillaged or occupied. We arranged to have our family furnishings stored in a warehouse outside the city, and I decided to bring family photographs with me, along with any official documents. Our homes had been leased, so we did not have to worry about selling the property.

Father had decided that his family — Mother, Wanhua, Kaihua, and Sonya — would remain in Shanghai. Jade had indeed left Father, and I did not know where to reach her before we left. I admit I did not try very hard. There had been a silent understanding that Jade's recent visit was a sort of goodbye between us.

In the chaos of impending war, my only thoughts were of getting my family safely to Hong Kong. The details were endless and I remember that I kept thinking that we were being overly cautious. Chiang Kai-shek would surely stop the Japanese before they invaded Shanghai. It would all be over soon. We probably would not even have to go to Hong Kong in the end. Things would settle down.

This was what I thought, even as I frantically ordered the older children's school transcripts, collected all the necessary documentation, arranged for movers, and sorted through various possessions for ancestral or sentimental value. Liankui had given me many exquisite pieces of jewelry over the past few years, and of course they would go, but the item packed most carefully was the hairpin Mother had given me on my wedding day. The one Grandfather had given her. As I held the lovely hairpin, I thought of Grandfather's words again. How had he known so very much?

In that first week in August, there were constant negotiations between the Municipal Council of the International Settlement and the Japanese government. The Foreign Settlements had always seemed like an oasis amidst the civil wars of China. Everyone feared the anger of the European actions, and did not disturb their settlements — until now. French and English governments were strongly recommending evacuation of their citizens. Liankui and I would be up before dawn, waiting for the newspapers to arrive, with reports of the negotiations. And on August 12, the Municipal Council ordered mobilization of the Shanghai Volunteers to maintain law and order in settlement areas.

The following day, August 13, 1937, Japan attacked Shanghai.

In the chaos of that first attack, two of China's warplanes were mistakenly hit by anti-aircraft fire, as they were defending the Chinese City of Shanghai against the Japanese. The Chinese pilots lost control of their aircraft, and accidentally dropped two bombs on the Great World Amusement Park in the heart of the International Settlement, killing hundreds of civilians.

My husband had been sitting in his car in traffic in front of the amusement park just minutes before the bombs fell. He was so badly shaken that when he arrived home, he ordered me to take the children and leave for Hong Kong immediately on the next available steamer. There was no more time to prepare.

Thus, I took seven children — Liankui's five children and our young two — board the SS *Conte Verti*, an Italian steamship, which was packed beyond capacity with other refugees who were all as frightened and sad and worried as we were. Everyone was leaving someone behind. Liankui remained in Shanghai to wrap up some business affairs; he would come as soon as he could. His daughter, Margaret, was heartbroken as she said goodbye to Henry Ho, a young man who had become most important in her life.

I did my best to appear calm and brave, even nonchalant, in the eyes of the children. But I was twenty-one years old, and was running from war in the only home I had ever known. I was going to a place I had never seen, and was responsible for seven children. And inside, I was terrified.

The sea was unusually rough as we sailed to Hong Kong. Most people on the ship were seasick so there was the constant smell of vomit. Each of the children took their turns being ill, and I found so much strength in the knowledge that seasickness is temporary. They would be well when we reached land. Everything would be fine.

It was pitch dark when we dropped anchor near Kowloon Pier in the colony of Hong Kong, after five exhausting days at sea. My husband's friend, Tanru, was indeed a gentleman — and a true friend; he was there, along with his three sons, to greet us as we stepped on that rocky land. He had hired a fleet of cars to take us to a house they had rented in Kowloon Tong, a beautiful residential area. Over the past month, Tanru had been overwhelmed with requests for sanctuary, and every room of the elaborate mansion was being used as a bedroom.

Historically Hong Kong was only a barren island when it was ceded by China to Britain in 1842. In the eyes of the British, it was an important strategic island, as well as a potential trading port, and they constructed a small town on the north side of the rocky terrain; the island's primary sources of revenue were opium and salt trading. The colony's size grew in later years when China was forced to allow the British to take over adjacent territory, but the population remained small.

But in 1937, as the Japanese invaded China, tens of thousands of Chinese sought refuge in the British colony of Hong Kong, and Hong Kong saw its population triple, swelling to more than one million. The Hong Kong economy was booming. The colony was a collage of past and present, as new buildings were constructed adjacent to old ones, creating housing for the hordes of refugees.

We had rarely slept on board the ship due to our own sickness, or that of others, and I was immensely grateful to Tanru for saving my family a room in his home. As we settled in and made our pallets on the floor, Margaret, Alice and the boys fell asleep immediately, despite the howling winds and thunderstorm that had started outside.

The younger children were more disturbed by the storm, but finally, Judie and Anthony were quieted and drifted into a peaceful sleep. I lay beside my children and I was so grateful to be off that ship. Although I was exhausted, my mind was filled with what might be happening in Shanghai. We had heard little news on board the ship, only that the Japanese were sending in more troops, and I was reluctant to discuss too many details in front of the children. As I lay in that room, I imagined I could hear the warplanes and the bombs showering down on Shanghai. I was so caught up in my visions, and sounds of the war, that I felt I was there. I was certain I could hear the bombs. Suddenly, a large tree limb came flying through the window over Margaret and Alice.

That same night, September 2 — our first night in Hong Kong — the island was hit by the worst typhoon in the history of the colony. First, the electricity went out. Tanru came beating on our door, urging everyone to the interior hallways of the house. The wind seemed to be everywhere; doors were blowing open, windows breaking. The winds took life-form that night, and the sound of their screams was deafening. When the upstairs windows started to shatter and explode, Tanru urged everyone to the bottom floor, and center of the house.

Anthony and Judie were crying, being awakened so suddenly in a strange place, and in the center of this fit of the earth. I groped for my primary bag — the one with Mother's hairpin and my jewelry, and our papers — and I draped the strap across my shoulder. I held Judie's hand, and carried Anthony, feeling my way down the dark hallway with my shoulder on the wall. Liankui's sons brought what they could carry of our bags. People were screaming, adults and children alike; some were trying to shout orders above the chaos, some were in a state of panic. I tried to feel my way carefully down the stairs — small steps — using my feet like a blind person's walking stick, and then, just as my feet felt the end of the stairs, we heard it — the ceiling had collapsed on the upstairs rooms. Everywhere there was water as rain sheeted in the shattered windows. Darkness. And screams.

I sat huddled under a table with my children, and I waited for the dawn.

Finally, we were greeted with a sunless dawn — and in that dark, foggy, wet dawn, we saw the devastation. It was as though the earth was ashamed and stayed dark to shield us from seeing all that she had done. Hundreds of fishermen had drowned. Twenty-seven steamers were sunk or blown ashore. Everywhere, houses and businesses were destroyed, trees snapped like twigs, cars lying on their sides — blown yards away from where they had been parked. Many were injured — or killed — as buildings collapsed.

I walked as though I were in an abstract living painting, my vision blurred by rain, fog, and chaos. And with utter physical exhaustion, I went to the telegraph office to let Liankui know that we had arrived just ahead of the storm. I wondered if I should thank God, or be angry with him.

Human beings are like ants, you know — when their mounds are crushed, they immediately set about rebuilding. After a day to absorb the shock and the reality of what had happened, we set about finding another place to live. With the help of Tanru, my family and I moved to an apartment of our own — the second floor of an old house on Hong Kong Island. I purchased some basic furniture — a few beds, mattresses, a kitchen table and some chairs, and some kitchen utensils. It is truly amazing how few 'things' it takes to survive.

I cannot begin to imagine what those first few weeks would have been like without dear Mrs Chen, our landlady. Mrs Chen was the matriarch of our neighborhood — she knew, and cared for, everyone. Having raised five children, she was most adept at seeing what was needed, and offering help or direction, often before I could organize myself to ask. She understood that if the children were bored, they would be more consumed with the war, the homesickness, and the terrors, through which we had just lived. So Mrs Chen set about immediately engaging the children. The boys were assigned tasks to help with the clean-up of the apartment, pending school arrangements. Margaret was to be tutored in English, and apply to continue her studies at the University of Hong Kong. Mrs Chen spoke with the administrators of the Sacred Heart School and gained admission for Alice. Sacred Heart was a Catholic school, just across the street from our apartment. And dear Mrs Chen was an expert at engaging young Judie and Anthony in 'helpful' tasks around the house, the primary help being the occupation of those small, inquisitive minds — and hands! By the time Liankui arrived, almost a month later, I could see the quiet admiration in his eyes as he surveyed my ability to function without him.

But Liankui was also devastated by what he had seen in Shanghai. The Chinese armies, under orders of Chiang, had tried to leave Shanghai just before the Japanese arrived. Many didn't get out in time and it is estimated that China lost over a quarter of a million soldiers in the capture of Shanghai. No, Chiang's army did not even fight against the Japanese; they simply followed Chiang's orders to retreat quickly. I read an interesting newspaper article, which quoted Mr Oskar Trautmann, a German Consul following Chiang's rapid retreat, "My name is Trautmann, the Chinese pronunciation is *tao de man*, which means 'running slowly.' I cannot compete with Chiang Kai-shek, who can *tao de kuai* — 'running fast.' "

It was then — drunk with easy victory in their capture of Shanghai — that the Japanese marched into Nanjing. And the atrocities committed in Nanjing are recorded in history. To this day I cannot reconcile the stories of these atrocities of the Japanese soldiers with my perception of humanity. The stories — and they are true — of the rapes, the tortures, the pillaging — they can only have been committed in the intoxication of the dark side of the human spirit.

We listened, and we hated the Japanese with every fiber of our beings, and I could not imagine the most primitive barbarian being more purely evil. War and rape are so much more frightening seen through the eyes of an adult — the eyes of a mother. I looked at my children — at Judie — and imagined her in the hands of these Japanese soldiers, and my blood chilled. I was glad that their young minds were consumed with sweeping Mrs Chen's porch, and arguing over the broom; that they were relatively unaware of the threat of Japanese soldiers.

When Liankui came to Hong Kong, it was as though Shanghai came with him. Many of his business associates had also arrived in Hong Kong, and soon they established a daily routine of tea in a suite provided by Du Yuesheng — the penthouse of the Gloucester Hotel. Du and 'Mrs Eighteenth Floor' had arrived in Hong Kong just before Liankui. Du's First and Second Wives had chosen to stay in Shanghai; Third Wife had taken her children and gone to London.

It was a difficult time for my husband, who was so professionally revered in Shanghai, and was — for the first time in his life — at a loss in how to spend his hours. He had never chosen to learn English, and, of course, he was not a member of the Hong Kong Bar. I suppose it was a natural choice for Liankui to indulge in his favorite pastime, gambling. Except in Hong Kong, it became his profession — gold bullion speculation. Yes, it's a much more respectable risk than *jai alai*. Still it held that element of risk, which my husband so required in his life. The British had outlawed gambling, except for wagers on the horse races, which were considered sporting events.

"I've opened an account with Hang Seng Bank, Zhaohua. Mr Lin, the principal owner of the bank, was most accommodating in his terms. It helps to have friends in difficult times. I had nearly forgotten that I helped negotiate the terms for Mr Lin's release when he had been kidnapped in Shanghai several years back — he still remembers it, and greeted me as a dear friend."

"You never mentioned a kidnapping to me, Liankui," I could hardly believe my ears, and the casual manner in which my husband spoke of his involvement in such an event.

"Oh, Zhaohua," Liankui smiled at me as he spoke, "there are so many stories. At the height of the warlord feuding, there were so many kidnappings, assassinations and secret alliances. But I love you too much, my First Wife, to share them with you. They are stories I will carry to my grave. Knowledge can be dangerous. Men have been murdered for a mere slip of the tongue." As my husband left for tea with Du Yuesheng, it suddenly dawned on me. Of course, my husband, as primary legal adviser, and personal friend to Du, widely recognized leader of the Green Gang, was deeply involved in the dealings of the Green Gang. Yes, of course, Du had always been a part of our lives; I had grown quite fond of him. I suppose I had chosen to stay naïve as to the extent of my husband's involvement. And now, to suddenly envision my husband negotiating with kidnappers, and knowledgeable of the mysteries surrounding assassinations, it was a revelation — and not a comfortable revelation. There was little in which to find comfort in those years.

The Japanese were securely entrenched along China's coastline, including all the major cities; most of China was now militarily occupied, and ruled, by the Japanese. Tensions were mounting around the world.

In spite of the occupation, by the end of the year, Liankui's sons had chosen to return to Shanghai to finish their education under the Japanese occupation. They had been deeply involved in their school, the Zhengshi Middle School. The school had hired foreigners to serve on the board of directors, so it was less likely to be attacked than those under strictly Chinese administration.

Margaret and Henry were married that year in Hong Kong. After a quiet ceremony, they left Hong Kong for Chiang Kai-shek's wartime capital in Chongqing.

Our lives in Hong Kong settled into a routine of sorts; my days were spent caring for children, preparing meals, and grasping at any news of Shanghai and the rest of China.

I was also pregnant again, much to the delight of my husband.

Liankui would have his daily tea with Du and other associates, and monitor his gold bullion trading; another associate, Rushan Zhu, owned a gold trading company in Hong Kong, so my husband's speculation activities increased.

Of course, gold speculation doesn't carry the thrilling intensity or the instant gratification of a mahjong table or a *jai alai* game. Before long, my husband discovered Macao to fill that void. Macao was a Portuguese colony about thirty-five miles from Hong Kong, comprised of a small peninsula and two tiny islands. Gambling was, and is, the primary source of revenue for Macao.

In an effort to take my mind off the war, Liankui suggested that he and I take a trip there in the spring following our arrival. Mrs Chen offered to look after my children, saying that I needed the rest. I was finding this pregnancy more difficult than the others.

When our boat docked in Macao, I could hardly believe my eyes. I thought it must be Liankui Ching's picture of paradise. We took a taxi to the Central Hotel, which boasted an elaborate floating casino, a world-class elegant restaurant, and a gorgeous cabaret. As the taxi drove through the city — everywhere — people gambled. They came from all over the world to Macao. Every business was centered on gambling, and even in the alleyways, people were huddled playing cards or throwing dice. It was an endless, decadent feast for those who love that feeling — that incredible rush — of risk.

Much to my husband's annoyance, I did not share his enthusiasm for throwing our money away. I could not imagine how these people could be so careless, as I watched thousands of dollars lost in one deal of the cards. I had never respected Liankui's addiction to gambling, but when I saw him cheerfully bet — often to lose — thousands of dollars, as our country was at war, and our home most probably destroyed, and our futures so uncertain, I could not hide my distaste. I sat in the corner of the grand Central Hotel and watched my husband, and I thought him selfish and juvenile in his fever.

I told Liankui that I was ill. Finally, he took me back to Hong Kong. Although I refused to return to Macao with him, he traveled there regularly. Of course, there were wins. But wins only provided more revenue with which to gamble.

I think that's when I outgrew Liankui Ching. He was more than twice times my age, and had a law degree and important friends and immense knowledge. But as I sat there in that plush chair of the casino, and watched my husband smoke and blink and bet incessantly, I felt infinitely older than him.

It was in the summer of 1938 that I gave birth for the fourth time in the Hong Kong Sanitorium, located in Happy Valley. Priscilla was adventurous from the first day — she was born, as we say, in 'the birth of a goddess with a leg on the lotus flower!' That meant that she had come out with her little leg first.

During the following year, tensions mounted in the political situation in Asia. My husband spent most of his days, and our money, in Macao. And I slipped into the abyss created by the arrival of an infant, into the midst of two toddlers, and an extended family — all huddled in a tiny apartment, hiding from war.

20

In September of 1939, war was declared in Europe.

There is always a profit to be made on war.

With that declaration, my husband's many investments in gold bullion increased tenfold. He made hundreds of thousands of dollars. Of course, he reinvested all his profits in more gold. I pleaded with him to hold some out — it was just a matter of time before Japanese soldiers would come for Hong Kong. He did not listen.

Hong Kong's currency was pegged to the English pound, and when the news of American support of the pound sterling reached Hong Kong, the gold market crashed overnight. Liankui lost everything he had made — and more.

Of course, it wasn't my husband's fault. Yes, I can feel positive or negative energy when I enter someone's home. I can tell if it is a home of comfort, or a home of pain. I can tell if positive energy is created in the home, or if positive energy is drained, leaving only negative. I believe in many of the theories of feng shui.

But when my husband was convinced that the entire world economy had shifted to send him into bankruptcy because our apartment was inhabited by unfavorable spirits, I could only shake my head in dismay, as I packed to move to our new home. I suppose that was the first real sign of my husband's paranoia. There would be more.

After a tearful goodbye with Mrs Chen, we moved into our new apartment on Robinson Road on Hong Kong Island. Even now, my mind holds a crisp picture of my young family in that apartment in the spring of 1940: my aging husband, my young Judie who was always with a book, young Anthony who was still suffering from occasional asthma attacks, and my happy baby Priscilla.

Although I knew I would also love the baby who would be born later that year — I was pregnant again, my fears for my family's financial security were coming to fruition earlier than I had anticipated.

We had next to nothing left. Liankui continued to gamble away anything he could get his hands on. Between caring for the children and another child to come, I had no time — and less energy — to continue my studies or get a job so that I could provide for our children.

Those were dark days for me, spiritually. At twenty-five, I was tired. Tired of motherhood, of being married to Liankui Ching, and tired of worrying about the future, when I received my first letter from Wanhua, with news of my family.

Wanhua wrote that Father had left with Sonya for Beijing. He was going to join the North China puppet government under Wang Keming. The Japanese had persuaded China's last emperor, Pu Yi, to act as leader for Manchuria — he was the same child emperor who had been dethroned when Dr Sun Yat-sen had led the people to establish the Republic, just before I was born. He was a traditional symbol to whom many Chinese would cling and obey without question, though the Japanese government instructed him what to do. He was their 'puppet.' The status of Father's scholarly ancestors had qualified my Father for the position of Commissioner of Customs in Qingdao. Kaihua and his family had moved with Father, all living in a grand home in Beijing.

Mother and Wanhua had remained in Shanghai, along with Little Tiger, Kaihua's youngest son, who had developed a special bond with Mother. Our home had been destroyed, but Father was having a lovely new home built on leasehold land, along with some extra houses, which he would lease for income.

Wanhua also wrote that she would be graduating from St John's University in two years. Yes, Wanhua was going to get her degree. She was free and thriving, even in occupied Shanghai. Tears dripped onto the letter as I read. Tears of relief, tears of love, tears of exhaustion, and tears for the life I would not know.

Then, as I sat there crying and indulging in self-pity, I felt that wonderful feeling, which is a gift of the gods meant especially for women, that feeling of the movement of another human life inside my own, that incredible feeling of life and the movement of my young fetus. I dried my tears, changed little Priscilla's diaper, propped up Anthony's pillows so that he could breathe more clearly, and found Judie's favorite book, and I persevered.

My desire to care for my children was enough to propel me through my days, but once again, I no longer listened with living eyes to my husband's gossip when he returned from his afternoon teas with Du. The political news rarely changed. The Nationalist government, still led by

Chiang Kai-Shek, was retreating further. The Japanese occupied most of eastern China, with Chiang Kai-shek and his Nationalist Party operating out of Chongqing, far west of Shanghai.

Du Yuesheng often traveled from Hong Kong to Chongqing; he had organized his Green Gang members to provide badly needed supplies from China to Chiang and the Nationalist loyalists on the black market, in exchange for rare minerals, which were plentiful in Chongqing. While there, he often met with the head of the Nationalist Secret Service, Dai Li, whom Du provided with information gathered from his massive network of Green Gang workers, still in operation in Shanghai under Japanese occupation.

It was fascinating dinner conversation, but even that which is most intriguing can lose its luster in hollow eyes.

I began contemplating speaking to Liankui about the possibility of returning to Shanghai — and trying to make a life under the Japanese occupation — at least I would have the comfort of familiarity. Yes, I thought of my mother, and the happiness she had found when we moved, for that brief period, to the Chinese City. It is fascinating, how much of our mothers we come to know, indeed to live, as adults.

During that week, as I was walking along the street in Hong Kong, looking for something economical to prepare for dinner, I almost bumped into another lady, holding the hands of her two children.

"Excuse me, please — Janet? Janet Xie? It's me — Zhaohua Ching! I thought you were in Chongqing! Oh — Janet," I embraced my friend with so much joy spilling from my heart. We both had to wipe our eyes as finally, we separated, and moved to a nearby bench to recover from our tears and shock.

"I thought James was with the Nationalist government in Chongqing. What brings you to Hong Kong?"

"My husband was transferred to the Hong Kong Office of the Ministry of Communication just about three weeks ago. I have wondered where you were — it is so difficult to get reliable information out of Shanghai. Oh, Zhaohua, I have thought of you so often and missed your friendship so very much. Tell me all about your life now."

I proudly introduced my children, who were all with me, and they met Janet's children, and I thought my joy could not be greater. And then Janet asked if I had been in touch with Nancy — she had been living in Kowloon for months — in fact she had just been released from the hospital.

Janet and I laughed and talked and stepped back into our friendship as though there were not a lifetime of experiences between us since we had last been together. It felt so wonderful, so very, very wonderful, to be chatting with my old friend.

Though it was late when I returned home, I could not wait to phone Nancy. My mood evaporated, however, when I heard the weakness in my friend's voice as she came to the phone.

"Nancy? This is Zhaohua, Zhaohua Ching, I have been in Hong Kong for three years. I just ran into Janet quite by accident and she gave me your number ... Nancy? Nancy?" I could hear my friend's soft sobs through the phone line. Yes, McTyeire, a lifetime ago, had provided the setting for three young women to bond so soulfully. I continued slowly, allowing my friend time to get over the surprise. "Janet says you have just been released from the hospital. Are you okay, Nancy?"

"The doctors think that everything will be fine, but they are guarded. I'm pregnant again. The past few months have been most trying ... we traveled from Shanghai to Chongqing, and then here to Hong Kong. The journey was so hard ... China, our China is so sad, Zhaohua, we have two young children who traveled with us. We all survived, but my body was so weakened — there was little food — anyway, they think that I will not lose my child, if I rest and get a proper diet. Oh, Zhaohua, I am sorry to go on about my troubles, it is so wonderful to hear your voice, my old friend. Please, tell me, fill me in on your life since those beautiful days when we were last together."

So I had another reunion — my heart was so warmed as my friend and I exchanged the details of our lives. Yet, I could sense the change in Nancy. She felt so incredibly weak.

Over the next few months, I rarely thought of returning to Shanghai, as the days were brightened by the occasional visits with my old friends. We would visit, and our children would play; there are photographs of the three of us that fall — Nancy and I with our pregnant bellies, Janet slender and beautiful, all of us smiling as though our lives were as carefree as they had been only a few short years ago.

In my happiness, my husband and I even managed to revive an element of friendship. I took new interest in his reports of his meetings, and he seemed to be home more. I thought perhaps he was realizing how absurd his persistent gambling had been.

Until he left one day for Macao, and did not return the next day.

I went into labor. While my husband was at the craps table, losing the last of our savings, I was alone with three children and about to give birth to his — our — fifth child.

I phoned the school and they sent Alice home to drive me to the hospital. Then she returned to care for the other children while I was experiencing a slow and excruciating labor. I tried desperately to ward off my anger and sadness at my husband's abandonment. I heard Mother's words, saying that it would bring poor health to me, and a melancholy spirit to my child, to display negative emotions during childbirth. But childbirth is frightening. It doesn't matter how many times you've been through it; a woman looks death in the face when she gives birth. And I looked death in the face — for the fifth time — feeling abandoned, frightened, alone, and not respected — indeed humiliated — by the father of my child. My husband.

I did not speak for weeks after my Frank was born. Perhaps that is why he was always brimming with words — I gave him all of mine.

Of course, Liankui was most eloquent in his apology. I kept my eyes on the window as he showered me with eloquence. I had forgiven this man so much — but not this. No. This hurt was too deep, or perhaps it was just that my soul had no forgiveness left for this man. I would never again be deluded into thinking that Liankui Ching would change. No, Mother, love does not always come after marriage.

I had given birth five times in eight years. And I resolved that there would be no more pregnancies.

Over that following year, I started trying to sell my jewelry. There were days when I did not have the resources to feed my children. There were no public schools in Hong Kong and often I could not pay the fees for Alice and Judie. Anthony's asthma became worse and there was no money for a doctor. The days were a blur of too little food, crying children, constant worry and utter mental and physical exhaustion.

In December of 1941, when I thought things could not get worse, Japanese planes bombed Pearl Harbor.

21

The phone rang in the middle of the night, waking us from a sound sleep. It was Tanru.

"Liankui, the Japanese have bombed the Americans — Pearl Harbor. The Sino-Japanese War is now part of the global war between the Allies and Axis powers. Hong Kong will be the first target of the Japanese. Prepare for the worst, my friend. Gather any essentials, especially food — I'll be in touch when I can."

My body started trembling as soon as I heard the news and did not stop throughout the night. I had not dreamed that war would follow us from China to Hong Kong. I waited, counting the minutes — one, two, three — both grateful and fearful with each passing hour. At last, it was dawn. I was banking on the fact that few Chinese-speaking citizens tuned into the BBC or Voice of America, and I phoned the shops as soon as they opened. The shopowners promised delivery of goods, but when the hour went by and they did not show, I knew word was out. I stayed with the children and sent Alice, accompanied by our friend Larry Wang, who was a student living in our apartment complex, with the last of our money to buy anything she could.

Again, I counted the minutes. This time until Alice returned. She had managed to bring back two dozen cans each of corned beef and sardines, and two bags each of oats and flour.

"The rice shops and grocery stores are all closed; people are selling all kinds of food in the street. You just buy what they have and pay what they ask. But there was no rice to be found." Alice was proud of what she had managed to purchase; many people had not been so fortunate. Then she almost cried as she opened the bags of flour, and found that cornstarch had been substituted. Her despair quickly turned to rage, and she was determined to return the bags to the swindlers. I told her it was no use arguing with them — better to be cheated than injured or murdered.

It was time to concentrate on survival. We set about rationing and hiding our food. First, we carefully divided our food into rations by priority. Preference was given to the old — Liankui; the sick — Anthony; and the young — Judie, Priscilla and Frank. They all received the rice, milk powder and oats. Alice and I would survive on a mixture of oats and cornstarch. One can of sardines or corned beef was to be our entire family's main dish. We would eat just enough to survive. Then we packed our valuable papers, Mother's hairpin and the jewelry I had left. Our final task was that of making black curtains for the windows.

The following day, the BBC kept repeating the same line over and over: "Britain and Japan are at war." Everywhere, the words resonated.

That afternoon, the first air raid siren sounded. The central market was bombed. Hundreds were killed. The sirens sounded day and night. We saw the planes — flying low — on the other side of Victoria Harbor; over Kowloon we saw the hatches open and we could actually see the bombs drop. When the bombs hit, it was like ten thousand thunderstorms at once. I could feel the reverberations inside my body as I tried desperately to nurse Frank. My children screamed and covered their ears.

Crowds of frightened people, their belongings slung over their shoulders in bundles, sought refuge under doorways and staircases; children were clinging tightly to their parents' clothes. Many were unable to comprehend what was happening to them, and fell into the mass chaos of war. Black smoke filled the air. At night the sky blazed red, lit by flames from the buildings hit by incendiary bombs and artillery fire. The stench of sulfur mixed with blood was everywhere. Words cannot describe war-torn Hong Kong. If there was indeed a hell, it abandoned its dark home and dwelled in Hong Kong, as in other parts of the world, in those weeks.

We huddled in our apartment in filth, hunger and fear — close to one another, quiet and on edge. Late one afternoon, there was a knock on the door. Alice answered, cautiously.

"It's me," our friend, Larry Wang, said. Alice opened the door to invite him in. Larry had been very helpful during the first few days of bombing. So when we saw him dressed in the civilian uniform of the Hong Kong Defense Force, we were both proud and saddened. "The Hong Kong Volunteer Defense Corps has issued pleas for recruits to help the elderly and children. It is voluntary, but I want to help. I've come to say goodbye." It was a tearful goodbye, full of best wishes for this young man who had come into our hearts.

As the sirens continued to sound, we found the energy to drag our bodies, time and again, to the damp basement of our building, which was used as an air raid shelter. Then, one night, in one of the worst bombings, as we mechanically gathered our things and grabbed our children, my Anthony looked at me and pleaded with me not to take him into that basement again.

"Please, Mom, I don't want to go there again," he cried. "I don't think I'll be killed by the bombing, but I am sure to be choked by the stuffy air down there."

I looked into Anthony's eyes and realized that he was probably right. His breathing had become almost impossible. I thought that yes, it would be better to die quickly, in an explosion, than to suffocate.

"Don't cry, Anthony; we'll let them go down. I'll stay with you. We'll be together." I hoped my son did not feel my arms trembling as I embraced him.

After that day, I sent the others downstairs. Every time the sirens blared, Anthony and I remained upstairs. We would go into the closet of our apartment and I would read a story, loudly, to my son. Trying to soothe his nerves and strengthen my own. And wait for the next bomb.

In just five days, five eternal days, Kowloon had fallen to the Japanese. The Japanese entrenched their armies and aimed their artillery across Victoria Harbor to Hong Kong proper, day and night, terrorizing the people. Our Robinson Road apartment was on the side of Victoria Peak overlooking the harbor and was an easy target.

I watched through the window as the building across the street from our apartment caught fire and was consumed in flames in a matter of seconds. My friends and neighbors were in that building. I smelled that smell of sulfur and burning flesh, and I vomited.

The following day, Liankui announced that we would not sit there and wait for death. We were leaving. An associate of his, Kwok Tong, whom Liankui knew from his afternoon teas in the Gloucester Hotel, had an apartment in Happy Valley; Kwok Tong had told Liankui to go there if our area was taken. We took only the bare essentials and began the long walk to Happy Valley. Alice carried baby Frank on her back while Liankui held Judie's hand. A friend of Liankui's offered to carry Anthony and I held Priscilla in my arms. As we walked, we passed body after body, lying on the road. Most were dead, but some were clinging to life. Dante's picture of hell was a paradise compared to what we saw on the streets of Hong Kong. We tried to cross to the other side of the road, or into the grass, and instructed the children to look in the other direction. I don't quite know how we made it. With each step, I was certain we could not make another. Yet we did.

At last, we huddled inside Kwok Tong's small apartment. People were everywhere — even sleeping under the beds to create more floor space. I forbade my children to look out the windows — there were always dead bodies.

We had fled to Happy Valley seeking refuge, but war, as so many know, is not predictable in its reach. We arrived to more paranoia; in an apartment on Blue Pool Road, which was in an exclusive area just above the road from Kwok Tong's apartment, a tragic and violent massacre had just taken place. The victims were friends of Mr Tong's — Mr Wang, the Hong Kong Manager of the Ministry of Communications of the Chongqing government, his family and his friends. Wang had kept guns in his home to protect himself and the seventeen people living there. One evening, he heard noises outside his home; he thought looters were coming. He fired a few shots into the sky and out the window, just to scare them off.

They were not looters. They were Japanese foot soldiers. They burst into Wang's home. First they raped the women, as the men watched helplessly. Then, they stabbed everyone, including the children, to death.

War reduces human beings to their primal elements. Simultaneously, it exposes the colors of the spirit. Some are light and shine with compassion and courage in the face of fear. Others are dark. But everything in the middle dissipates and you see the essence of the human.

I have tried to tell myself that men must leave their humanity behind when they go to war. That they must call on the dark side of their spirits, in order to shield their minds from the fact that they are taking the lives of other human beings — men, and women, and children. I try to tell myself that the Japanese soldiers, like other soldiers in other places and times, became consumed in that darkness. But still, if I am honest, I cannot forgive them.

Despite the rapid fall of Kowloon, Japanese demands for the island's surrender were flatly rejected by the Governor of Hong Kong. But finally, on Christmas Day, nearly three blood-filled weeks since the fighting had begun, the heroic defense of Hong Kong Island came to an end. Hong Kong fell to the Japanese.

As a reward for victory, it was the custom of the Japanese military to grant soldiers a three-day pass to indulge in the conquered cities. The atrocities of Nanjing, now called the "Nanjing Massacre," were in everyone's mind. Soon, Hong Kong had its own atrocities to contribute to this dark year in history.

For three days, and three nights, as the Japanese began their celebration, I did not close my eyes. If one child had to use the bathroom, we all went. I kept picturing the door of that apartment being flung open by Japanese soldiers, and I was determined that when they came, my arms would be around my children.

We were spared the indulgence of the Japanese soldiers, but others were not. I suppose I should be thankful that my family and I have only the visions, and the stories, and the nightmares to carry with us.

Following the three-day 'celebration,' with Japanese soldiers now firmly in control of Hong Kong, patrolling on foot and on horseback, we set out for the long walk back to our Robinson Road apartment.

Crowds of Chinese, expressionless and silent, holding children or elderly relatives, with bags hanging on their shoulders walked back to what had been their homes. We, like the others, kept our heads bowed, and remained silent during the walk back. Still, we could see and hear, and feel, the Japanese soldiers, as they paraded through the streets, some in huge tanks, others in military trucks, still others on horseback. They gloated and reveled in their roles as the new masters of Hong Kong. Of course, with our heads bowed, we could not hide our eyes from the mutilated corpses on the ground — Chinese corpses. But we felt it better to look upon dead Chinese than the eyes of those Japanese soldiers.

When we found our Robinson Road apartment still standing, that tiny lice-ridden apartment felt like heaven. Home. Our own home.

It was a fleeting joy, however. The atrocities of the Japanese soldiers did not stop. Alice and the children hovered inside our apartment, not daring to venture out for fear of being shot or raped. After a few more days of fear, we decided that the children and I would be safer if we could take refuge in Alice's school — we felt certain that the Japanese soldiers would not invade the convent. Some friends in our building would look after Liankui — he would be safe in the apartment. I disguised myself as a Cantonese maid, complete with the old garments and a fake bun at the back of my head. As I rubbed my face with dirt, I saw the past few months staring me back in the mirror. The fatigue and stress indeed gave my face the years it needed to pass as that of an old, weathered, laboring woman.

The nuns graciously gave us refuge, although they remarked that Alice's stepmother, meaning me, would probably have been safe from the Japanese soldiers — their rape victims were limited to young and attractive women. At that time, I had just turned twenty-six.

I think it was the first time I had slept for more than a half-hour consecutively in over two months. My body embraced that sweet solitude of rest with every fiber it contained; I slept for almost twenty-four hours straight in that lovely haven. The nuns cared for the children as I slept, and when I awoke, it was with a start, and I immediately jumped up — in a panic search for my children — certain they were safe, lying next to me.

When I saw that they were fine and indeed playing, I bathed and cleaned my hair and felt as indulgent as an Empress when I emerged, clean and rested. In fact, the nuns didn't even recognize me when I joined them for dinner.

Two weeks later, the lust and intoxication of the Japanese soldiers seemed to again subside, and we decided it would be safe to return to our apartment. I had to turn my attention to clothing my children, and again scrounging for food. It is interesting to note that I did not even consider Liankui as a possible source of help in these matters.

There was no clothing to be found on Hong Kong Island. Food was scarce. It was not safe to try and sell my jewelry at the time, and I sat and watched as my starving children huddled in our apartment. Sometimes I would feel something wet on my chin and realize that a tear had escaped my eye.

Of course I prayed. But after days, I no longer prayed for food. Or clean clothing. Only for sleep. It was the only escape from our misery. I counted each minute that my children slept as a blessing.

Finally, we heard it — that knock on the door. We all held completely still. It was not the code knock of our neighbors, designed to immediately calm fears. I was certain that the Japanese had finally come. Liankui slowly opened the door — his head was down and I knew that we were both holding our breath.

But it was not the Japanese soldiers — there stood his dear friend Zhu Wenqi, with whom he had passed so many carefree hours playing chess. Zhu was actually smiling. I had not seen anyone smile in so long. He spoke fluent Japanese and had been hired by the Japanese as part of their Peace Patrol, so he wore a white arm band which identified — and protected — him. He had been living in Kowloon. As the first area taken by the Japanese, it had been the first to recover, and form a base for the Japanese army. So things had settled down there much more quickly — there was electricity and food, and law and order. Our friend Zhu had come bearing gifts — wool sweaters, milk powder, and biscuits.

At first, we couldn't even move. The children went to him shouting with joy and excitement, "Uncle Zhu! Uncle Zhu!" He embraced each of them, one by one, as I wiped tears from my eyes. We had a friend who came to us in need.

While accepting his gifts, I cried with joy. "Thank you ever so much. All the gifts are just what our children need right now. Please convey my thanks to your two wives."

Liankui was so excited to see his chess friend and they talked about their mutual friends and political affairs. Zhu said Du's wife, Mrs Eighteenth Floor, in disguise as a country woman, had taken her children and left — on foot — for Chongqing, where Du had remained since before the Japanese invasion. Other friends had also gone to Chongqing, or returned to Shanghai.

"Liankui, Zhaohua — everyone will be so happy to hear that you are well. Please, come to Kowloon tomorrow. Things are more settled there. You can see some of your old friends and possibly hear news of others. Many in Kowloon are wondering about their friends and relatives and would like to hear what you have to say. You will have to walk most of the way. The Star Ferry has resumed operation between Kowloon and Hong Kong, but there is no other transportation. Still, it would be good for you I think. My wives would love to see you, and we can give you more supplies for your family."

"Thank you, Zhu. Assuming things are peaceful here, we would love to come."

The following day, we started our journey walking from our home in Hong Kong to the Star Ferry terminal, crossing the harbor to the Kowloon side, and then we walked to Zhu's house, not far from the Kowloon terminal.

The difference between Hong Kong and Kowloon was staggering. The people of Kowloon seemed to live as though they were still under British administration, rather than the rule of the Japanese.

Zhu's two wives welcomed us with open arms. They had prepared a feast for us, and the apartment was filled with friends offering smiles and warm greetings.

Liankui and I stared at the merry gathering in amazement. It was Liankui who articulated our bewilderment, "It's incredible that here, just across the harbor, you're enjoying Chinese chess and telling war stories. In Hong Kong, we are still surrounded in the misery of war."

In Kowloon, the loss of life and property was minimal; the city had been taken quickly by the Japanese, and the residents had sat and watched — helpless — as their friends and relatives were being bombed on Hong Kong Island.

We exchanged news of friends and loved ones as we dined on crisp chicken, orange beef sauteed with scallions, sweet and sour pork, rice and red bean pudding, green vegetables and fresh fruits — a feast of delicacies compared to our meager rations in our Hong Kong home. As we ate, and chatted, and even occasionally laughed, there were actually moments when we momentarily forgot about our recent traumas.

On the way home, I became violently ill. I had not had rich food in so many months; my body rejected the very notion. But I made it.

As the days wore on, Hong Kong resumed law and order under Japanese rule, and life resumed a resemblance of its previous existence. Liankui even resumed his teatime visits to the Gloucester Hotel, although there were only a few of his friends left.

Things in our area of Hong Kong did not improve. Food was in short supply and the Japanese were urging Chinese citizens to return to China. So when my husband came home from tea one day with a mysterious smile on his face, I knew that something was about to change.

He didn't say a word as he handed me five hundred Hong Kong dollars. I accepted it immediately; I didn't care where the money had come from. I only knew that my family would eat. As we danced in our joy, my husband continued with his mysterious mood.

"There's more, Zhaohua." He smiled, teasing me with his good news. Yes, it was nice to savor — and slowly consume — this taste of happiness.

"What, Liankui? What? Please" I smiled playfully in the moment.

"Okay, okay. Du has not forgotten us — I knew he would send help when he could. Our mutual acquaintance, Xu Caichen, has contacted me. You met him briefly in Shanghai, but it is best not to mention his name to anyone. Xu, you should know, Zhaohua, is a double agent for Du. He has connections both with Chiang and with the Japanese."

I remembered Xu immediately. He was tall, thin, and about the same age as Liankui. Xu was also a heavy smoker, and — like Liankui — Xu always looked very nervous. When he entered a room, his eyes always darted about, inspecting every corner, as though he was constantly on the lookout. In Shanghai, he was well respected as a wealthy and generous textile tycoon. I would never have suspected him of being a double agent.

"Yes, it is dangerous," Liankui continued. "But he has arranged passage for you and the children on board a Japanese cargo ship. You can return to Shanghai, where things are much more stable. Besides, you will have your mother, and other relatives to help you."

"Liankui, you said the children and I; you will not be going?" No, I had never been in love with this man. Since Frank's birth, things had been more distant, still, Liankui Ching was my husband, and we had walked the streets of hell together, and I could not imagine leaving him behind.

"I am going to help some others get out, Zhaohua. I will not be far behind. I promise. We have other friends here, and I have the names and information to help them now. Do not worry, my First Wife. Xu can get me out when it is time." In the few tender moments we shared in our marriage, Liankui always called me his First Wife, a romantic gesture of honor. No, Liankui Ching never doubted his lifelong belief that we were the reincarnation of Ching Guan and his beloved concubine.

On a bitterly cold winter day, Alice, my four children, and I, went to the Kowloon Wharf to board a Japanese cargo ship, flying a flag identifying it as a part of the Refugee Evacuation Mission from Hong Kong direct to Shanghai. This evacuation was a part of a goodwill gesture by the Japanese. Every now and then during the war, the Japanese had extended feelers to Chiang, still in Chongqing, to see if a separate peace treaty was possible. They understood that it would be impossible for them to conquer all of China.

Before boarding the ship, all the passengers had to line up while Japanese soldiers examined their travel and medical documents. Most passengers were Nationalist Party family members, almost exclusively women and children, some of whom I had met with Liankui. Baby Frank was running a slight fever — Alice carried him on her back and held Judie's hand. I carried Anthony, whose chronic asthma rarely abated these days, and I held Priscilla by the hand. I trembled with fear as we approached the Japanese soldiers — fear of the Japanese and fear that they would discover the illnesses of my two children and deny passage. Though I was not yet a Christian, I prayed without stopping as I stood in that line, awaiting clearance to board the ship.

As we were granted passage, I was certain that I was dreaming. I had left Shanghai over four years ago — and now, I was actually going home with my children.

On the ship, there were two sleeping areas divided by a long passageway. Actually, the space was designed for storing cargo. This time, it was carrying human cargo instead. On the other side of the ship was a large dining area with a few long tables and wooden benches. Although everything was spartan, it was also neat and clean. Contrary to the vicious occupation army in Hong Kong, the Japanese sailors were disciplined and polite. Because of the freezing temperatures on the rough sea, the journey was very tough, but all the passengers were hopeful to have a better life in Shanghai.

Because of the stormy weather, the journey took ten days. Silently, we celebrated the Chinese New Year on board, wishing one another a happy and prosperous life, despite our uncertain future for ourselves and our country. On ordinary days, we visited one another in the holds. If the sun shone, some would go to the stern of the ship for a little fresh air, others just stayed in their holds, praying and waiting for a safe arrival. To console themselves, the Buddhists counted their beads, Roman Catholics recited their rosaries, and Protestants repeated the Lord's Prayer aloud. In moments of desperation, religion seemed to provide an element of peace — a peace badly needed to heal the scars these souls had incurred. But each day, we counted the hours before our arrival in Shanghai. The journey felt endless.

At last, one bright sunny morning, we awoke from our separate nightmares, and all the passengers were treated to a vision — the shore of Shanghai on the horizon. The stately gray buildings along the waterfront had never looked so beautiful to me. The Sassoon House, the Custom House, and the Clock Tower stood tall and elegant. As the ship approached the pier, happiness mixed with relief surged within me. I relished every moment, and held my breath before I once again breathed the familiar air. Alice had to prompt me to hurry.

I walked down the shaky gangplank, a child held tightly in each hand. When I reached the dock, I had to restrain myself from kneeling to kiss the ground.

Home! Sweet home! Whatever difficulties lay ahead, we were home.

22

China was exactly as the Japanese hoped it to be — divided. Under the Japanese occupation there were so many governments: Manchukuo, the North China government, the North Hebei government and the Nanjing government. Chinese leaders, in whom the people had trust and the comfort of familiarity, were placed in power. And these leaders took their orders from the Japanese government. They were puppets. The greatest fear of the Japanese was the unification of China, and they worked hard to keep the various parties pitted against one another.

Officially, Chiang and the Communists were united, and working from Chongqing to overthrow the Japanese. But there were always rumors of Chiang Kai-shek meeting secretly with the Japanese. Many Communists did not trust him and began to form independent guerrilla groups.

Father was named Commissioner of Customs in Qingdao, working for the northern Chinese puppet government headed by Wang Keming. Father maintained two households — one in Qingdao and one in Beijing. The Beijing home was primarily for his own father, who was very old and ailing. My paternal grandfather lived with Father and Sonya, along with Kaihua and his family, in the sprawling Beijing home, though Father also maintained a vacation home above his office in the luxury seaside resort town of Qingdao.

Father had built Mother's home — actually, it was a cluster of homes — in Shanghai, for his retirement. The group of buildings in Shanghai consisted of a large house surrounded by a wrought-iron gate, plus three semi-detached Spanish-style townhouses. These townhouses were leased at a small profit following the Japanese occupation; although there was a housing shortage, people could not afford to pay high rent. Entire families crowded into one bedroom, sharing a kitchen and bathroom with other families. The income received from the three townhouses was used to support Mother, and Little Tiger, as well as Wanhua.

It was in the Shanghai townhouse that I first saw my mother and sister; I had been in Hong Kong for over three years. My reunion with Mother was, at first, tearful and silent. We simply embraced.

Then Mother and Wanhua met Priscilla and Frank, and made such a fuss over Judie and Anthony, commenting on how much they had grown. My children played with their cousin, Little Tiger, Kaihua's youngest son, who still lived with Mother. I basked in the comfort of this unfamiliar home.

Shanghai's suburbs had been bombed and the Japanese held tight control, but still, I was back in Shanghai. My Shanghai was hardly recognizable; there was no sign of Westerners — some had been sent back to their own countries, while others were in concentration camps. The shops were empty or drably displayed only local products. I had more children than I had money, but I was filled with the energy of Old Shanghai from the time I entered the city, and I felt quite invincible.

Mother was most gracious and invited us to stay with her until I found a place to live, a task I enthusiastically set about doing immediately — only to become most discouraged. I looked for weeks, to no avail. Though Mother and Wanhua were wonderful — and Alice and Wanhua were even becoming good friends — Mother's home was much too small for all of us to stay there indefinitely.

Just when I felt I had no options left, Mother received notice from the tenant in the townhouse adjacent to their home that he was moving out. The only obstacle to our moving in was Father. Mother could not offer the townhouse without Father's permission. I had not spoken to Father in nine years — since he had publicly disowned and humiliated me when I married Liankui.

"I couldn't possibly ask him, Mother. He ... Father would never accept me. He has made his feelings quite clear."

"Of course your father still loves you, Zhaohua. He had to save face when you married a Ching — you know that. It went directly against Confucian teachings. Write him, Zhaohua. It is time — you are as stubborn as he, you know!"

Mother was right. It was time. So I swallowed my own pride and I wrote to Father. But I did not apologize for my marriage. I told Father that Alice, my stepdaughter, his four grandchildren and I had all arrived safely from Hong Kong. I gave him details about the children, news of Hong Kong and Liankui, as well as news of some of their mutual acquaintances. I told him that it had been difficult to find housing upon my return to Shanghai, and the news of the vacating tenant. I suggested a straightforward business arrangement. I insisted on paying rent every month — market price. And I signed it, 'your daughter, Zhaohua.'

To my surprise, Father's reply was equally conciliatory. He thought it would be a wonderful arrangement for my family to move into the townhouse — he even invited me to bring the children for a visit with him and Sonya in Qingdao — saying that the fresh sea air might be good for Anthony's asthma.

He signed his letter, 'Your father, Ching Tongli.' Yes, I thought, holding Father's letter, it is time.

Thus, we moved into the townhouse next door to my mother; it had three stories, with a lovely front yard, bordered by a low, wrought-iron fence. The first floor had an airy sitting-room, a dining-room and kitchen — complete with servants' quarters at the back. The second and third floors had almost identical layouts, each containing two bedrooms, a bathroom, and storage space. And there was a lovely terrace on the flat roof of the building.

I immediately set about making a home, realizing that my two younger children had never known a real home — only temporary refuges — and of course the older two did not even remember the home they had left as toddlers. After the horrors of the past three years, I felt like I had stepped into a fairytale, in a vaguely familiar place, and that none of these wonderful events were actually happening.

I had our old furniture delivered — yes, it had survived the bombings and was still in storage, and as I placed the familiar pieces, I was reminded of that grand home in which I had lived the first four years of our marriage. My memories, however, brought no desire to ever visit that hollow building again. It represented confinement, despair, Tommy and sadness. No, there was no fond reminiscing as I unpacked those relics of the young bride I had been. Only the knowledge that these hands were stronger now.

I sold some of our most valuable paintings, so grateful that I had wrapped them well; they showed few signs of their years spent in storage. With the money from the paintings I had a telephone installed, and I planted colorful flowers around the front of the house and in boxes on the terrace. I steered Alice through her applications — and admission — to Aurora University, and had Judie enrolled in McTyeire Primary School, and signed Priscilla up for nursery school. I hired a housekeeper, Mrs Bei, who was a wonderful and hard-working woman to help with Frank so that I could look after Anthony's home studies — he was too weak to attend school. When Liankui arrived, almost two months later, he could see that the young naïve girl he had married was nowhere to be found.

Liankui finally recognized that our relationship had reached a turning point. True, that point had actually come when I gave birth to Frank in

Hong Kong alone, while Liankui was losing the rest of our savings. But, at last, I was free from the bombs, the paranoia and the fear, to actually be that new person and exercise the resolve I had reached. I think Liankui realized there was no alternative but to accept his mature bride — and I could feel his respect.

"Zhaohua, this is remarkable; you have created a lovely home — everything, everyone is settled. I had heard such terrible stories of the state of things in Shanghai. And I fully expected to find our family in shambles when I arrived." Liankui actually played with the children when he arrived that afternoon in Shanghai. I can still see him tossing little Frank into the air — little Frank roaring with laughter. Liankui rarely displayed any affection — let alone playful interaction — with our children; I suppose that is why that memory is so vivid.

With my family settled, I began — with more than a little trepidation — the task of locating old friends. Nancy and Janet had returned to Shanghai, and we immediately made plans for a visit. Jade had not been seen since before the invasion. As I expected, Madame Sheng and Sheng Seventh had fled with Chiang's supporters to Chongqing. All in all, it was a positive report. Amazing, in fact.

"Liankui, my friend Janet Xie, and her husband James Woo, have also recently returned from Hong Kong. He is a stockbroker, you know. They're coming for tea after dinner." I waited anxiously after the announcement. Liankui had not objected to my few visits with my friends in Hong Kong, but I suspected that since we were 'home' he would attempt to revert to his old habits of isolating me from my friends. I had braced myself to stand up to him.

To my astonishment, Liankui smiled widely, "It will be lovely to see them!"

Yes, things had changed. And that evening marked another milestone in my life.

"I'm afraid I know nothing about the stock market, James — although I must say, I'm intrigued. Liankui, what do you think? Should we open an account with James?"

"Well, we have lost most of our money, James, but I do have five hundred shares of World Publishing Company, which have been lying in my safe for years. They weren't worth very much when we left Shanghai — what do you think?"

"Liankui, nowadays, even worthless stocks are worth something. The 500 shares would be perfect to open a new account!"

My husband continued to surprise me, leaving me quite speechless, with his next words. "Zhaohua, I will trade some of those shares and purchase a few shares in Asian Realty — real estate is in demand right now, so it should be a valuable stock. James, I want those in Zhaohua's name. Zhaohua, you can start your own account, if you'd like."

Our marriage had changed. I smiled at my husband. And I began reading the material James had left — about stocks and trading — that very evening.

——— ——— ———

Wanhua and I grew quite close during that time. She had continued to thrive at the university, even getting involved in the drama department at St John's. Our relationship seemed to finally reach a level of support and friendship, as well as that unconditional love of a sibling.

"Zhaohua, I'd like for you to meet someone. This is Jin Honglin, a fellow student of mine from St John's University; he is majoring in English." Wanhua's eyes and tone told me that Jin Honglin was most definitely more than a fellow student, and I smiled with intrigue, slightly embarrassing my 'little' sister.

"So, Honglin, do you wish to teach when you graduate?"

"Oh yes, I have wanted to teach English for as long as I can remember." Honglin immediately gave me the impression of being straightforward and direct, and also very sincere. I was intuitively pleased for what I suspected he meant to my sister.

We chatted at length over tea and my first impression continued to be confirmed. When Honglin mentioned that my sister's performance as the heroine in *Thunderstorm* had been most captivating, I agreed and smiled playfully again and was pleased that my sister's feelings were reciprocated.

Wanhua and Honglin were married soon after that — a quiet wedding, as Shanghai was still in a mood of mourning. They had a brief honeymoon in Qingdao, where they visited Father and Sonya.

"Liankui, Anthony is getting worse every day. I'm so worried about him. The humidity of the summer makes it so difficult for him to breathe. I have decided to accept Father's offer to visit him and Sonya on the coast. Anthony can't be much worse off — I'll take Priscilla as well, it won't matter if she misses nursery school. Frank will be fine with Mrs Bei. He's a bit young for the trip. Judie would probably enjoy it, but I don't want her to fall behind at McTyeire."

"I'll write to your father, Zhaohua, and tell him of your plans. You've been through a lot, my lovely First Wife, and have worked so hard since we returned to Shanghai. It would please me to see you relax and enjoy the coast." That was my best year with Liankui Ching.

Anthony seemed to recover as soon as the train left Shanghai Station. Though it was midsummer, the journey by train from Shanghai to Qingdao was a pleasant one. As the train rolled northward, the stifling, humid climate of the city gradually changed to a dry and breezy, lighter air. Priscilla and Anthony pressed their faces against the windows, enjoying the rapidly changing views of the countryside — like a live moving picture show. They were full of questions as we saw fields of rice and green vegetables in the south, shifting to wheat, corn and soybeans in the drier northern soil. They stared wide-eyed at the strange sights — the sights of women and children and water buffaloes working in the irrigated fields. Those sights were what most people in the West associate with China, and which my children, indeed I, had never associated with our homeland.

Of course, travel involved wartime precautionary measures. At night, the trains were certain to stop only in large cities, for fear of guerrilla attacks from the Communists, who had been known to derail — or even blow up — passenger trains in protest. The trip took three days, and, as is the way with young children, it did not take long for the thrill of the new, confining surroundings to wear off. By the time we arrived in Qingdao, we were all ready to say goodbye to our tiny compartment.

Father and Sonya were waiting at the station when we arrived in Qingdao. My former student, and friend, Sonya — now my father's concubine — took charge immediately, smoothing over the awkwardness Father and I felt. We were meeting for the first time in nine years.

"Oh, Zhaohua, you look wonderful. How are you? Here, let me hold Priscilla. Hand your luggage to Tongli, and you hold on to Anthony. We have a car waiting outside … come on, Tongli … don't just stand there … give your daughter a hug and take her bag!" Father obeyed Sonya, grateful to be relieved of the responsibility for his actions.

"Thank you, Sonya," I said shyly, as Father and I timidly embraced. "Both of you look well." It was true. Sonya was barely recognizable — positively elegant and mature. She had learned well. But then, Jade Wang was a remarkable teacher. Father also appeared well and happy — he was the picture of health.

"We are, indeed, my daughter. The climate is wonderful here." Yes, he had said the words, 'my daughter.' We both knew that the reconciliation was complete.

Qingdao was a former German colony and had evolved into an elite summer resort. It is situated on the Shandong coastline overlooking Jiaozhou Bay and the Yellow Sea. In 1898, when most European powers rushed to China to gain a commercial footing, Germany leased it for business purposes. With Germany's defeat in the First World War, Qingdao reverted to China.

But the lovely brick, tree-lined streets had retained their German heritage, especially with regard to cleanliness. The town was impeccable with only a few tasteful billboards advertising American jazz. The elegant shops had a cozy European flavor and looked like those illustrated in travel books on Germany. Father's driver took us along a lovely downtown boulevard and then turned onto an avenue, which was bordered on the east by the wide beach. Eventually, we stopped in front of a building marked 'Office of the Commissioner of Customs in Qingdao.'

"Are we going to your office first?" I asked.

"We have a lovely apartment upstairs — come on, we have your rooms prepared." Father seemed truly eager to welcome us into his home.

Our days in Qingdao were spent basking in the sunshine, enjoying the cool ocean breezes, and the serenity — and in being together. Father and I never mentioned a word about the past; there were no recriminations, and no apologies. We had both chosen to simply enjoy these days. Sonya and I would get up early and watch the sun rise and spend the morning hours riding bicycles on the boulevard and humming popular songs and recalling stories of so many years ago.

I watched my son, Anthony, actually play, child's play, with his sister — without gasping for air.

And I rested. For the first time in what seemed like years — and indeed probably was — I slept. I missed my baby Frank, but realized that between his reluctance to sleep through the night, and Judie, my studious and stubborn daughter, and Anthony's routine waking several times due to shortness of breath, I had forgotten the mental clarity and physical energy, which accompanies a good night's sleep. I watched years fade from my face in those two restful weeks.

I think Father was reluctant for our visit to come to an end, so he suggested that we all travel on to Beijing — we could meet Kaihua's family and spend some time in Father's home there, saying I could visit my paternal Grandfather, whose health was failing rapidly.

I was high on the warmth of Father's reception, and eager to mend relations with Kaihua. True, we had never been close and as we grew older, Kaihua had openly resented the fact that I had surpassed him academically. Then when I married Liankui, Father's reaction had made it convenient for my brother to ignore me completely. But I was encouraged by my growing friendship with Wanhua, and even Mother and Father. I thought it was time to work on my relationship with Kaihua as well. Yes, it was time for our family to heal. So I agreed.

By the time our train pulled into the enormous Beijing Station, the nerve center of all transportation in Northern China, I had high hopes of finally building a relationship with my brother. The trip had been exhausting — taking twenty-four hours in a tiny compartment, which had been stifling with heat and humidity. As we stepped off the train, it felt more like Japan than China. Everywhere there were Japanese men and women in their kimonos and two-toed sandals. The station was more crowded than the streets of Shanghai and I held the hand of each of my children tightly as I followed my father closely along the passageway leading to the front gate.

Japanese soldiers were checking everyone's travel documents and asking questions about their medical condition — apparently there was a cholera epidemic. It was most intimidating. By this time, Chinese were treated as second-class citizens — yes, in our own country.

The Japanese feared that Chinese passengers might be carrying unsavory germs, and with the cholera epidemic, they were taking no chances, so they sprayed the crowd, without warning, with a strong liquid chemical — a disinfectant. The chemical was cold and it tasted like metal, which instantly made me nauseous and dizzy.

The next thing I knew, Father was bending over me, "Zhaohua, Zhaohua … please, Zhaohua — wake up!"

I tasted the metal as I opened my eyes, hoping I would not vomit on my worried father.

"I … I … am fine, Father … the chemical …"

"They almost took you away — saying you had the cholera — I told them you were just exhausted from the trip."

Father carried me to the waiting car, Sonya skillfully bringing Anthony and Priscilla, and finally we arrived at Father's Beijing home.

I could feel the negative energy in the home even through my nausea and weakness, as my brother's wife, Zhihu, greeted me — she was mistress of this household. I did not even ask where Kaihua was, and gratefully accepted the gesture when Father suggested I go right to bed. I followed Zhihu to my room, leaving my children to Sonya's cheerful care.

The next morning, I felt completely refreshed as I slid open the door made of framed rice paper. I was greeted most graciously by a lovely young woman. She was Lin Yanzhu, my brother's Second Wife. Yanzhu was such a soft young woman. Yes, that is the word that best describes her — soft — but not weak, and I liked her immediately. When she addressed me, her manner was polite and yet completely genuine. She was lovely and meticulous in her appearance, and I soon noticed that Yanzhu performed even the smallest task with patience and attention. There is a *Dao De Jing* teaching which says something to the effect of 'when you eat — eat; and when you drink, drink; and when you listen, listen.' Yanzhu seemed to embrace that teaching. I could see why my brother had fallen in love with her.

Yanzhu gave me a tour of the house, which was built in the traditional Beijing style — a main house with many wings separated by small courtyards. All the windows were pasted with thick, opaque rice paper. The furniture, furnished by the landlord, was made of hardwood in traditional Chinese fashion — low and clean lined.

We also passed my paternal grandfather's bedroom and saw that he was soundly asleep. So I did not enter and just left a short note there.

Yanzhu stopped the tour, however, when she gestured toward the wing that she occupied with Kaihua. That's when I realized that Kaihua would not be joining Father in welcoming me and my children into his home. I tried to hide the tears as they stung my eyes, but Yanzhu reached out and took my hand as if to say she understood. Of course, she said nothing negative about my brother, and I found it an additional statement of her character that she did not join him in his rude behavior.

When Zhihu entered the dining-room for breakfast, I realized where the negative energy had come from. My brother's First Wife was consumed with jealousy and bitterness. She relished her role as mistress of the Ching household in Beijing, and was not about to extend equal footing to Father's daughter. Sonya told me that Zhihu had refused to grant my brother a divorce so that he could legally marry Yanzhu. Although Yanzhu was well educated and came from a highly respected family, she had chosen to live with my brother anyway, accepting the inferior status of Second Wife, which by this time in China was nothing more than a live-in girlfriend and was socially, but not legally, still acceptable. Apparently, Yanzhu truly loved my brother. And I felt glad for my brother, despite my sadness at his rejection.

Father and Sonya did their best to make up for Kaihua and Zhihu's rudeness. They rented a horse carriage and took us on a tour of the center of the city. Of course, Beijing too, had changed drastically since Liankui and I had visited there on our honeymoon. In Tiananmen Square, we saw many Japanese men in military uniforms and Japanese women in kimonos, dominating the ancient, revered space. Many Chinese still consider this a holy place. The Japanese soldiers strolled around this sacred ground so arrogantly, as if to demonstrate that they were the rulers of China.

Beijing had also become a collage of ethnic backgrounds; there were Mongolians, Manchurians, Koreans, Tibetans, Laotians, and others — probably officials of regimes who were collaborating with the Japanese. Few native Chinese could be seen.

The shelves in the stores were conspicuously empty. Unbleached flour and broken corn, the staple food for the Chinese in Beijing, had to be bought with ration coupons. Restaurants did a booming business as they catered to Japanese customers, as well as to those puppet regime officials and their families.

My father was one of those puppet regime officials. I knew that he was doing what he had to do to provide for his family. My husband had been spared that humiliating choice because of his connections — dangerous, but lucrative connections. Those connections, along with the valuable paintings and jewelry, which the Japanese and their puppet officials anxiously purchased, were paying our bills.

So my honorable Liankui had flatly refused to register to practice law under the puppet regime. It would mean acknowledging their legitimacy. He was a Chinese patriot and he would not sell out. Though his decision contrasted startly with my father's choice, I both admired my husband's patriotism, and understood my father's lack of options. Money provides an element of freedom; freedom for conviction and patriotism and principles. If one has no resources and is faced with starving children, patriotic convictions don't go very far in the eyes and stomachs of those hungry children.

After a week in Beijing, Anthony had a mild asthma attack. By this point, Zhihu was openly hostile and disturbed by our presence. It was the day following his attack that I overheard my sister-in-law's acidic words.

"Father, you have to send Zhaohua's son to the hospital. We could all catch what he has."

"Nonsense; Anthony has asthma — it is a chronic disease, but it is not contagious." Father was trying to whisper.

"He has a cold first, then an asthma attack — a cold is contagious and can be passed to anyone. Either he goes to the hospital, or they return home at once!"

"Zhihu, I pay the expenses here. My daughter is welcome for as long as she wishes to stay. You will not speak of this further." Father's tone was not to be challenged.

They did not know I had overheard — they had been standing in the courtyard, and I was behind the rice paper window. I waited for two days in order to save face for everyone, then asked Father to book us on a train to Shanghai.

"Why now, Zhaohua?" Father's tone was light; he gave no indication of Zhihu's venomous words. "In another week, Sonya and I are leaving as well; we can go together. Besides, the coat you ordered for the winter is not finished yet. Kaihua has a friend in the fur trade and I have asked him to see to it." It was the first time anyone had spoken to me of Kaihua — I had not even seen a glimpse of him during our week there.

"Anthony is feeling better; we really should leave before he has another attack."

"Let's speak of it tomorrow, Zhaohua. I have dinner reservations this evening; let's go out and enjoy ourselves, shall we?"

When we returned from dinner, late that evening, Zhihu was waiting for us.

"Zhaohua, I have your train tickets. You leave at 8:30 tomorrow morning."

Father was openly outraged. "No, Zhaohua — you cannot possibly go that soon — you don't even have time to pack."

"I've already paid for the tickets. They are not refundable." Zhihu sat expressionless and determined.

Father was furious. "No! How could you make such a decision, Zhihu. You have gone too far this time ..."

"No, Father, please ... it is better that I go. Anthony is feeling better and it is a good time to make the trip. It has been so lovely to visit with you. Thank you for everything. Good night, Zhihu."

I went to my room and packed, and left the money for the train tickets in an envelope for Zhihu. I stayed up all evening and left before dawn, leaving notes of goodbyes and thanks, trying to spare my father more embarrassment.

As I sat at the train station with Priscilla and Anthony, choking back my tears of humiliation at Zhihu's rudeness, I could no longer hold them in when I saw my brother approaching, carrying a large package.

"Your coat, Zhaohua ...you will need it in Shanghai this winter. It is well made and will keep you very warm." I knew my brother — he was spoiled and self-absorbed, and so this goodbye had cost his pride all the more. I was most grateful for his kindness.

"Thank you, Kaihua. I shall think of you when I wear it." We did not embrace, nor did we acknowledge our awkward moments. My brother just touched my hand for a moment and then turned and walked away.

In years to come, I was to be immensely grateful for that brief encounter with my brother and the fact that we had parted on cordial terms. That was the last time I ever saw my brother.

23

I returned to Shanghai inspired to embrace life. Despite my unhappy departure from Beijing, the physical rest of those four weeks in Qingdao had been tremendously uplifting, both physically and mentally. But then, the entire summer had been somewhat of a reprieve from sadness. I stepped off the train with an awareness of all that was positive in my life. True, Shanghai no longer resembled the bustling city in which I was raised, but ours was one of the few families who had not lost loved ones during the Japanese invasion. My family was so happy in our home next to Mother and Wanhua — it was a dream come true in a war-torn city. My relationship with my mother and sister had grown so much closer. I had reconciled with Father and Kaihua. Even my husband had shown me measured increments of respect. I felt invincible and anxious to bask in all that was good.

But I knew when I saw Alice at the station — she had come to meet us — that my reprieve was about to come to an abrupt end. I could see it in her eyes.

"What is it, Alice?" Anthony and Priscilla quickly let go of my hand, and ran with that beautiful uncensored joy of children, to embrace their half-sister. Alice greeted them with hugs and kisses, interrupted occasionally with glances in my direction. I understood that we would wait until we got home, and the children were settled, to talk.

Liankui was not there when we arrived, which I found surprising. But Mrs Bei, our housekeeper, had done a wonderful job — the children were thriving. Little Frank clapped with toddler joy when he saw us and eagerly showed me his latest trick — climbing up and down the stairs. I held my breath as he started down but he was most meticulous, scooting down backwards, feet first, and being certain of his position before looking over his shoulder to find my eyes. I clapped for his accomplishment when he reached the bottom, which of course inspired him to do it all over again.

Judie was consumed in school, and took time from her studies to tell me that her grades were in top marks. I was so proud of her hard work.

Alice said that Mother and Wanhua were preparing dinner for us as a welcome home celebration, but she needed to speak with me privately for a few moments. We settled the children and retreated to the kitchen.

"What is it, Alice?" I was both anxious to hear what my stepdaughter had to say, and yet I was aware that I had been savoring those moments watching Frank on the stairs, and listening to Judie's exclamations about school — avoiding what I could feel would be bad news.

"Much has happened while you were away, Zhaohua. And Father is not taking the news well, there has been news — a telegram — from Suzhou ... Jiaxiu ..."

We had written to Jiaxiu, Liankui's oldest daughter in Suzhou, many times since our return to Shanghai. Communication was difficult and unreliable, and we had not heard from her since before we left for Hong Kong. I held my breath, seeing the words in Alice's eyes before I heard them.

"Jiaxiu is dead — they say there has been an extended illness, but there are no details. She had four young children, Zhaohua." Tears streamed down Alice's face as she relayed the news of her sister.

Jiaxiu and I had never had an opportunity to grow close. We had not seen one another since her wedding in Hangzhou, where I served as her maid of honor. But I had written to her often and had, over the years, come to feel a special bond with Liankui's oldest daughter. I had immersed myself in the role as stepmother to Liankui's children, and had, over the years, unconsciously assumed a great deal of emotional responsibility for their well-being — the girls, at least. Though I felt a sense of responsibility toward Liankui's sons, he had always gone to extremes to keep them separated from me.

I crossed my arms at my stomach and sat down numbly, unable to speak. I felt an overwhelming empty sadness at the news of my young, beautiful stepdaughter's death. I thought of her four children, left without their mother, and then of Alice. Jiaxiu had been like a mother to the family before her own marriage. My heart ached for the pain Alice must be feeling. I embraced my stepdaughter and let her cry in my arms. After a while, Alice dried her eyes and cleaned her face; she looked down before she spoke, "There's more, Zhaohua. My second brother, Chiajin, has left for the other side of the river to join the New Fourth Army. Father is, of course, very upset."

'The other side of the river' was the code phrase for saying that someone had shifted their support to the Communists. The New Fourth Army was a secret Communist force operating within the borders of Japanese occupation — sending information to the Communist leaders who were supposedly allied with Chiang Kai-shek in Chongqing, still working to overthrow the Japanese.

"Where is Liankui, Alice?" I knew my husband's loyalty to the Nationalist government was so intense that he would be angered by his son's action — as well as concerned for Chiajin's safety.

"He has been taking long walks every afternoon, often not returning until late evening. He ... he is not handling the news well, Zhaohua. Ever since Hong Kong, Father has been so different ... he is often irrational and seems to withdraw more and more from his family. I'm worried about him, Zhaohua."

I sat there absorbing the pain of my husband's family — my own family — and I thought of how happy and full of life I had been, just a couple of hours before, stepping off the train.

Alice was right; over the past year, I, too, had noticed a change in Liankui. In some ways he had become more timid, especially in his interactions with me, but often he was completely withdrawn and angry. My emotions surrounding Liankui Ching were never to be simple; there were always layers and layers of shifting feelings, ranging from disgust and rage to partnership and loyalty, sometimes even heartfelt compassion. But, as I have said, I was connected to this man. At that moment, I felt his pain, as well as my own.

There was to be more pain. My dear friend Nancy had died while I was away. Her body had never fully regained its strength following her difficult pregnancy in Hong Kong. Janet said that Nancy had entered the hospital again, and Nancy's husband had come to her, requesting a divorce. In China, it is believed that one can die from a broken heart, that the soul and the body are connected in a way unfamiliar to the minds of most Westerners. Although the doctors had predicted a complete recovery, Nancy had simply given up. She told Janet, from her hospital bed, that she had released her will to live. Yes, our beautiful friend Nancy had died from a broken heart — died too early, leaving three young children behind with sad hearts of their own.

The death of Nancy hit me hard. To lose a friend with whom you have laughed, and grown, and confided, and shared pregnancies and private griefs — I had not felt so much pain since my dear Tommy died. Of course, it was a different pain, and in some ways I was stronger emotionally, but I was also so very tired of grief.

Again, my eyes went hollow, I lost interest in everything around me, and spent many days and nights in that dark room of grief. At least this time, grief had the element of familiarity.

Shanghai continued to deteriorate. The Americans had sent support to Chongqing to help fight the Japanese and they quickly recognized the dissension between Chiang Kai-shek and the Communists. While the Americans could not support a Communist regime, they had grave concerns about the leadership of Chiang Kai-shek.

More and more young people 'crossed the river.' Duanduan and Song-song, both of Aunt Liming's children, left 'for the other side of the river.'

Liankui still refused to acknowledge the puppet government operating in Shanghai, and would not register to practice law with a government which he insisted was merely a fabrication. He made some money on his investment accounts with James Woo, but the idleness got to him. And Liankui was such an intellectually energetic man. To be denied the opportunity to practice a profession he had loved, and in which he had excelled, was a private torture for my husband. Granted, it was mild in comparison to some of the tortures the Japanese inflicted, but it was enough to sow the seeds of mental deterioration and madness in my husband.

Yes, many Nationalist loyalists, as well as Communists, were tortured and imprisoned by the Japanese. There were stories about 'Jessfield Road,' an infamous detention center for political prisoners. Many of Liankui's friends had been sent there, including Wu Kaixian, who had worked underground in Shanghai for the Nationalist government.

Wu had been one of the lucky ones; he was released when he convinced the Japanese that he could be effective in persuading Chiang in the advantages of peace with the Japanese. But the stories he told my husband of the tortures he had seen while detained on Jessfield Road were utterly horrific. Wu said that, months after his release, he still heard the screams of the men every hour of every day. It was a constant ringing in his head.

When I look back on those years, I think the fear of the consequences of Liankui's actions also contributed to his increased paranoia. As I have said, I was connected to Liankui Ching. I felt his pain and his fear, though he rarely spoke of his emotions. It was soon after I returned home from my vacation, and once again embraced grief and darkness — and my husband's grief and fears — that my nightmares started.

The most frequent nightmare was of the Japanese soldiers bursting into my bedroom in the middle of the night — they laughed as they tossed me from my third-story bedroom window. I could see myself land — certain of imminent death — but something broke my fall. It was a large mound of bloody corpses, some with their eyes open, some holding severed arms, others holding dead children. The Japanese were sending giant machines to roll over the bodies, trying to crush those who refused to die. When that didn't work, they sent hundreds of soldiers, still smiling, to fire machine guns into the mounds. Thousands of rounds of artillery would pass through my body. My head would turn slowly to watch the bullets go through. And still, I could not die. I could smell the blood. Then I would see the faces of my children in the mound — just out of my reach. And they would call to me with their eyes and I would try to move, but my body was in fragments.

Then I would hear a child screaming, and slowly I would crawl from the mound of bodies and leave that black fog, and realize that Anthony was waking again, with another asthma attack. The attacks had grown steadily worse since our return to Shanghai and I was getting up with him many times through the night. I would hold my child as he wheezed and gasped for air and thank him for bringing me from that mound. And often I could not distinguish between which nightmare was real.

The doctor in Shanghai had taught me to give Anthony shots of adrenaline to help relax his closing airways, so I was always certain to have the syringe prepared before I went to bed. It is interesting that nightmares and daily brushes with death can actually become an unremarkable part of our routine.

As the political conflicts intensified and I sank deeper into my haunted, sleepless fatigue, Honglin suggested one evening that we should make use of our minds and our time after dinner in learning to play bridge. I thought it an utterly ludicrous idea.

"Bridge? You want us to sit in the middle of this madness and learn to play bridge, Honglin? What possible good could that do? Win or lose, nothing will change — we will all be lost in the end." I was aware that my tone was incredulous and defeated. I did not care.

It was my passionate sister who responded, "True, Zhaohua, it will not help anything outside these walls for us to play a card game. But Honglin is right — it will help those inside these walls. You cannot continue to raise these children in the midst of such somber sadness. The dawn will come, Zhaohua. This will pass. And we have to resolve to come through it with as few scars as possible. We cannot give the Japanese any more of our spirits — it is handing them victory on a platter!" I looked at my timid, quiet, baby sister, who pushed me from hopelessness that day.

As I looked at Wanhua and Honglin, I could sense a comfort between them, and I knew that their spirits suited one another and provided a mutual source of strength. They had been so kind to my family since we had returned from Hong Kong, so out of gratitude for their kindness, I forced my reluctant body to Mother's house after dinner one night to play bridge. I told myself that it would be good for Mother — she too had declined in health and spirit lately.

Wanhua and Honglin had suggested the game in an effort to cheer me, and I went to avoid hurting their feelings, and providing some cheerful comfort for Mother. And it is true, when we turn our attention to others, we can more easily forget about our own sadness. That first evening turned out to be quite grand.

There was something in the air that night and Wanhua and I quickly fell into a childish sisterly game. We giggled as we signaled our hands to one another — not at all discreetly.

My dear brother-in-law was so serious. He tried to teach us bridge as though we were students in his classroom — and we drove that sweet, gentle, methodical man to near madness with our snowballing giddy indulgence in pure play.

"Zhaohua! Stop making faces. You girls are openly cheating! Did you even read the book on the rules of bridge that I gave you last week?"

"Well, Mr Honglin, sir, I did try, but I, uh, didn't have time to finish it, you see." Wanhua tried to suppress the smiles at my playful response.

"Okay, one more time. There are proper ways to signal your partner, but first, I think it would be wise for us to review the glossary — it really should be committed to memory. Remember, 'practice makes perfect.'" Honglin ignored my playful reference to him as a teacher, but his voice took on that lift and tone of an exasperated teacher speaking to his students.

I think our playfulness did cheer Mother for a while, although she was not convinced that bridge was going to be her chosen way to spend the evenings. After about an hour, she announced that she was going to prepare tea — Uncle Sha, with whose family we had shared a house in the Chinese City, and who now visited almost every evening, would be arriving soon. Aunt Sha had grown very ill; she was bedridden and asleep most of the time. Uncle Sha and Mother had found immense comfort in their mutual history and friendship.

At last, Honglin conceded and finally joined us in our playful spirits; he threw the cards in the center of the table as he laughed and suggested we go out for an evening bike ride, and drop in on the fortune-teller,

Wang Xianren. Honglin's colleagues at St John's Middle School had been full of enthusiastic reports on the capabilities of Mr Wang.

"They say that he can look in your palm and tell you details of the past as well as predict the future. Everyone is astounded by his accuracy."

"Yes, let's go. It's been so long since I've seen the streets of Shanghai in the moonlight!" I went for my sweater and to check on the children, whom Mrs Bei had most ably tucked into bed while I was enjoying my playful evening.

With Honglin leading, we rode through the elegant tree-lined streets of the French Concession on our bicycles. We passed Rue Retard and wound around the corner of Rue Albert onto Avenue Joffre, the main thoroughfare of the French Concession. A few of the expensive shops and restaurants were still open, but of course there were no European goods available, and instead of the usual imported goods, the windows now displayed a sparse selection of local products. No, my Shanghai no longer resembled the vivacious, crowded and charming world metropolis it had been. Even the sounds of the city were different. No longer did I hear thousands of automobiles loudly honking their horns, stagnant yet hurried. On that evening, there was only the light *dling-dling* of the bicycles, and the *hehoheho* of the pedicab drivers to be heard on the streets. I looked at the full moon and I wondered how it could have possibly remained the same, when so much on which it shone had been so devastated.

The fortune-teller's house was located in a narrow lane on the east side of Avenue Joffre. We parked our bicycles in the courtyard and Honglin rang the bell; the door was opened by the fortune-teller himself. I was taken aback by his appearance; Wang Xianren's spine was bent and swollen — 'hunch-backed' — he was labeled. In his long, faded, handmade, navy blue Chinese gown, and his handmade black cloth slippers, Wang gave the impression of humble elegance. As I entered his sparsely furnished home, I could feel that his name suited him — Xianren had been given this name by his admiring clients. It means 'demi-god,' a term derived from the Daoist tradition of immortals who lived as recluses far from civilized society. True, Shanghai was hardly the wilderness, but neither did it feel particularly civilized under Japanese occupation.

We entered his simple sitting-room and Wang offered us a cup of green tea and passed a box of cigarettes around. Despite wartime shortages, Wang was not the sort of person to overlook traditional Chinese courtesies. He spoke the Shanghai dialect fluently, without a trace of a provincial accent.

The room was cozy in its simplicity. On the walls were drawings of two palms, right and left, and of human faces accompanied by rows of Chinese symbols which explained the significance of various lines on the palms, as well as the lines on the face. Dominating one entire wall was a huge diagram of the magical Eight Trigrams, or *ba kua*, consisting of different combinations of straight lines arranged in a circle. On another wall there were two red scrolls, with black characters:

> Destiny is predetermined by Heaven.
> The future is foretold by Wang Xianren.

There was no small talk. Politely, Wang asked Honglin to open his left hand. After a careful examination, Wang wrote the Chinese character *da*, which means 'large' on the palm and said, in a very soft voice, "Is your father a merchant? Do you have two mothers and many brothers and sisters?"

Honglin swallowed before responding, "Yes, my father is a jewelry merchant and the only son in a big family. He was also adopted by his uncle. Since he was shared by two families, he was allowed to take two legal First Wives. I have five brothers and two sisters."

"As for the future, don't worry so very much, Mr Jin. There is nothing to be done about destiny. Yes, yours will be a long and difficult life, but you will ride out your many storms and survive."

The fortunes of women are hidden in their right palm, so Wang politely turned to Wanhua and asked her to please open her right hand. Again, after studying it in silence, he wrote the Chinese character *da* on her palm.

"You are the youngest child in the family. Physically, you are rather weak, but you are indeed intelligent. I can tell that you are Mrs Jin as you have the same future as your husband. The good news I have for you is that you will stay with your husband as long as you live. Wherever he goes, you will follow. Your marriage will provide the blessings in your life."

Those words, in China where husbands so often took concubines and mistresses and marital fidelity was rare, were joyful words for a wife.

Wang then turned to me and I extended my right palm without being asked. As with Honglin and Wanhua, Wang studied and then inscribed the familiar character on my palm. Then he moved my palm up and down, right and left, many times. His eyes would grow intensely serious and then he would eye my palm suspiciously. I grew impatient and concerned as he bent over my hand, again and again, without saying a word. When he spoke, it was a whisper.

"May I please look into your left palm?" A most unusual request. Chinese know that the fortunes of women are held in their right palms as well as Americans know that the sun sets in the west.

After a consuming eternity, Wang broke his silence.

"Madam, it is most extraordinary. Your two hands are those of a man. You have had an unhappy childhood. And you married at a very young age. Though you have a husband, you will not depend on him. You will have your own career in the future, a long and successful career. You have had your children and all of them will do well under your guidance and care, but you will not depend on your children in your old age.

"Listen to me carefully, madam," and Wang looked into my eyes, demanding my calm and focused attention, "despite many adversities, you will endure and outlive your misfortunes. You will prosper. And you will change the lives of others." Wang looked into my eyes as though he was actually glimpsing pictures of me — years from that moment.

"Mr Wang, I'm afraid there must be some mistake. I did not even finish high school; it is most impossible for me to have a career, sir, let alone be prosperous." I laughed and smiled lightly, I found Mr Wang's words — actually the intensity with which he spoke them — to be most unsettling.

But Wang was firm. "Madam, I say only what is held in your own hands. I cannot question what I see. All that I have said is according to the *I-Ching*, the Book of Changes, which has proven true for thousands of years."

We paid Wang's fees, as he silently sipped his tea and mumbled our polite goodbyes.

We were all quiet as we rode our bicycles back through the quiet streets. We felt the truth in Wang's words.

Truth can be a frightening thing. And Wang's truth did indeed strike an element of fear deep inside me.

I am an ambitious woman. I faced my ambition again that night. I wanted my passion back. I wanted Zhaohua Ching. The real Zhaohua Ching. I wanted that essence to come alive again. I wanted to be a good mother and I wanted to be a respectable wife and an honorable daughter, but I also wanted to nurture my own essence. I wanted my education, and I did not wish to follow in the footsteps of my mother — a victim of the feudal society of male dominance and conservatism.

I craved independence. I had smothered that essence when I married

Liankui Ching because it was too painful to watch it go hungry. But Wang had read my way correctly. And I knew it. I also knew that the work involved in realizing that truth was staggering; I wasn't at all certain that I had the energy or the stamina left to go after my way. But Wang breathed life back into that which I had smothered, and my hands shook on my bicycle as I realized the implications of embracing the fortune-teller's words.

We cycled home in moonlit silence, and as we pulled into Mother's courtyard, Honglin came over as I was putting away my bicycle. He spoke softly, and with purpose.

"Zhaohua, he was right, you know. I have always felt your strength."

I did not respond to Honglin. I walked quietly back to my own home, and I kissed each of my sleeping children and lingered by their beds. Before I settled into my own bed, I prepared Anthony's syringe of adrenaline, and then I opened my windows, framing that lovely full moon. And that night, for the first time in months, I did not have nightmares of Japanese soldiers.

24

'Paris Liberated ...' 'Athens Freed by Allies ...' 'USSR Agrees to Friendship Pact with China ...' 'Mussolini Killed at Lake Como ...' 'Hitler Commits Suicide ...' 'Berlin Falls ...'

This was the news that dominated the world. Of course, we heard none of these reports; news in China was tightly controlled, and if the Japanese caught families trying to tune into the BBC, they were executed on the spot. But the Japanese soldiers heard the reports, and with each headline, they became more desperate to annihilate the Chinese people.

And that was all we knew.

Officially, the two parties in China, Nationalists and Communists, were still united against the Japanese. However, everyone in China knew the alliance was false and tenuous, and that it would not last. The Communist Party had continued to grow in numbers and power; they worked from the 'ground up' in their campaigns, focusing their energies on the peasants and the laborers and in the schools. The Nationalist loyalists were primarily composed of those who had been obedient and friends of Chiang Kai-shek, our dictator.

The Japanese, however, had made the mistake of underestimating the tenacity of the Chinese people. True, the Japanese had conquered our eastern coastline, and major ports, with relative ease. But the Chinese, in meticulously simplistic maneuvers, moved inland and took anything of value with them. Businesses dismantled machines, universities dismantled libraries and laboratories, and they packaged each item, each piece carefully, and shipped it by river — inland, where they rebuilt their factories and their universities, and continued as China.

The Japanese controlled all of our enormous lands along the coast. But not our vast interior. Also not our hearts and minds. Anti-Japanese songs were taught in schools, as early as kindergarten. *The March of the Volunteers*, with its bouncy tune and spirited words, was a popular favorite at the time. Later, it was adopted as the national anthem of the People's Republic of China.

It was a state of anarchy. The Wang puppet regime underwent dissolution. Some banks and schools were closed. People hoarded food and other necessities, such as toilet paper, cooking oil, and fuel. US planes bombed military targets in Zaibei. Some stores refused to use the banknotes issued by the Wang regime.

As the war dragged on, Shanghai continued to crumble. Of course, as more and more Chinese moved out, taking businesses with them, property values plummeted.

Thus, Father, still in Beijing, decided he had no choice but to sell his Shanghai properties. Under Japanese occupation, their value would only continue to decline. If the Nationalists were victorious — which looked possible with Allied assistance — Father would be labeled a traitor, since he had worked for the puppet government — and he would probably be stripped of his property anyway.

At the time, I wasn't aware of all the reasons behind Father's decision — we were so isolated from news in Shanghai and communication was strictly controlled. All we knew was that Father had telegraphed Mother, instructing her to sell all properties immediately at any price. Mother, Wanhua and Honglin were to join Father in Tianjin, where he was being transferred. Our home was being sold, and we would have no place to live. I was faced with a new crisis. I had sold almost all of my jewelry — our last resort as income. Moreover, I would no longer be near Mother, Wanhua and Honglin. Yes, I had come to know the comfort to be found in family. Even a family that had not been particularly close in its beginnings had come together to nurture, support, love and laugh. It is true, you know, family will be there in need and I was still in need.

When I recall that day, watching my family pack and prepare to separate, I wonder when the leaders of nations will realize how barbaric the notion of war is? War kills sons, brothers, fathers, mothers, daughters and babies. And war tears families apart. It is primitive, base and not civilized. War took me from my family that day — and our goodbye was so painful, like each of the millions of goodbyes at the hands of war.

Yes, I know the *Dao De Jing* would say that war was the reason I found my family. Were it not for the war, I would not have had the opportunity to mend our breaks. But no, I can find no justification for what China endured at the hands of war. Though I know that every country has had her taste, those of us who have lived it, we know war is something the human race must outgrow.

As I watched my mother, Little Tiger, my sister and brother-in-law leave the house, I did not embrace my grief. I hated war — and all those responsible — with every fiber of my being.

But people do what they must do.

It is most fascinating how past, seemingly disconnected, acquaintances play into the web of our lives, weaving their way back in to become essential to the pattern.

"My friend Old Li has offered us the use of his house in Suzhou, Zhaohua. There are some tailors who have a shop in the front part of the house, but he says the back half is empty and we're welcome to use it. Besides, I think it's time to leave Shanghai for a while — perhaps the change of scenery would do us all good. Another friend, Yang, a wealthy bond trader, has plenty of room in his second wife's house — it isn't far from here, and he says we can store our furniture there." Liankui's voice sounded so old as he relayed this information. I was reminded of his playfulness just before we left Hong Kong — yes, in Shanghai, watching our beautiful city turn to a wasteland, had aged us all — but I think they gave my husband more years than the rest of us. He had continued to decline in spirit, growing more detached from our family, more hostile and more paranoid. And I found myself hoping that the change would indeed do him some good. So we prepared to leave for Suzhou; there was little left, so it did not take much time.

———   ———   ———

Suzhou is the Venice of China. The ancient city is situated around canals and lined with lovely stone bridges and garden villas, a picturesque backdrop for the hundreds of small boats filling the waterways. Next to Hangzhou, it was supposed to be the most enchanting city in China, and like Hangzhou, Suzhou held its own legends of magic. The women of Suzhou were said to possess a mysterious element of beauty — their features more delicate, their complexions more fair, and the eyes of the women of Suzhou were known to be enchanting. Many poets had written about the excellence of the eyes of the women of Suzhou.

The images of my family there, during that summer of 1945, feel surreal as I conjure them, like the mood of a sad but lovely poem.

We moved into the back section of Old Li's house — a traditional courtyard separated the back half from the front. Everything in Suzhou had an antique feel to it, and our lodgings were no exception to the mood of the city. The house was partially furnished, and if the dust on the furniture was any indication, it hadn't been occupied for years. Alice and I immediately set about cleaning the place a bit. The children were filled with the excitement and that wonder which accompanies new surroundings and so they set about exploring. Much to their delight they discovered an obscure pull-up stairway, which led to a roomy attic. Liankui decided the attic would be a good place for all of us to sleep — if the Japanese soldiers came, they might not even notice the attic. So we made nests of down quilts and blankets, and the children and I spent our evenings curled in that antique attic, reading and telling stories and playing games. Liankui stayed to one side of the attic and did not join us in our evening entertainment.

Like our nights, our days in Suzhou also held an element of enchantment. The children and I planted flowers, and played outdoor games in the courtyard, and spent hours just walking the lovely stone streets and visiting the old shops and ancient temples. The people of Suzhou indeed embodied a tranquil element; their spirits seemed to reflect the element of water in which they were surrounded. It was contagious. We all relaxed and absorbed an element of tranquility.

Even Liankui seemed to be more comfortable, spending his days with a couple of associates who had also retreated to Suzhou, Peng and Young. Peng was a collector of Chinese paintings, old books and antiques. Indeed, he had either purchased or helped to sell some of our own paintings in the previous years. And Young had amassed fortunes in the textile and flour industry in Wuxi. The three of them spent their afternoons playing Chinese chess, or frequenting the traditional tea houses lining the canals, or in trading rumors of news of the war. It was an idle existence for men who were accustomed to the fast paced world of finance and business. Under other circumstances, their time in Suzhou might have been savored. At the time, however, in that surreal summer of 1945, it was a solitude and a city to be simply endured.

It was in this enchanting setting, that Liankui brought us the news of the arrival of the dawn.

The arrival of the dawn was the sustaining hope of every Chinese citizen in Japanese occupied territory — the end of Japanese rule. The return of our own Chinese rule, albeit Chiang Kai-shek's distorted version of democracy.

When it was announced, on August 15, 1945, that Japanese Emperor Hirohito had unconditionally surrendered, it became one of those historical moments forever engraved on the minds and hearts of citizens around the world, but especially in China.

I remember that I was preparing dinner when Liankui came home with the news. I can still see every detail in that antique kitchen in the floating city of Suzhou, where I heard the news of the end of the war. I can feel the breeze coming through the window and I can smell the fish I was preparing for dinner. And I can still feel the silent tears as they dripped down my eyes, and from my chin onto the threadbare green dress I was wearing.

We did not embrace and we did not dance. We just stood — stunned — in motionless, exhausted relief, as we absorbed the arrival of the dawn.

We immediately made plans to return to Shanghai. And the kindness of my husband's friends continued; the same Mr Yang in whose house our furniture had been stored, offered us stay in the first floor of that house until things settled. Mr Yang had exercised keen foresight and invested in Nationalist government bonds. With the surrender of the Japanese, he not only amassed fortunes as the Nationalist government was reinstated, but he was also above suspicion of collaborating with the Japanese puppet regime during the occupation.

Others were not so lucky. The dawn for many Chinese was to be simply another storm on the horizon. As if in confirmation of this fact, during the first two weeks of the dissolution of the Japanese puppet regimes and the arrival of Nationalist officials flying from Chongqing to Shanghai, the sky remained covered with dark clouds and every day there were thunderstorms and lightning. The black skies and the storms were a fitting backdrop for the return of Chiang Kai-shek to Shanghai.

The Nationalists behaved more like conquerors than liberators. Chiang's first order of business was to declare 'Traitors' Laws.' A traitor was defined as anyone who had used Japanese-issued banknotes, eaten rice grown in the occupied territories, drunk water controlled by the Japanese, or paid taxes to the Wang puppet regime. Virtually anyone who had lived under the Japanese occupation could be charged as a collaborator. There were thousands of trials; most of those charged were convicted and either exiled or executed. The end result was that large numbers of puppet officials, as well as army officers and their troops, fled in fear of persecution by the Chinese government. Their only refuge was to join the Communists, who were quietly and rapidly dissolving their alliance with the Nationalists now that the Japanese had been defeated.

The arrival of that bleak dawn on Shanghai brought the return of corrupt government, runaway inflation, and critical housing shortages as Nationalists returned to the coast. Those officials would move into the loveliest homes left standing, declaring the owners traitors. The

Communists had no need to actively recruit members — the contempt of the people for the 'victorious' Nationalists accomplished that goal. The Communists simply had to sit back and welcome those thousands who feared their Nationalist 'liberators.'

My husband's refusal to practice law during the Japanese occupation turned out to be a wise decision. Many attorneys who had practiced were denied the right to practice law for the rest of their lives. Indeed, our dear Uncle Sha, who had become my mother's dearest friend, was stripped of his license to ever practice law again. I listened as the wives of those who had worked under the Japanese to feed their families and then been imprisoned as traitors, came pleading for the assistance of my husband, who had quickly resumed his practice in the front sitting-room of Mr Yang's house. Liankui had always practiced law with integrity. This integrity came into conflict with his national loyalty as he repeatedly declined to represent those charged by the Nationalist government. It would have been quite lucrative for him professionally, had he accepted the cases, as payment was being made with gold bars or American dollars. But I can still hear him as he contemplated the appeals of the wives of his friends and former colleagues.

"If I should win the case, I will do my country a disservice; if I lose, I will do my client a disservice. I would prefer to remain poor rather than suffer from a bad conscience."

But my husband did not remain poor. The principal players in the financial, political and legal network of Shanghai sought their familiar business associates and alliances. I watched my ageing husband embrace his work with enthusiasm and fervor. He desperately wanted to believe in the success of the Nationalist government and committed himself to rebuilding his life and his country.

Of course, Du Yuesheng returned to Shanghai and quickly enlisted my husband's legal expertise in re-establishing the new stock exchange. They were successful and Du was named Chairman of the new Shanghai Stock Exchange, and my husband was given a brokerage seat on the exchange, a highly sought-after prize.

In those first few months, we tried with all our hearts to believe in the propaganda of Chiang and the Nationalists. My husband was elected as one of the representatives of the Shanghai Bar Association to draft the new constitution. He often traveled to Nanjing, where the conventions were scheduled. But we both saw the mounting strength and animosity of the Communists. And we both saw the corruption and lack of sound policies of the Nationalists.

Still, we tried to contribute to the rebuilding of our country, in spite of the fact that our position in political circles was difficult. My husband's loyalty to the Nationalist government was never questioned, but the general attitude of those who returned from Chongqing was that anyone who had lived under the Japanese occupation had compromised their national loyalty. Because we had stayed in Shanghai, and survived, we were treated as second-class citizens, despite my husband's connections and his loyalty to Chiang's Nationalist Party.

As our days began to settle into a shell of a resemblance of our past lives, I also set about rebuilding my family, financially and spiritually. Alice resumed studies at Aurora University. The children resumed studies in what was left of their respective schools. And much to our delight, Liankui's other daughter, Margaret, and her husband Henry Ho, returned to Shanghai. But Margaret brought hard news for my husband. Her brother Chiajin, Liankui's second son, had died in a battle with the Japanese in Northern Jiangsu.

My heart ached for my husband as I watched this proud man's eyes cloud with tears. It is a most painful sight to see a man mourn for his son.

I tried to comfort my husband, and though we had reached a new level of partnership and respect, Liankui seemed more distant and unfamiliar to me. I tried to ignore his troubling patterns of behavior, which grew worse when we returned to Shanghai — his fluctuation between being possessive and then respectful, and his often irrational paranoia — attributing it to the residual horrors of war.

Still, as Liankui and I discussed political events, my husband continued to give me measured increments of respect; he even enlisted my help in some of his cases. His practice, with the help of Du and other loyal friends and clients, was quickly revived, giving us enough to live on in the face of sky-rocketing inflation. Still, we could not afford our own home and with four young children, and Alice, and a law office, all functioning out of the generosity of Mr and Mrs Yang's cramped quarters, I tried to save every penny in the hopes of moving within the year.

When Liankui was asked to represent the children of Silas Hardoon in the dispute over the division of their father's estate, I was overjoyed. The famous case marked the return of my husband's professional recognition in Shanghai, as well as an opportunity for us to rebuild financially. I eagerly agreed to help my husband research the history of the case and became fascinated with the family.

Silas Hardoon was one of the wealthiest men to have lived in Shanghai. There were streets and parks and temples named for him — many still exist. Perhaps my fascination with the Hardoon family had something to do with the fact that theirs was a Western story. Yes, it all took place in the East, but it is the story of a family that achieved so much, against all odds. I suppose those rags-to-riches stories are always fascinating, whether one is in the East or the West, but as I researched and recorded the details of the case, I felt as though I knew the family on an intimate level even though I never actually met them. And the Hardoon family confirmed my conviction, though sometimes an elusive one, that anything is possible. I remember thinking that money can be a sort of freedom, if you are not ruled by it, and that money can also bring so much sadness.

Silas Hardoon arrived in Shanghai as a refugee from Baghdad, fleeing Jewish persecution. He arrived young and quite penniless, and went to work as a night watchman in one of the Sassoon Company's warehouses. He quickly worked his way up and became a rent collector for the many properties owned by the Sassoon family. Silas watched and learned, and he saved and worked. He invested in real estate, then in opium, and made millions.

Then he met the lovely Jialing Luo, a beautiful Eurasian, born in the Chinese City to a French police officer and a Chinese mother. When she was three, her father returned to France, and her mother died when she was nine, leaving Luo to survive in a poverty-stricken area near the Old West Gate. It was rumored that she survived by selling flowers, and also that she sold sexual favors, when Silas met her.

It is said that Silas fell completely in love with Jialing Luo the first time they met and that he married her within weeks. He designed a lovely estate, situated in the heart of the International Settlement and named it Aili Garden — using his wife's Chinese name. It was referred to as Hardoon Park and its twenty-six acres were designed as a miniature of the Empress Dowager's Summer Palace in Beijing. It contained an elaborate, Gothic mansion whose entrance was guarded by two tall, vermilion iron gates. Also beautifully spaced on the grounds were guest houses, a magnificent Chinese garden, pavilions, pagodas, rock gardens, bamboo groves, and arched bridges over artificial lakes and hills. At the many docks were tied graceful, traditional Chinese boats, all painted red and decorated with classical Chinese inscriptions. Yes, it was just as magical and enchanting as it is described.

Silas and Luo had no natural children of their own. They built an orphanage on the grounds and eventually adopted many children from the orphanage. Mrs Hardoon was greatly influenced by a famous Wumu Mountain monk and scholar named Huang who persuaded her to undertake the printing of the Buddhist canon; it ran 8,416 volumes, with Huang doing the editing. Mrs Hardoon's picture appeared in the first volume. Following the publication, Huang retired to a monastery near Nanjing, but Mrs Hardoon remained a devout Buddhist. Though Silas never abandoned his Jewish faith, he gave generously to Buddhist temples in honor of his wife, while also spending a sizeable fortune on building the Beth Aharon Synagogue, a most interestingly designed structure — combining sharp corners and smooth curves, on Museum Road in the International Settlement.

I learned that Silas Hardoon was a man of contradictory nature, often most eccentric. He had millions and their home and lifestyle was quite lavish; they were always followed by an entourage of attendants, assistants, and servants. Their many adopted children were always surrounding them. He had one of the best curry cooks in Shanghai, an intelligence network, even two bodyguards. Yet his office was the antithesis of wealth. No curtains on the windows or rugs on the floor — even on the coldest days, he would work in his office and refuse to have it heated — he sat there bundled in his overcoat.

When Silas Hardoon died in 1931, his funeral service followed both Jewish and Chinese rituals. He left everything to his wife.

Mrs Hardoon was said to have found comfort in the constant companionship of her chief steward, Ji Jiami. Of course, it was rumored that he was also her lover.

When Mrs Hardoon died a few years after the death of her husband, there was a bitter legal battle waged by some of the adopted children over the division of the estate. The battle had begun before the Japanese occupation, so it involved rulings in various courts — some no longer recognized. Under the Japanese imposed legal system, the adopted Chinese sons had lost their claim in the estate to one of their Caucasian 'brothers' who had collaborated with the Japanese.

The seven Chinese sons who had been adopted by the Hardoons — they all used the Chinese name of their adopted mother, Luo — had hired Liankui. My husband was deeply committed to their cause and took the case without a retainer. He was to be paid with property once his clients' right as heirs was re-established.

I think that when we look closely, there is something we can learn from everyone's life. The many late evenings I spent consumed in the letters and records of the Hardoon family were engrossing.

I learned from Silas Hardoon — a man whom I had never met — or perhaps, I simply reaffirmed what I had always known — that there is a richness to be found in diversity. He was not intimidated by his wife's different religious values; indeed, he seemed to embody the goodness to be found in both Buddhism and his Jewish faith. As I came to know the Hardoon family, I admired that trait.

As Liankui and I worked together into the long hours of the night, we tried to believe all the indications that everything was going to be fine.

Chiang Kai-shek kept reassuring the people that China was stabilizing. Even as he ran from the Communists, who were marching south.

25

"Zhaohua, the time has come to make some decisions," Liankui spoke softly after he closed the doors to our tiny bedroom in the Yang home. I could tell by his tone that he was concerned. I nodded as I sat down on the bed, waiting to hear what my husband had to say.

"I have saved enough for us to move to our own home, Zhaohua. It is time for us to leave the Yangs. My practice is continuing to grow and Chiang Kai-shek insists that China will be unified. But still, Zhaohua, I cannot dismiss everything I hear about the Communists. I think you should consider the option of returning to Hong Kong with the children — making a home there. I would stay in Shanghai and see some of my cases through, and then join you — or perhaps it will soon be safe for you to return to Shanghai. Du has offered me some suites in the Chong Wai Bank Building. I could practice law as well as live there until … until we know more. What do you think, Zhaohua?"

The fact that my husband was even considering allowing me to go to Hong Kong without him spoke volumes of his uneasiness regarding the political climate. I contemplated his words and felt completely torn. Shanghai was my home, the city in which I was born and the city I loved. I wanted to believe that China would embrace her long-awaited freedom and democracy and that the Nationalists would fulfill their role as democratic leaders. But even as I voiced my hope for my country, I could feel my intuition as it surfaced. I, like my husband, could not turn a blind eye to the mounting discontent of the people. However more comfortable that blindness might have felt.

"I think that I have a wise husband, Liankui. You are right. If the children and I go, we can always return when Shanghai settles down. And if things do not settle down, we might not be as fortunate if there is another war. I will begin the arrangements; the children and I will leave next month." Liankui nodded quietly and turned over to go to sleep.

"Liankui?" he turned again to look at me. "Thank you, Liankui."

"I wish to always protect you, my beautiful First Wife."

It is interesting. It had been fifteen years since Liankui Ching first called me his 'beautiful First Wife,' and the words had fallen on a young girl filled with fear and pain and disgust. Fifteen years later, I could not say that I had ever loved Liankui Ching, but those same words were soothing and carried honor and comfort.

Somehow, I knew that Shanghai would never again be home. Yet it would always be home. In the coming weeks, I said goodbye to Uncle Sha — the only member of my own family left in Shanghai, a broken man, still barred from practicing law under the Nationalist regime as his punishment for 'collaborating' with the Japanese. It was never taken into account that his family might have starved had he not 'collaborated.' I said goodbye to Margaret and Henry, yet again. We had spent so little time together, but we had grown close in those weeks. And I said my goodbye to Mrs Bei, who had been with us since we had returned to Shanghai; she had loved my children as her own and had been an integral part of those wartorn years. She had become a part of my family, and it broke all our hearts to say goodbye.

I knew leaving Shanghai was the right decision. I also knew that I was leaving a piece of myself behind.

So it came to be that, in the summer of 1946, Alice, Judie, Anthony, Priscilla, Frank and I sailed on an American steamer and arrived at the familiar docks of Kowloon. Liankui had made arrangements for his friend, Mr Guang Xu, President of the Xinya Medicine Company, to meet us at the dock. Guang had been one of the few who had not starved under the Japanese occupation of Hong Kong, as the Japanese had needed drugs desperately during the war. The Japanese had given Guang and his family special rations in return for pharmaceutical supplies.

As we left the ferry that had transported us from Kowloon, across Victoria Harbor, and to the city of Hong Kong, I could scarcely believe my eyes. We had heard no news from Hong Kong during our time in Shanghai, and as I surveyed the devastation of Hong Kong, I became more aware of the impact this war had inflicted on the rest of the world. I had mourned the destruction of Shanghai, but as Guang's driver took us through the streets of devastated Hong Kong, I realized — as one can realize only through direct experience and not just news reports — that others, in other parts of the world, were mourning as deeply as the Chinese.

The Allies had bombed Hong Kong heavily in an aggressive campaign to recover the British colony. A shortage of building materials had resulted in crumbling ruins serving as residences. As we drove, I continued to survey the crumbling buildings and devastation lining the streets. I'm not certain there is a sadness similar to the one experienced in the ruins of a city after a war; it is both universal and utterly filled with personal grief.

"So, Xu, tell me, has it been difficult for you? With the British government, I mean?" My mind was filled with the trials in Shanghai of those who had 'collaborated' with the Japanese.

"No, Zhaohua, the British are handling things very differently from what I read of Chiang Kai-shek and the Nationalists in China. The British realize that most 'collaborators' lived at the point of a gun during the occupation, and did not cooperate with the Japanese of their own will. In supplying the Japanese with their badly needed medicines during the occupation, I was in a position to help many residents who might have otherwise starved. Many of my friends who traded with the Japanese did the same. The British know this. They are only prosecuting a handful, those who used their Japanese influence to extort, or who were unnecessarily cruel. The rest of us are encouraged to assist in the rebuilding of Hong Kong." Guang's words were filled with a sort of painful honor. It had obviously cost his pride to provide the Japanese with supplies, yet in the end, he had little choice.

"And what of the new banknotes? I have heard so little of Hong Kong, but I recall that when we left, the Chairman of the Hongkong Bank, under duress, had issued the new banknotes. The market price was much lower than the old ones because people were afraid that the British would not recognize them."

"Ahh, but the British did recognize them; the new notes were held by the people. The British knew that the economy would be more severely devastated if the notes were declared worthless. Of course, some who bought the notes at a lower price have made a handsome profit. But I think most will use their profits to reinvest in Hong Kong. It is ironic, in the aftermath of war and all its inhumanity, there seems to be a strengthened sense of humanity in the people."

As Guang relayed the approach of the British government, I saw more clearly the contrast with Chiang Kai-shek and the Nationalists in China. I was saddened for my China in the hands of their Nationalist 'liberators.' And I knew, at that moment, that China would fail in her dream of democracy.

Mrs Xu welcomed us into her apartment with warmth. There was a delicious lunch all laid out on the table when we arrived and we ate every bite! By the end of our lunch, I felt completely comfortable in accepting Mrs Xu's gracious offer to stay with them until I found a home for my family.

No small feat. There was a serious housing shortage in Hong Kong; anything available held those visible scars of war. Broken windows, partially collapsed ceilings, doors removed to be used on exterior walls. The buildings in Hong Kong were tangible representations of what I saw in the eyes of the people. If we could glimpse inside the people who had survived the past six years, we would see pieces missing and collapsed.

Finally, I found a three-room apartment in a rambling old house on Kennedy Road. Even the windows were intact! In spite of the fact that the house was built into, and near the top of, a steep hill, and we had to share the bathroom and kitchen with another family, I took it immediately. Once again, with the help of my nearly grown stepdaughter, Alice, I set about rebuilding my family, weary of repeating the same tasks, but filled with the determination and energy — inspired by new, if slightly discouraging, surroundings.

Judie, Priscilla and Frank were enrolled in St Francis School. Anthony was still too weak to attend school, and the tropical climate of Hong Kong did not help his breathing. Household help was very inexpensive and I hired two Cantonese maids — Ah Yen and Ah Yu — who had been born into the tradition of devoted domestic servants from the village of Shunde, near Macao in Guangdong province. They took pride in their work and were meticulous in their appearance, always dressed in clean white shirts over black trousers. They embodied the traditional ways of their village and each wore a single long braid of hair down their backs. Were it not for their presence, I could not have pursued the plans, which I had postponed for so many years.

It was time, and I knew it. I assessed my options and knew that I did not have the luxury of time required to pursue a university education; in fact, I had not even completed my high school diploma. I resolved not to dwell on what I could not do, and explored the alternatives.

After careful deliberation, I enrolled in classes of my own — English, business correspondence, shorthand, typing and filing. I decided these skills were the quickest avenue to a job and an income. Other interests could be pursued with time and attention.

I surveyed the syntax of our lives, and I felt pleased — with one exception — Alice, my stepdaughter, who had become my dear friend. Her father had insisted she come to Hong Kong with us, leaving Aurora University without her degree. Although generous enough in spirit to allow me to bring the children to Hong Kong for the welfare of our family, Liankui still had possessive qualities and had made it clear that Alice was to be with me at all times. She was to be my watchdog in his absence.

"Alice, it is time to focus on your life, now. I thank you so much for all you've done to help us get settled in Hong Kong, but it is time for you to return. You still have time to enroll in the beginning of the fall semester at Aurora," I spoke with the authority of her father's wife, knowing that she would protest.

"But, Zhaohua, Father insists that I stay with you. You will be so busy with your own schooling — I could not possibly return to Shanghai." Alice was so honorable, but I knew how much she wanted, indeed needed, that degree. My recent assessment of my own life, and limited choices, strengthened my resolve for my stepdaughter.

"Alice, we both know that your father wants you to watch over me. And we both know that I do not need watching over. I am both honorable and capable, and I will not allow you to sacrifice your future on my behalf. I have booked you on a ship for Shanghai. I will continue to prepare a home here in case of the worst — come back anytime if you feel that things are becoming unbearable in Shanghai. But, for now, you will be safe at the university. You leave in two days." She did not need to say thank you — I could see the friendship and appreciation in her eyes as I handed her the ticket. The matter was settled and Alice ran eagerly to pack.

The following day, we received a telegram from Liankui with strict instructions for Alice to remain in Hong Kong until he arrived. I told my stepdaughter that if it came up, I would lie to my husband and say that we received the telegram after she had boarded the ship — too late.

"There are sometimes matters more important than blind obedience, Alice. The traditions of our country are to be questioned — not necessarily abandoned, but questioned. Just go. Do not mention the telegram to your father."

Change is the only constant. And life goes on.

I looked up old friends and made new ones in my classes, and I happened to come across Betty Tseng, a cousin of my friend Nancy who had passed away while I was in Shanghai. I had met Betty at Nancy's wedding of course, but she was younger than us and just a child, then. I hardly recognized the elegant and refined young woman whom I walked past in a shop in Hong Kong. But Betty recognized me; we chatted for a while and then she invited me to join her in meeting her parents for tea at the Hong Kong Hotel.

Betty's father was educated in England; a fact immediately obvious in his dress, manners and meticulous pronunciation of the King's English. Mrs Tseng was a perfect compliment to her husband in English dress and styling; they had spent many years living in London while Mr Tseng was studying for his doctorate. He had subsequently been appointed as a member of China's embassy in England. Upon his return to China, he had held the position of Deputy Minister of Railway, and then Deputy Minister of Foreign Affairs.

We chatted comfortably and had an elegant tea, and I enjoyed their company immensely. When I mentioned to Betty that I had just completed my courses and was looking for a job, Betty suggested that I go to work for her father. She had been assisting him in the Central Bank of China's Representative's office in Hong Kong, but was ready to return to Shanghai to join her husband for a while. Her father hired me on the spot.

The Central Bank Representative's office was on the mezzanine floor of the Hongkong Bank Building, located in the center of downtown Victoria, overlooking the harbor and the Kowloon peninsula. Two huge stone lions guarded the bank entrance on each side, along with a couple of uniformed guards. The mezzanine floor was reserved for the bank's own use, with the exception of the Central Bank Representative's office.

The first day I started to work accompanied by Mr Tseng, and we were welcomed by a charming lady, Daisy Shen. She spoke fluent English and Mandarin and greeted us by saying, "Good morning, Mr Tseng. This must be the lady you mentioned to me over the phone yesterday." Immediately we liked each other and became good friends.

I returned home that day having made new friends, and with my first job. I was most pleased as I climbed the hill to our apartment in Hong Kong to tell my children the news.

Thus, I became a working mother of four. I worked with Anthony in the evenings, helping him to keep up with his studies. He was never well enough to attend school, but he managed to do well on the examinations. Judie, Priscilla, and Frank adjusted to their new surroundings with that phenomenal resilience of children.

Alice graduated from Aurora University in 1947 and returned to Hong Kong, quickly securing a job as a ground hostess with the China National Aviation Corporation. Alice had been grounded in the traditions of China. It is the way in China, as in other Asian countries, for the young, as they establish their own financial independence, to help growing families and the elderly parents. It is a tradition somewhat foreign to Western minds, but an integral part of the lives of the families in China. She contributed so much toward creating a stable family life for my children.

It was Alice who took the children to the Kai Tak Airport to watch the planes take off and land on Saturdays. Afterward, they would all go out for a special lunch, always remembering to bring a lunch box back for Anthony, who was not up to such outings. I would stay at home and catch up on my studies or make clothes for the children or spend time with Anthony. Yes, life goes on.

Alice had left Shanghai as the city was bracing for another civil war. By the end of 1947, war between Chiang's Nationalist forces and the Communists had spread from Manchuria to the other major cities in Northern China. Mao Zedong's sweeping victories were due mainly to the support of the peasants whom the Communists had won over with the promises of a new world order of economic and social reform. Chiang Kai-shek continued to run from the Communists and to undermine his support by raiding villages and destroying the lives of the peasants in his quest for power.

Alice had relayed sadly that the very air in China seemed heavy with the pain, war and ill will.

I waited patiently and apprehensively for news of my family — Mother, Wanhua and Honglin had all moved north to be with Father, and the north held the wars that year. Finally, after almost two years in Hong Kong, I received a letter postmarked from Shanghai, in my sister's handwriting. It was April, 1948.

Wanhua wrote that Chiang Kai-shek had finally been officially elected as President of China. It was odd that this was Wanhua's only comment on the political situation. She then proceeded to fill me in on the family. Everyone, including Father and Sonya, had returned to Shanghai — though she was careful to mention that she did not know where Father was living and that she had had no contact with him. I understood that Father was in danger of being prosecuted as a collaborator.

The good news was that Kaihua had finally been granted a divorce from Zhihu, and he had then legally married Lin Yanzhu, who had been so kind to me in Beijing.

Wanhua also wrote that our paternal grandfather had died at the age of 84. I stopped reading for a moment to privately mourn my grandfather. Although there was an intense sadness at the news of his death, I was aware that it was an appropriate sadness. Death, after a long life, and a life of children and grandchildren, is the intended way. It is sad, but it is also the natural order. It was a different grief than that which I had felt for

Tommy, Nancy, and Liankui's son. A sort of peaceful grief, not weighted with anger and injustice.

As I resumed reading Wanhua's letter, more tears fell. Mother was not well. She complained constantly of aches and pains, but refused to see a doctor. Wanhua's tone was urgent as she closed, full of words of family and precious moments and hoping to see me.

The following day, I asked Mr Tseng for a two-week leave of absence and bought a plane ticket to Shanghai without even consulting Liankui. Communication with Shanghai had been difficult, and we had heard only sporadically from Liankui — he sent money with friends who came to Hong Kong, when he could. No, there would be no need for him to know I had left Hong Kong. I would visit my mother and my sister and not even contact him while I was home. Yes, I still thought of Shanghai as home.

During those days in Shanghai, I was so conscious of every precious moment spent with Mother and Wanhua. I think I could sense that my days in this city were truly and finally over.

I could also see that my Mother had finally lost all will to live. She was no longer alert or interested in anything happening around her. She sat in her tiny bedroom, with Little Tiger often by her side, in the attic apartment that she shared with Wanhua and Honglin, and she stared at the drab walls. My mother had endured such heartache in her life, and through both lack of choice and circumstance, she had never found the means with which to heal. I think that Mother's constant pain, and indeed, her obvious impending death, were the result of a heart broken and shattered and, like tiny shards of glass, strewn throughout her tired body.

So I cherished the moments and was glad that I had come, in spite of sadness.

Alice was right; the pain of China could be felt in the air. It was tangible, heavy, gray and somber. The city was in shambles, flooded with refugees from the north as Chiang Kai-shek's Nationalist forces retreated from the Communists, city by city, creeping southward. Mao Zedong's forces were about to take Nanjing, and everyone knew that Shanghai would not be far behind.

People lived in the streets as the millions had fled south, seeking refuge from the civil war. The Nationalists, still in control in Shanghai, in their rage and continual defeats by the Communists, lashed out more fiercely at the 'traitors' who had collaborated with the Japanese. I suppose it was an effort to turn attention away from the mounting strength of the Communists, but it was a politically suicidal maneuver. At a time when they should have been building strength and alliances and loyalties, the Nationalists continued to inspire fear and disgust in the people.

Though I wished to see Father, it was impossible. My Father had held a high post in the northern puppet regime. He was now a traitor and in hiding; he had made no contact with Mother and Wanhua. It would have put them in danger, to be associated with a traitor.

Honglin, my sister's husband, was his familiar self and tried gallantly to lighten the inherent sadness of the visit.

"I think we should celebrate tonight, Zhaohua — the fact that we are here together again, in spite of everything around us is worthy of a special evening. We don't know what will happen to all of us in the future. Let's go to dinner." I watched in amazement as Honglin loaded a large basket with stacks of paper currency, tied together in bundles about the size of bricks.

"What are you doing, Honglin? Is dinner now the price of a house?"

It was Wanhua who explained to me, her tone matter-of-fact, about the tenuous state of the economy under Nationalist rule. "It will all be worthless in a matter of days, Zhaohua. Chiang Kai-shek has issued his New Emergency Economic Law. His son, Chiang Ching-kuo, holds the title of Special Economic Envoy — he has full power to implement this so-called New Emergency Economic Law." Wanhua rolled her eyes as she repeated Chiang's economic policy. "Under Chiang Ching-kuo's leadership, all police, both civil and military, are on duty in the streets and have the authority to search every store, market, company and public place for gold, silver and any foreign currencies, which should be surrendered to the government banks. Everything is to be surrendered in exchange for a new currency — the Gold Yuan." Again, my sister's tone was mocking, as though Chiang's Gold Yuan would amount to nothing more than play money.

"Chiang Ching-kuo is enforcing the law with an iron fist — anyone resisting is imprisoned."

I couldn't believe my ears. There had been no news in Hong Kong of Shanghai, and I had no idea things had deteriorated so drastically. The people were living in a police state under the Nationalists.

"What does Du Yuesheng have to say about the state of affairs?" Economically, Du had always been the most powerful person in Shanghai; considering his strong connections with Chiang Kai-shek, I could not conceive of him endorsing and supporting such a policy.

"You're not going to believe it, Zhaohua, but Du Yuesheng's own son has been arrested. Nothing is as it was."

Wanhua's words spoke volumes. If the son of Green Gang leader, Du Yuesheng, had been arrested, then that meant that the Green Gang had lost its power. Du was no longer in a position of influence and control. China had, in recent years, seen a turbulent political history, but through it all, in Shanghai, the Green Gang had been the constant, the one consistent 'governing' influence. Yes, I had witnessed the end of an era for Shanghai. Indeed for all of China.

After a somber dinner, which cost my brother-in-law what would amount to thousands of dollars, which might as well have been dried leaves, we returned to their tiny apartment, and again, I found myself waiting for the dawn. A different dawn. I knew that I had to see Liankui, to see how he was holding up under such turmoil, and to let him know that I had come to Shanghai to visit Mother.

I was prepared for the worst when I went to Liankui's office. I had thought that he would be furious at my coming to Shanghai without consulting him. But my husband just stared at me, as though I were another facet in a surreal world. When I look back, I see that that one year alone in Shanghai had greatly changed my husband. Liankui Ching had been born in Old China. His China had revered and worshipped the Emperor, as had his ancestors for thousands of years. He came from a line of scholars and poets who had been honored in these dynasties. And in spite of this historical placement of his birth, he had supported the Revolution and always believed in the rights of the people. Liankui Ching had seen, in one lifetime, his people struggle and cling to a long craved democracy. And then he watched them cower in fear of those who had professed false words of democracy. Indeed, Liankui Ching himself feared those he had helped bring to power. It was a tragedy for my husband of great magnitude.

"Zhaohua ... How? ... When? You look lovely, Zhaohua." I could feel the sadness in my husband as he spoke. Though ever handsome, my husband had aged in that way that people age without lines and outward change in appearance. He felt beaten and weak.

"I arrived over a week ago, Liankui. Mother is very ill and I knew that I had to see her, and I knew that you would object." I lowered my head as I spoke to my husband; I, too, was ingrained in the traditions of Old China, and in spite of my quest for independence and my Western spirit, I was also an honorable wife. I did not find peace in defying my husband.

Liankui and I lived in a time in history when the ways of our ancestors were no longer valid, and yet, the ways of our children not yet defined.

We embodied a turbulent and pivotal generation in which traditions and customs of thousands of years were abandoned, and we weren't at all certain what was to replace them. I felt it all, in both of us, in that office in Shanghai.

"I have a job, Liankui. In the Central Bank of China's Representative's Office in Hong Kong. The children are settled in St Francis, except for Anthony of course. Alice is back and an immense help. We have a pretty good apartment by Hong Kong standards — it's built on a hill, but considering available housing in Hong Kong, I felt fortunate to find it. Mother is not well, Liankui. I had to come and Shanghai is so very sad, Liankui. I can't believe you are still here. When will you be coming to Hong Kong?"

"Zhaohua, I knew you would be strong, but you have become so independent, my First Wife." I could feel that my husband was both impressed and somewhat intimidated by my ability to function without him.

There was a knock on the door, and in hindsight, I can still see the utter fear in my husband's eyes with that knock. It was one of those telling gestures which registers on some level, but on which I did not dwell, putting it off to the tense political climate of the time. But, as I look back, it was a gesture to which I can tie a turning point in my husband. Yes, his paranoia had begun to set in by that time, and as is the case with mental illness, it would grow.

His eyes blinked wildly and he looked around the room like a caged animal.

"That, Zhaohua, will be your father. You must not have contact with him; it is dangerous enough for me. If he is prosecuted, they will require him to list anyone with whom he has spoken. Please, hide here." Before I could absorb what my husband was saying, he motioned me to go into a sitting area of his office, sectioned off by thick red, velvet curtains, which he drew, nearly closed. "Please, Zhaohua, do not come out. I know you will wish to see your father, but it would be too dangerous. I think it would be embarrassing for your father, Zhaohua. The war — it has changed us all."

My father was indeed changed. Heavy tears streamed down my face as I saw my father — barely recognizable — through a crack in the curtain. My father had, I later learned, taken a bad fall in Tianjin; he struggled into the room bent, and on crutches. Though I could only feel how my husband had aged, it was to be both felt and seen in my father. My father had always been so incredibly handsome and proud and gallant. On that day, he sat before me as a beaten and shriveled, old, old man. To this day, it is one of my most painful memories.

I was proud of my husband in the honor and friendship he continued to show my father. Yes, I had, in the early years, resented the fact that my husband continued his relationship after my father had disowned me. But on this day, I could feel only gratitude as I watched my husband hand my father money, and my father so humbly accept. Yes, it would have been humiliating for my father to have faced me.

I wanted to say all those words we had never spoken in our beautiful days by the sea in Qingdao. Yes, pride disintegrates in the elementary and unselfish awareness of love, and it is only then that we can see how much needless damage that silent pride can inflict. We think that there is strength in pride and in holding back words of comfort and forgiveness in the name of honor. But I have learned that pride is evil, childish and not honorable. I wanted to hold my father and say that I did not blame him for having disowned me — thousands of years of Chinese tradition had made him do it. I knew that now. I wanted to tell him that I knew he was not a traitor. That he had done what he had to do to support his large family. I wanted to thank him for turning his back on those thousands of years of tradition and for the gift of those lovely days in Qingdao and for allowing me those happy times in his house in Shanghai, with Mother and Wanhua. But my words, drowning in all their unspoken pride, just rolled down my face in silent, heavy tears. It would have brought no comfort to my father to know I was there, seeing him bent and accepting money from my husband.

Liankui arrived in Hong Kong the following year — in April of 1949. He had tried to hold out for the money from the sale of the property in the Hardoon case. Du Yuesheng, and other friends, also arrived that same week.

Shanghai fell to the Communists the following month, in May of 1949.

All land was declared as owned by the state, and Liankui received nothing for his years of work on the case.

Chiang Kai-shek with his best-equipped armies fled to the island of Taiwan, along with his loyal followers, taking all the gold, silver, and foreign currencies, which he had collected under the New Emergency Economic Law.

On October 1, 1949, Mao Zedong, Chairman of the Communist Party, stood atop the rostrum of Tiananmen Gate and declared the establishment of the People's Republic of China. The capital would be Beijing.

"The Chinese people have arisen!" Mao Zedong proclaimed victoriously.

And, God, how I wished it were true. But we had risen so many times in my short lifetime. Only to stumble and to fall, and to be beaten back down, often, by our own people.

26

Hong Kong was chosen as surrogate homeland for thousands of Chinese. I suppose it held a sort of geographical comfort, this colony still, in part, attached to our homeland — within sight — yet displaced and nearly severed from our history. It seemed fitting for a people caught in limbo. We did not belong to the past, nor were we able to define our future. We were without a country of our own. We were not allied with the Communists, and we could no longer support Chiang Kai-shek in his version of 'democracy', as his followers re-established themselves on the island of Taiwan. Families were both separated and reunited; Margaret and Henry did not remain allied with the Nationalist government, and they chose to stay in Shanghai.

It was as though we were actors, playing the people we had once been, when we came together later that year in the apartment of Du Yuesheng and Mrs Eighteenth Floor in Hong Kong. Du and Mrs Eighteenth Floor were hosting a 'banquet' in honor of his fifth wife, Miss Man Xiaotong, also a well-known opera singer and a good friend of Mrs Eighteenth Floor.

As we entered the small apartment, I could not keep from my mind the contrast with the grand home, which had held my first celebration with this man who was once, arguably, the most powerful man in China. We walked through the narrow hallway of the Hong Kong apartment, and I thought of the marble floors, the live music, the winding staircase and those brilliant chandeliers of Du's grand home in the International Settlement. This plain hallway was lined with stacks of oxygen tanks — bottled life — made necessary by Du's opium addiction, combined with an asthmatic condition.

In the center room, there were three simple round tables set for dinner. Mrs Eighteenth Floor was, as always, genuine and gracious. Though her natural warmth was still obvious, her spirit, like the rest of us, carried an air of defeat.

I sat in this apartment and listened to the somber conversations, and I recalled the mahjong games, the clinking of the tiles, and the women cursing and laughing and so decadently smoking opium on those couches designed for extravagance. I could feel life saying to us, over and over, that we had seen the end of a time in history. Yes, the men wore their traditional robes — robes the colors of night, and they drank their tea. And I think I cried night tears on the inside.

For Du Yuesheng and Liankui Ching, who had known such power and such vitality and such wealth, this gathering, so near what everyone knew would be the end of both of their lives, was a peace-making with all that happened, I think. Without words, they said goodbye.

Du Yuesheng died in Hong Kong in the following year. From Taiwan, Chiang Kai-shek sent Du's family a telegram of condolence, praising Du for what he had done for his country.

My husband spiraled into his idleness and his paranoia, and would disappear for days at a time. I knew he was in Macao, losing money we didn't have.

I had lost my job. When the People's Republic of China had been established, that Communist government was soon recognized by the British government. The Representative's Office of the Central Bank, which belonged to the Nationalist government, and with which I had worked for two years, was booted out of the Hongkong Bank Building. We moved to another building and struggled for ten months before closing down completely. The money Liankui had managed to bring from Shanghai was almost gone.

Hong Kong was now flooded with refugees. Unemployment was rampant. I took any job I could get. Some lasted for weeks. Others, with bosses who knew that young, attractive assistants were desperate for employment, would last only days, sometimes hours. Though pressured, and yes, desperate, I refused to succumb to their overt advances.

The recession progressed and the jobs came and went; my husband continued with his gambling and I began to shrink. I took more classes at night, determined to hold fast to my commitment to educate myself and work my family out of this hole, but again, life had stolen my breath. It was all motions. My self-esteem plummeted, my exhaustion mounted, and my hopes withered. Still, my body, with some shreds of my spirit, did go on.

Alice, and my own children, who all found solace in the Catholic religion taught in their schools, encouraged me to join a class in Catholicism; it was being conducted by Father Cronin at the Catholic

Center near our home. Finally, I mechanically followed their advice and did eventually embrace the Catholic faith. I was baptized in the Catholic Cathedral and indeed found a great deal of peace and, I suppose, a spiritual soothing. This, I think is one of the prime elements in any religion — that ability to provide a voice of comfort, when one most needs comfort. I heard that voice, and, as the years went on, found more and more comfort in my faith. Yes, I can still see that exquisite, looming statue of the Virgin Mary in the Hong Kong Catholic Center, on the day of my baptism. And I am reminded that all can be endured.

——— ——— ———

Thus life went on in Hong Kong. Although communication with the rest of the world had been re-established, news from either China or Taiwan was scarce. Yet, in a rare successful attempt at communication, I received a letter from my old friend Janet Woo. The tone was flat and the content of the letter was straightforward. She, her husband, and their two children, had left Nanjing to go to Taipei, following Chiang Kai-shek, when the Nationalist government fled the mainland. Before leaving Nanjing, James Woo had surrendered his considerable fortunes in gold bullion and foreign currencies to the Nationalist government as required by the Economic Emergency Law and received the equivalent in Gold Yuan, the official currency of the Nationalist party. It had all turned out to be worthless. James had suffered a severe nervous breakdown and was no longer able to function — all decisions, as well as the livelihood of their family, were left up to Janet. Janet asked about the possibility of coming to Hong Kong, but would need our assistance. Her only other option was to return to Shanghai.

I wrote Janet the day I received her letter and told her to come to Hong Kong immediately.

Then, encouraged by the communication from my old friend, I wrote to Wanhua. I urged my sister and her husband to leave Shanghai — I had found Honglin a job with a bank in Hong Kong — and to bring Mother and Little Tiger with them.

After several anxious weeks, I received my sister's emotional response.

Dear Zhaohua,

After careful consideration, Honglin and I have decided not to come. It was the Opium War that cost our China the property of Hong Kong, and it is our national disgrace. For many years, we have lived in a foreign settlement, in our own homeland, because we had no choice. And now we have a new China. A China different from our old, corrupt country.

This past year, 1950, has marked an historical transition for us from struggle to reconstruction. We have been busy rebuilding our country, which was left in ruins when Chiang fled to Taiwan. There was no money in the coffers; bridges and roads were destroyed, farms and fields had been abandoned, and the cities and villages were devastated.

You, Zhaohua, have always embraced new ways, new things, and new ideas. I know that you would embrace our New China, as well.

Liankui is getting old, Zhaohua. But you are still young and you have four children. In our new society, the government would take care of you and your children. You would be given a job as soon as you arrive. Education and health care are provided free. Rent is only a few dollars per month. All foreigners and capitalists are gone. It is no more, 'big fish eat small fish.' We are liberated, my sister! 'The Chinese people have arisen.'

Please consider my words carefully, Zhaohua. Your future depends on it — and also the futures of your children. Our New China is your motherland, Zhaohua. She awaits you. She needs you. She loves you. And she, like your family, will welcome you, always.

Your loving sister,
Wanhua

The tears started falling with the first line of my sister's letter and did not stop for many hours after I read it. Tears of confusion and questioning and a longing for home. I felt like a traitor, like a coward, hiding in Hong Kong from the turmoil in my homeland. Oh, my sister knew me so well — and she was right. I was not intimidated by new ideas. I embraced them, in fact. But my future in Hong Kong was so uncertain. Any money we had brought from Shanghai was almost gone. I knew that I could no longer rely on Liankui to support us. And yes, those who were thriving in the capitalist society of Hong Kong seemed selfish and uncaring about the livelihood of the masses. Her words rang in my head all that day and late into the night. I could not fall asleep and my head ached from crying.

The thought of going home and having the government of my homeland take over the burdens of my family seemed to be the solution for which I had prayed and waited. Perhaps I could even attend the People's University in Beijing and use my degree to find a job I actually enjoyed. I pictured myself back in Shanghai, joining my family and friends in the rebuilding of the city and country I had so loved. I saw myself joining them and standing up, straight and elegant, as a free Chinese. Even Janet, in her letter, had mentioned returning to Shanghai. Indeed, many Chinese had left Hong Kong to return to Shanghai.

I saw us as we had been in my father's homes in Shanghai. My children surrounded with the love and support of their aunt and uncle, easing their grandmother in her last days. I was captivated by the comfort of home and family and I decided that, of course, it was the most logical answer. I would write Wanhua and accept her offer to return. I would then write to Janet, whom I had invited to Hong Kong, and tell her of my decision. I had not heard from her since my letter, although I had secured for them the apartment above us, when the family who lived there had become discouraged with the job situation and had themselves returned to Shanghai. For all I knew, Janet had not even received my letter and had gone to the mainland as well.

Yes, every indication was that Shanghai was the best place for my family. It was the logical decision.

It was near dawn when I finally got out of my bed, having not slept at all. My hands trembled as I held my pen to write to my sister. Yes, it was the right decision.

It was then, sitting at my writing table, in that apartment on Kennedy Road, that I heard a voice. I know it was a voice. A woman's voice. The voice said that I should have confidence in myself and faith in the God in whom I had professed to believe; that I was not listening to my own words: the words that came from within.

Even as I recall these words, so many years later, I know that something on a spiritual level occurred in my tiny bedroom in Hong Kong that night. Whether God is in his Christian heaven, or inside us, or in our intuition, or in Buddha, someone spoke to me that night. I watched as the words spilled from my pen, and I answered my sister's letter.

I told Wanhua that I loved them all. And that I would not be returning to Shanghai.

I did not hear from Wanhua for several months. Though it hurt me to know that I would be labeled by my family as a traitor and a capitalist — whom the Communists considered the embodiment of evil — I knew that I had made the decision I was supposed to have made. The decision that was to fulfill my way. And the decision that felt right in my prayers.

Finally, a letter arrived. It was short.

Wanhua said that our mother had died.

The magnitude of my grief caught me by surprise. When Father's father had died, I thought I had defined and accepted grief that I was experiencing the inherent sadness in the cycle of life. But when one loses one's mother, it is a grief of its own. Because she is the one who gave us birth and held us as infants, the one who has connected us to the past and given us the future. It is an emptiness for which there is no metaphor. No words. A hollow inside. And pain on a level of its own.

As grief once again claimed my precious days, my mother came to me. I had always heard stories of such encounters and wondered at their reality. My response vacillated between belief, but, if I am to be honest, laced with the suspicion that these were apparitions born of grief and exhaustion and despair, and not of reality. Until I saw her. My mother. She was standing in front of my bed and she was quite lovely. She spoke softly — she had come to say goodbye. To say that she loved me. To say that she was so sorry that her despair had sent me to Liankui Ching to borrow money, cementing my sad fate with this man. That she was sorry that she could not help me during her lifetime. That she had been born with the traditions of China in her bones and maybe someday I would understand how powerful they could be.

I sat up in my bed and I heard her words and I saw her. She was as real as the sheets touching my skin, and the frame of the bed, and my hand on my face, as I touched them all — my sense of touching assuring me that I was indeed awake. That my mother was real. I got up from my bed and walked to my mother, and I told her that she had nothing to do with my marriage. I thanked her for standing up to my father that day and for not sending me to Nanjing, and that it was not her fault, that my life was my fate, as her life had been her fate.

My mother disappeared.

As life wore on, Janet and James Woo did indeed arrive in Hong Kong. I was just about to let the apartment upstairs go — it was an expense I could no longer afford — when I heard from them. Janet arrived looking tired, but still lovely. James's hardships were more obvious in his appearance, and his eyes did not seem to see us when we talked, though Janet said he was doing much better and felt well enough to look for a job in Hong Kong.

They had sold what jewelry and valuables they had left, the proceeds of which dwindled quickly as James went out, day after day, looking for work — we could tell in the way he climbed the hill to the house that he was having no luck. He and Liankui would spend the warm afternoons playing Chinese chess — when my husband wasn't taking off for Macao, that is.

I went from job to job; Alice was a great source of pride and help in those years. She had continued with her job with the airline, though even that situation looked to be tenuous. China National Aviation Corporation was state-owned, but precisely which state was the legal owner was in question. It had been formed under the Nationalist government and Chiang Kai-shek insisted that the airline belonged to his government, now based in Taiwan. Others thought that since Communist China had been recognized by the British, the mainland government was the legal owner.

Alice insisted on contributing toward the cost of rent and household expenses while she worked at the airline. As the dispute over the airline worsened, I could tell that Alice had a lot on her mind.

"Zhaohua, I know how difficult things have been and my job has been the only consistent employment, but I don't quite know how to say this, Zhaohua, but the turmoil is tearing the airline apart. I think I am going to have to …"

"To what, Alice? You can speak freely with me."

"I have been offered a full scholarship to Fordham University in New York, Zhaohua, to work toward a master's degree. I hate to leave you and the children — I know you need my help …"

"You will accept, Alice. Immediately." I made certain that my tone carried no room for argument from my honorable stepdaughter.

When the time came, it was another emotional goodbye, but this sadness had an underlying joy. Of course, I would miss Alice who had become my friend and confidante, and a great source of strength and support during these difficult years. But, at the end of the day, I wanted only what was the best for her.

We all went to the pier to say goodbye, including a special young man, K. C. Liang, who had worked with Alice at the airline. Our family had grown fond of K. C. during his increasingly frequent visits to see Alice. When I saw how Alice looked at him, and the look returned in K. C.'s large, pained eyes, I admired my stepdaughter all the more for her courageous choice.

"Alice, may I have a word with you, please?" Alice joined me and we walked a short distance away from the others.

"Zhaohua, I do not quite know how to say goodbye — you have been such a — "

"Alice, I have something for you. Here." I placed in her hands a neat roll of American dollars.

"Zhaohua — no — you do not have this money to give —"

"Alice, it is your money — the money you have so diligently handed me over the years for household expenses. I have never used it, Alice. I knew this day would come. That you would find your own way, and that you would need it. And I have always planned for you to have it."

"Zhaohua, thank you, Zhaohua. I will not forget, Zhaohua. I will help you — from America. I'll send money and I'll help your children, when it is their time. Thank you, Zhaohua."

We turned to join the others quickly, neither of us wishing to display our immense sadness at parting amidst the large crowds at the dock. Both knowing there was no need for an emotional display and knowing how very deeply the other felt.

The year wore on. The jobs came and went. I continued taking classes, English, accounting and bookkeeping, and maneuvering money and jobs and children like a desperate balancing act, wondering when it would all fall down around me.

My husband declined in mental, as well as physical, health. He had recurrent nightmares, following which the entire house would awaken to his screams. My once proud and handsome husband looked like a skeleton; his eyes, though still plagued with that familiar, nervous blinking, were completely alien to me. Liankui no longer referred to me as his lovely 'First Wife.' There were to be no more tender moments. And then he sank into a near constant state of utter paranoia, accusing all of us, but mostly me, of planning to kill him.

I became his enemy. He watched my every move with suspicion and, try though I may, I could not allay his fears nor soothe his paranoia. Eventually, I did not try. I simply watched him leave for his afternoon walk and did not say a word as he departed, spouting accusations and rambling on in his private, impenetrable, madness. And often he would not return. He would check himself into a hotel, sometimes for days at a time. Of course, at first, we would go to look for him, only to be humiliated as he told the workers at the hotel not to admit me — that I was plotting to murder him for his money. The hotel workers just shook their heads. They knew, as well as I, that Liankui Ching had no money. I would scrape enough together to pay his bills and go home without my husband.

Even in his more rational moments, he was convinced of my plots to murder him. It was then, during one of those more lucid moments, that I came up with a plan to allay his fears. I told Liankui to draw up divorce papers. If we were divorced, I would receive nothing in the event of his death. In fact, my husband had absolutely nothing to bequeath to anyone upon his death. Fortunately, he agreed.

Liankui Ching and I divorced. Yet, of course, I continued to care for him and he continued to live in our home, for which I paid the rent. My frightened children watched as he regressed more deeply into his paranoid madness — painting his windows black to keep out the light and sometimes staying in his room, which became filthy and which he would not allow to be cleaned, for days at a time.

Alice and I corresponded regularly. She insisted on sending money to hire a servant to care for her father. It was a gesture of respect for her father; a gesture of kindness for me.

My dear Alice was true to her word, and she worked diligently at securing opportunities for my children as they reached their high school graduations. She helped to get Judie a full scholarship to study at the College of New Rochelle in the United States.

Judie had been a marvelous student at Sacred Heart Canossian School. She had embraced the Catholic faith with her heart, going to church every day. I was always so proud of her commitment to hard work and thought perhaps she would become an excellent writer or an English teacher someday — she had written an essay which had been chosen for publication in her school journal.

Next, it was my dear Anthony's turn to leave. My son whom I had held so many nights as he gasped for air. He had continued to miss school because of his asthma, but we kept up with his studies at home and when examinations were held, he was determined to go. And he always did well. Finally, he, too, graduated from St Joseph's College. He applied for, and received, a scholarship to Universite Catholique de L'ouest in Angers, France.

Once again, I stood on that pier in Hong Kong and watched as a piece of my heart, indeed my own flesh, boarded a ship. I knew the climate would be so much better for my son and I knew that this was the intended way — for our children to reach their time to pursue their own destinies. I was so happy for him and so very, very proud of him. Still, I felt an intense, primal sadness when I said goodbye to my son.

Following Anthony's departure, there was another brief letter from Wanhua. Father had died. I mourned, but if I am to be honest, I mourned out of duty. Though I respected my father and had yearned for his acceptance and his affection, the bond between us had not been nurtured.

Priscilla and Frank were a source of joy in the vacuum of so many goodbyes. Together, the three of us would climb that hill each day and return to what had become home.

Over that next year I worked for a South African jewelry merchant, and then as a bookkeeper and secretary in an import and export company. It was there, in that tiny office, that I got his call.

"Hello, may I speak with Zhaohua, a Zhaohua Ching, please?" His words were spoken with a crisp English accent, and that lilt — that melody, which so often accompanies that graceful pronunciation of the upper-class English.

"Speaking. May I ask who is calling, please?"

"Oh, Ms Ching. I'm so glad I've caught up with you. My name is Sandy Smith. We have a mutual acquaintance — actually I believe she's a distant cousin of yours — Mrs Susan Ma, in Toronto. When she heard I was visiting Hong Kong, she requested that I deliver a gift from her to you and to bring back news of the family." I barely remembered Susan, but felt honored by her thoughts.

"Ms Ching? May we arrange to meet — perhaps for lunch? The truth is also that I know no one in Hong Kong, and nothing of the area. I'm here on vacation and would appreciate a few tips. Susan suggested that you might be gracious enough to give me some information — something other than the standard tourist propaganda — on the area."

"Of course, Mr Smith, I'd be happy to offer suggestions, but I'm afraid that I rarely take lunch — my job keeps me very busy."

"Well, then, perhaps an early supper; I could meet you when you finish; give you Susan's gift, we could have a bite together and take care of everything. Would that work with your schedule?"

"Certainly. Perhaps around 5.30 tomorrow?" I gave Sandy directions to my office and thought again how thoughtful it had been of my distant relative to remember me.

I had no idea that Sandy Smith was about to change my life.

27

I can still see Sandy, exactly as he was on that first day. Middle-aged and not too tall for a North American. He wore a well-tailored suit and a patterned silk tie; I also recall the way he walked as he approached — long strides confident and sure — and yet his mind was obviously occupied. I can feel his hands as he took mine — a polite, yet warm, handshake. I can see the subtle, somewhat surprised smile in his lovely blue eyes as he introduced himself; he was obviously and immediately pleased with Susan's cousin, though Sandy Smith never overstepped the boundaries of a gentleman.

"Well, Ms Ching, your cousin said that you would be a most attractive lady, but I must say, her description hardly does you justice," he said in mellifluous English. Sandy Smith smiled and bowed his head slightly. Though his manners were impeccable, and Sandy obviously had that sophistication of worldly experience, there was also an unmistakable element of the genuine and the undisguised in his manner.

I felt myself blush and could not hold his gaze; I was not at all prepared for the compliment, nor the effect of this charming man.

Our attraction was instantaneous, as was our comfort, and our relationship was balanced in the intensity of each of these elements.

We were seated at a corner table in a small restaurant in Hong Kong. There was soft music, white linen table cloths, glasses clinking, and all of those accessories portrayed in great detail in novels and movies. Though each of those details is completely unnecessary and unrelated to what happened between Sandy and myself over dinner that evening, I remember them all. Especially the waiter — he came back three times, only to hear that we had not even opened our menus, too absorbed in our conversation, until finally we laughed and ordered for the sole purpose of not being interrupted again.

I got to know Sandy before we even ordered, both in detail and essence. And I sensed, immediately and most completely, that this man was kind and fair and genuine. He was an attorney for the Bank of Montreal in Toronto; he was in Hong Kong for vacation and would be leaving at the end of the week. I remember feeling such immense sadness upon hearing him speak of leaving Hong Kong, then realizing that we had not yet been acquainted for an hour. On behalf of my cousin Susan, Sandy handed me a small bottle of perfume and said, "Ms Ching, you look so young. Your cousin Susan told me something about you. She said you were a most attractive lady, and I must say, you match her description perfectly."

"Thank you, Sandy," I felt my cheeks turning red, and stared at the tablecloth. "Susan hasn't written me for a long time. By the way, is this your first visit to Hong Kong?"

"Yes, I am a real tourist," he smiled, but not boldly. "I'm single."

"What would you like to do and see here?"

"I'm interested in shopping, touring the countryside and also seeing the New Territories," he replied. "In fact, everything in Hong Kong is fascinating."

As dinner progressed, we both knew what was happening, and there was no attempt to disguise it.

"Zhaohua, could you possibly take some time off and show me around Hong Kong while I'm here? There is so much to see and to do. Besides, I'll be leaving next Sunday."

An impossible suggestion, of course; I was immediately dropped back into the syntax of my life. My children, Liankui, and the desperate need to hold on to my current job.

I was confronted, in vivid detail, with all of the obstacles to Sandy's suggestion. And I have come to know that it was strength, and not weakness, that inspired me to accept his invitation.

I stared at him. Then I smiled at him and slowly nodded.

The following morning, I phoned my office and said that I would need a few days off for a personal matter. I had awakened early, so full of life and energy, and I bathed and dressed carefully, and went to meet Sandy.

Sandy had hired a car and we spent the morning exploring the New Territories. I felt as though I was seeing Hong Kong for the first time; never had it held such an element of joy. We had a picnic lunch; he had planned ahead and packed cheeses and breads and even had a cooler with a chilled bottle of white wine. I told him of my children, and of my life in Shanghai, and of the war, and even of Tommy. I hadn't spoken of his death in years, and I found, with Sandy, that finally I could remember my baby and get through it. When he asked about Liankui, I told Sandy simply that we were divorced.

Sandy loved the water, so we spent that enchanted afternoon swimming in Deep Water Bay. Lovely sailboats sat anchored out in the bay, and occasionally a tour boat would go by in the distance. I was certain that the people on the boats could take one look at us and know that, as our bodies danced in the water, we were two people utterly consumed in content and joy.

That evening we dined and danced in the ballroom of the Hong Kong Hotel. It was a lovely jazz band; the music sounded just like a summer breeze. He was a beautiful dancer, and I felt, I think for the first time, safe. Yes, that was it. I felt safe and completely alive. I knew that I was exactly where I was intended to be. When he asked me if I would come to his room, I smiled and said simply, 'of course.'

I had been married for over twenty years. I was a mother. But I had not, until that evening, experienced an element of pleasure in physical love. For both Sandy and myself, as he touched me so gently, it was one of those rare consummations in which the pleasure surpasses that which is physical and becomes a sort of spiritual union. I knew in that moment, that moment of unique pleasure, that Sandy Smith and I would always be connected. Whatever happened in our lives, there would be an undeniable union, and that it was wrapped up, intrinsically, in a physical attraction of the most intense passion. But ours was a relationship that went far beyond that attraction and entered that realm of serene harmony. Sandy said that when he was with me, in that hotel room, in a foreign city, on the other side of the world, that he felt as though he had come home.

Every day we swam. In Deep Water Bay, then in Repulse Bay, then in Clear Water Bay. Sandy said that he thought our spirits were happiest in water that he had always found an immense peace and freedom in water, and that it seemed an appropriate place for us to dance. We even swam by moonlight one special evening. I can still see the lanterns glowing on the boats, like the stars had come down to play with us.

We spent five glorious days, basking in that balanced contradiction of intense desire and perfect peace.

Now as I recall the days, I wonder, for a moment, if my mind chooses to embellish the romance and the peace. But the days were as beautiful as I describe them. Indeed, mere words cannot do them justice.

Every minute dripped in that supremely powerful consumption of fresh love. Until that last evening, of course, just before he left. Yes, the peace was shattered that evening.

"Zhaohua, I will be leaving tomorrow morning. And I want you to come to Toronto; I want you to be my wife, Zhaohua. I want to help you with your children. It would take some time, I know, to make the arrangements, but ..." And then I knew. I knew that I had been strong enough to grab these days of happiness with Sandy, but I could not turn my back on tradition.

What Sandy and I had was supreme. It was that type of love we all crave. What I had with Liankui Ching had never resembled what I shared with Sandy. Yet, in the end, it was more binding. Liankui and I had shared the birth of children. We had shared the death of a son. We had lived through wealth and wars and poverty and now, mental deterioration. I could not desert him now. Not at the end of his life. I loved Sandy completely, in the purest sense of the word. But my bonds with Liankui Ching, though infinitely less beautiful, less peaceful, and somehow — less right — were stronger.

"Sandy, please stop. I ... I ... it is impossible, Sandy. Yes, I have my children to think of, and ... but ... I cannot desert Liankui, Sandy. He is my husband. Yes, we are divorced, but I still care for — look after — him. He has no one else, and he is quite old and not well. But I cannot ... Sandy, I am Chinese — to the bone — and I did not realize, until this very moment how ..." Saying that, I broke down. Sandy took out his handkerchief to dry my tears.

"Zhaohua, do you love me?"

The tears started then, and for every degree of joy I had felt with this beautiful man, I experienced the opposite extreme of pain. A balanced, widely swinging pendulum.

"You know that I do, Sandy," I whispered, my heart in my throat.

"Then we will make it work, Zhaohua. Oh, my sweet girl, do not cry. I am not that easily discouraged. You will be my wife, Zhaohua. I am a patient man."

Sandy held me, and I could feel his love. It was so tangible and vibrant. No, we would not be together, and yes, my life would go on as before. But I was calmed that night and thought that I could survive anything — even losing him — with just the knowledge that Sandy loved me.

——— —— ———

Sandy did leave for Toronto. But he wrote letters regularly over the next year. I began to dream of my life in Toronto with him, though I told no one of the affair. These were not expectations that turned into day dreams, to dwindle and wither into forgotten hopes. No, Sandy's friendship and love grew in that year. He was determined that we would be together.

During that year there were more jobs and financial stress, more evening classes, more problems with Liankui, and worries because I had not heard from Judie. But through all of these, it was my supreme pleasure to find, every week, without fail, a letter from Sandy in my mail. We exchanged our views on current affairs and our wishes to be together again. There were moments when I felt I could almost touch him, and I knew when he was thinking of me — I could feel it with an intuitive certainty.

That next summer, he wrote that he would send me pictures from Athens, where he was travelling on business, and that he could wait no longer, and that he would return to Hong Kong as soon as a couple of things were wrapped up in his office.

When I did not hear from him, as expected, I knew something was wrong. I wrote to him in Toronto.

I heard nothing for four weeks.

Finally, a letter — postmarked from Toronto — arrived. The return address was that of Madame Marie Pascal, and my fingers trembled as I opened it.

She had enclosed my letter to Sandy, unopened.

It was with sadness and regret that she informed me that her brother, Sandy Smith, had been killed in a car accident while away on business, in Athens.

The stars no longer played. The sight of the water around Hong Kong made me ill. And I thought life to be unfathomable in its cruelty.

Sandy's death, coming on top of my personal mountain of grief, was my breaking point. I mourned privately for several days, feigning sickness. I had told no one about Sandy, so I had no one with whom to share my grief. As I emerged and saw my family and the world going on, as though the most beautiful man I had ever met had not just been killed, it felt like a boulder on my chest. I saw that life goes on. It simply goes on. And it carried me away, like a current of the gods.

There were more refugees than jobs in Hong Kong. Still, I dragged my hollow body out of bed, and I dressed and combed my hair. I went into town and took anything I could get. Extra typing, temporary positions, but the last of our savings, and my reserved pieces of jewelry were almost gone. My only hope now was Judie. She would be graduating soon, and employed. She would help. She would send me American dollars every month. I knew she would help as it came time for Priscilla and Frank to apply to universities. I felt I had to keep going until I got them settled. Then I could give in to that exhaustion which had plagued those blurry, heavy days after Sandy's death.

Liankui grew increasingly difficult to deal with. He even suspected Priscilla and Frank of aligning themselves with me against his life. He refused to allow his room to be cleaned. And he would wander the streets during the day, with not the slightest resemblance to the man he had once been.

Then I got a letter from Judie; she had decided to leave the College of New Rochelle to join the Ursuline Order. She was going to become a nun. She had decided she could do more for me, her brothers, and her sister, and for China, through her prayers.

I was heartbroken. I had expected her to help me financially after she graduated, like so many other Chinese students in the States who took care of their parents and siblings in Hong Kong. She was my only hope. I wrote her numerous pleading letters asking her to change her mind. Pleading, on behalf of my children and her father. And I received no reply.

Then came the sins of the mother. Margaret had entrusted me with two thousand dollars when I left Shanghai — for safe keeping, should they need it. I had experienced some success with my limited investments with James Woo in Shanghai; inspired by that success, I had invested Margaret's money in a Chinese company stock, and I was so looking forward to the day that I could tell her that her money was worth so much more. Then the company declared bankruptcy and the owner fled to China. And the stock bottomed out. It was all lost.

Shanghai had become unbearable, and Margaret and Henry returned to Hong Kong. Margaret came to visit and said that they needed the money.

That was the day I began to steal Liankui's sleeping pills, a few at a time, until I had accumulated twelve, which I thought could help me die in peace. A long sleep without waking up.

The day arrived. I came home, again without a job. I was very tired and depressed. I climbed that hill and did not fight the exhaustion. I went to my bedroom and locked the door, and I found immense comfort as my body melted on the bed. I opened the drawer of the bedside table and took out the pills. Sleep was the only thing I cared about. I took the pills, one by one. I was conscious of being absolutely certain of my choice.

As I felt each pill slide down, there was no fear. I didn't think of my children. I didn't think of Liankui. I didn't think of Sandy or Tommy or of Mother. I felt only comfortable anticipation of the peaceful sleep to come.

I remember it coming, slowly, like a satin fog. And I was so very, very ready.

"Mother! Why have you locked your door? I need help with my homework — please, open the door, Mother." It was Priscilla's voice, slicing through my lovely tranquil gray.

"Mom, what's going on? Why is the door locked? Mom? Mom?" I heard Frank pounding on my bedroom door.

I tried to speak, but my mouth no longer belonged to me.

"Mom?! Mom!!!" I could feel the terror in their voices. They knew. They knew and they would find me like this — wrapped in gray satin. Their mother.

I found my voice. "I, I just need some rest before dinner. Please leave me alone for a while. I want to sleep."

"Mom ... mom, please, open the door."

My body rolled over. I began to feel sick to my stomach. I became dizzy and vomited on my bedroom floor.

My children saved my life that day. Eventually, I was to be grateful.

28

Stamina is acquired only through endurance. As I passed my fortieth year, I privately noted that I had become a woman of immense stamina. It was not an arrogant realization; it was simply an honest self-assessment.

I eventually resumed my life with the strength that comes in the realization that I had endured almost any cruel blow fate could deal. True, I had not endured it without scars, and I had not always been willing to go on enduring it. Nonetheless, I was still there. I was still caring for my children and my demented husband; I was looking for work — I was going on. Not through choice, granted. But I was standing, nonetheless.

My sister, Wanhua, had spent those years cultivating her own stamina as well, though her trials were different.

Aside from Wanhua's two brief notes, announcing the death of our parents, I had not heard from my sister. I did not know where she and Honglin were living, indeed even if they were still alive. The Communist government was erratic in its policy regarding travel and communication. Sometimes, travel between Hong Kong and China was strictly forbidden; at other times, enormous numbers of Chinese from Guangdong would pour into Hong Kong. There was always the expectation, on some semiconscious level, that my doorbell would ring and I would again be united with some members of my family. But expectations dissolve into daydreams, and daydreams into silent hopes, and silent hopes into memories of those hopes.

As I sat having my tea and reading my paper early one Sunday morning, automatically scanning the want ads first, I was slightly annoyed when the doorbell rang, interrupting one of my rare moments of solitude in the quiet house.

The ringing intensified. I opened the door to find a solemn woman, who looked to be in her mid-thirties, wearing a faded blue cotton *qipao* and cloth shoes. Her hair was cut bluntly and short, and she was holding a black umbrella. She held out a large, stuffed envelope. I recognized Wanhua's handwriting on the front of the envelope immediately.

She spoke quickly, and I could tell she was nervous. "Hello, Mrs Ching. My name is Wang Fei — I am a friend of your sister, Wanhua. She asked me to deliver this in person; they are letters to you — she says she is sorry she has not written. It is dangerous … all correspondence is read by the authorities now."

I quickly recovered from my shock and invited her in for a cup of tea, but she declined and said that she had other people to see and turned to leave.

"Please … wait … how are they, Miss Wang? My sister, and her husband — they are okay?"

"Don't worry too much, Mrs Ching. They are as fine as any of us, I suppose. I'm sure she says everything in her letters. I'll leave you with her words." She left quickly, in that cloud of sadness that I had felt on my last trip to Shanghai.

Wanhua's letters were clearly dated and organized, journalizing her life in China since I had last seen her. I made a pot of tea and settled in to hold these pieces of paper, which had so recently been held by my sister. I remember that I smelled the letters first, hoping to get a whiff of that familiar scent of home. I wanted to experience this tangible piece of my home in every possible way. The comfort of a familiar script, something as unique as a person's fingerprint, can be so soothing. I soaked in my sister's signature, running my fingers across it, as though I were seeing a piece of Wanhua. I think I procrastinated beginning actually reading the letters for several minutes — knowing the sooner I started, the sooner it would end. Finally, I could wait no more. And I read of my sister's life in China.

My Dear Zhaohua,

As you know, before liberation by the Communists, Honglin and I lived a relatively quiet life with Mother and Little Tiger in a small house in front of the former French Park. It seems so long ago, when you visited, before Mother's death. Honglin working for the Jincheng (Golden City) Bank, and I was working for the Nationalist government in the Import/Export Committee office. After you were here, we hired a maid to take care of Mother, Little Tiger and the household work.

But as Shanghai became surrounded by the People's Liberation Army, and the Nationalists were preparing to flee to Taiwan, everything changed. The streets grew eerie in their quiet, with sporadic rifle shots and explosions breaking the silence. There was a time when I wasn't certain which was worse — the silence or the explosions. The silence, after all, was only a time in which to wait for a shot or explosion. At least in the deafening noise, I could cover my ears and know that I had survived the last one.

On May 25, 1949, the eve of the collapse of the Nationalist army, the city was a ghost town. Everything was closed — stores, schools, banks. The streets were completely empty. I went to bed early, and left Mother and Honglin playing Chinese chess in the sitting-room. I was awakened, around midnight, by the maid rushing in and saying that the People's Liberation Army was stationed at all the cross streets. She said there was a group at the gate of the French Park. They were all barefoot and in straw sandals, and were sleeping and eating on the sidewalks. They refused to accept food or housing from the people.

The last of the wealthy and elite had left Shanghai that day and we felt that, indeed, the 'people' were at long last in control of China. Ours has been a country governed by the corrupt and the rich for so very long, Zhaohua. I know that you can understand our hopes for China at last. To finally be governed by the people. It was the arrival of a long-awaited dream. We were all prepared to make sacrifices for our new government.

In Shanghai, the celebration of the Communist takeover took place at the former race course. Mayor Chen Yi, who had been the head of the New Fourth Route Army during the Japanese occupation, delivered an emotional speech to millions of people who crowded around, both inside and outside the racecourse. The enthusiasm was tremendous, Zhaohua, and the passion of patriotism stirred in all of us. Shouts and cheers deafened our ears.

The Communists were well organized and did not waste time launching their movements. There was the Thought Reform Movement, the Three Anti, and Five Anti Movements and the Land Reform Movement. Any relic of the past — pictures, letters, even furniture — was destroyed in the hope of annihilating anything that represented the oppression of the people. All land became owned by the government.

They reformed the private banking system by sending their cadres to run the banks with supreme power to hire and fire people who had been employed for years. The old management had no choice but to carry out the orders of the new management, and concede their positions to it.

The Jincheng Bank where Honglin worked was one of the banks to be thus nationalized. In the name of patriotism, the government launched a campaign encouraging the bank's employees to go voluntarily to China's most backward Northwestern provinces — Gansu, Shaanxi, Qinghai, Ningxia, and Xinjiang — where experienced workers were needed to start an efficient banking system. The plan was to educate and use all of China's resources, in the hope that China might some day become a world economic power.

In the patriotic spirit of serving the people and country, most of the bank's employees, including Honglin, responded to the campaign. Those who signed up — and their families — were honored as heroes. They were praised for giving up the comfort of their city homes and leaving their loved ones, and going to these barren mountainous areas, taking only some limited clothing, and the barest of necessities. In the Jincheng Bank alone, there were about 8,000 employees and family members — four out of five chose to relocate.

As it turned out, I could not go with Honglin because there was no one to replace me in my own job.

My husband was born and raised in the city, you know, so this was a drastic change for him. It was difficult, Zhaohua. I must end here … . I will resume when there is time …

Love, Wanhua

———————

Dear Zhaohua,

As there has been no opportunity to send my previous letter, I will simply pick up where I left off …

To Honglin, the move to the countryside was a tremendous challenge. He was assigned to work in Lanzhou, the capital of Gansu. His colleagues went to various other places, primarily small towns, in the five provinces. The Communists endeavored to separate those who had worked together under Nationalist rule, especially those who had not formally joined their party before the takeover.

But wait, I did not speak of the trip. Honglin left in October 1952 by chartered train to Xian. Although the scenery along the railway was spectacular, yet to Honglin, the trip was most difficult. He traveled across the renowned Loess Plateau of Northwest China, and he was occasionally engrossed in the bleak expanse of yellow earth and bare brown hills. It was so very different from Shanghai. From Baoji to Tianhui, he traveled through the mountains — there were hundreds of tunnels. In some places, the train could go only five or ten miles an hour because of the danger of sudden landslides. The tracks were built on the sides of steep mountains, and there was a cliff on one side and ravines with brooks on the other side. The journey took many days and food could only be purchased when the train stopped at a station; peasants would come up to sell various items. No one even cared whether or not the food was clean; they were so weakened with hunger and exhaustion. Did I mention that the trains were packed and they had to stand in the cars?

Finally, the train arrived in Lanzhou, a city surrounded by mountains. Honglin was assigned to work in the People's Bank there. We thought we had experienced poverty in Shanghai, Zhaohua, during the occupation and then the war between the Nationalists and Communists. But in Lanzhou, the people lived in huts made of mud, with dirt ceilings and floors. When it rained, the huts would leak. Honglin was assigned a room with no furniture — there were four wooden benches and some boards. At night, he propped the boards on the benches to create a bed off the ground.

There was no running water. Everyone drank directly from the Yellow River, with the water being full of sand. Before drinking, he had to separate the sand from the water with a sieve. Most families bought water from vendors who sold untreated water from barrels mounted on carts. One of the first major purchases for each worker was a large crock or jar in which to store water. His meals were generally comprised of steamed bread made of bran, corn and millet, with tiny shreds of pork and vegetables.

Life in Lanzhou felt primitive to my husband, Zhaohua. He heard stories of those living further in the countryside. In many of the villages, the girls did not wear clothes, accustomed to walking around completely or partially naked. With the arrival of reform, the girls began to hide in barrels, ashamed of their nakedness.

Because of low wages of the local employees, all the people coming from Shanghai had to accept a 60 per cent salary cut, starting from the tenth month after their arrival.

Some of Honglin's colleagues could not take the drastic changes and the isolation, and requested to be reassigned back to Shanghai. All petitions were refused.

Some became ill and died, having never returned to their homes or families. Others tried to simply leave, on their own. They were arrested. And they disappeared.

So Honglin stayed.

I will write again soon.

Love, Wanhua

It is most interesting to reconcile the words of my sister and the life of my dear brother-in-law with the austere reports of history, which I would come across many years later. '... Lanzhou, the capital of Gansu, was governed by the Muslim Ma family — warlords — who also controlled eastern Qinghai and Ningxia. For generations, the Muslims had lived peacefully with the Chinese. In 1949, the Ma warlords surrendered Lanzhou to the Communists after six weeks of bitter fighting. As a result of the 1953 decision of the Communist Party's Central Committee to develop Lanzhou into a major industrial center of Northwest China, a population explosion erupted in this area, further straining the region's resources.'

Again, Wanhua's letters found no opportunity to be safely delivered, and her next entry was another continuation.

———— · ————

Dear Zhaohua,

In June, 1953, I was allowed to join Honglin in Lanzhou and was assigned to work in the same bank. I accepted a demotion to the position of a bookkeeper, as there was no other position for me.

I will not dwell on our time there except to say that we were glad to hear that we were being transferred. We were sent to Xian together, to teach English in a medical college. As we were both English majors, it was thought that we could serve our country best in this way. We were overjoyed with the thought of leaving Lanzhou and moving to an historical city.

Upon our arrival in Xian, we were assigned a small room in the dormitory of the medical college. The dormitory is actually an old house, which we share with several colleagues, each family living in one room. We all cook in the hallway.

It is difficult, but better than our life in Lanzhou.

Do not worry about us, Zhaohua. We are adjusting and I think we will find happiness here. In fact, I wish to close with good news: I am expecting a child, Zhaohua! Yes, it is true.

I will write again, whenever possible.

Love, Wanhua

P.S. I enclose some materials on Xian, which you may find interesting.

In the distant past Xian had been the capital of the Chinese empire for about one thousand years. During the reign of Qin Shihuangdi,

China's First Emperor, an administrative system which was the model for all successive dynasties was introduced. As a tyrant, the First Emperor did both good and evil. He started the building of the Great Wall to keep out the barbarians. He also ordered the burning of Confucian books and classics, and buried hundreds of scholars alive.

Later, when Xian was the capital of the Tang dynasty, it was known as Changan, 'Everlasting Peace.' During that period, it was called the Golden Age of China. It opened its doors to many cultural and economic influences of Persia, Arabia, Turkey and India. This was due to the founding of the Silk Road, a route along which both goods and culture were exchanged.

———————

That was it — the end of my sister's letters which I had both craved and dreaded. I had expected to get answers in Wanhua's letters, but, instead, there were only more questions. Questions about my family and about my China. I looked around my tiny home in Hong Kong and suddenly I liked it much better. It was placed on a steep hill; it was small; it was war-scarred. But I had chosen it. Choices were limited, but they were mine. Choice is a good thing.

And I got dressed that morning and went for a walk by the harbor.

29

My husband died in January of 1959. He was seventy years old. I was forty-three, I tried to let my eyes cry, but my body just went numb. Numb with grief — for this man whose life had become so intertwined with mine — and numb with grief for what had not been.

Margaret had moved in with us by the time her father died. It was my way of reimbursing her for the money I had lost, and her way of showing respect to her father. Margaret had cared much for him in those last months; she remembered her father when he was in his prime, I suppose. My children were born to an aging man, and they saw him, I am sad to say, in his worst years.

I think that my son Frank, who wrote the following words years after his father's death, summed up my husband very well … .

The following account appeared in a Hong Kong magazine in 1960:

"Two years ago one often saw an old man on the streets of Hong Kong and Kowloon. He was of a withered appearance, thin and emaciated. He wore a Chinese robe and a felt hat, and carried a rattan basket. He walked by himself, looking lonely and desolate. This was the famous Shanghai lawyer Liankui Ching."

It was an accurate portrayal of the man I knew as Father, a man who was eccentric, unhappy, sick, querulous and, toward the end, paranoid. This was almost the only side of him I knew; certainly the side I remember most vividly …

When I first discovered that Father was dead, my immediate feeling was one of relief. I felt that he had made life difficult for all of us, Mother as well as the children. When I returned home with the death certificate, I saw Margaret at a distance, her face contorted. I thought she, too, was showing relief at his death. But as I got closer, I realized that she was torn by grief. It came as a surprise to me that Margaret could have loved Father so much, when I thought of him only as a self-centered old man who was nothing but trouble. But then, of course, Margaret had known him when he was at the height of his career, and all I saw was his shell.

Looking back on those events, I see Father in a very different light. He was, I think, a man of many contradictions; a man who was loyal to his friends, yet neglected his closest family members; a man who cared deeply about principles, yet was practical enough to stay out of political entanglements; a romantic willing to defy convention, yet cruel to the women in his life. He was a brilliant lawyer who had achieved great success in his career in a turbulent period of Chinese history. But flaws in his personality, evidenced by his addiction to speculation and gambling, caused him to be controlled by events rather than to be master of his own destiny. In the final analysis, he was a tragic figure.

Yes, Frank, he was a tragic figure. Yet Liankui Ching, in all of his tragedy, contributed — in his way — to the lives that each of you — Judie, Anthony, Priscilla, and yourself — have made today. Indeed to my life, as well. I think it is best to focus on today.

If I am to be honest, Liankui's death, though leaving a deep sadness in me, also released me. I was no longer bound to Hong Kong.

Judie, despite my pleadings, had joined a convent in New Rochelle, and I did not hear from her. Anthony, who had overcome his asthma in France, was completing his studies there, while waiting for a visa to America. Alice had assisted Priscilla in securing a scholarship to study in the United States. Then Priscilla was a charming, intelligent, understanding young woman. Her heart was as good as gold, but a little too soft. I remember when she was working as a substitute teacher, she lost all the cash just received from the school one day. She did not want to report the loss to her superior because she thought that the thief might need the money more badly than she did.

On the day of Priscilla's departure, I gave a tea party inviting some of her friends: Taty Kuo, my friend Daisy Shen's cousin, and Ruby Gafoor, a charming pianist, Priscilla's best friend.

Frank was eighteen and studying at St Joseph's College on Kennedy Road in Hong Hong; he was also waiting to secure a university scholarship in the United States.

My life, at the age of forty-three, was once again my own. To a certain degree, anyway, that a mother's life can ever be reclaimed as her own.

Most applications for temporary visas to the United States were being declined. There was so much international confusion at that time as hordes of wealthy Chinese refugees crowded into Hong Kong, hoping to immigrate to the United States. I read an advertisement in the *South China*

Morning Post, a well-established English-language newspaper, about an office position available with the North Borneo government. I sent in an application, as I had done with countless other positions, and heard back in three days; they offered me a three-year contract working as a personal assistant for the government. The job sounded wonderful — paid vacation, a regular salary, transportation provided between Hong Kong and North Borneo, annual vacation and even a small living allowance.

I had never been free to make such a move. Until now.

As it happened, my landlord was preparing to tear down the house and build a modern apartment building on the site, so he was willing to pay relocation expenses for all the tenants. This windfall enabled me to repay all the money I still owed Margaret, who could then get an apartment of her own. Also, she promised to watch over Frank while he was in Hong Kong. So I accepted the offer right away to work for the North Borneo government.

I must admit that I did not feel particularly sad to leave Hong Kong. Aside from my memories of Sandy, which were always tinged with sadness, my years in Hong Kong had been years of endurance.

My last order of business before I left Hong Kong was arrangements with a bank there to receive a portion of my pay, and to forward that money to my brother every month in Shanghai. He had written that he was in extremely poor health, yet unable, financially, to retire from his job working on a farm. In his letter, he thanked me for a gold bracelet, which I had sent him through a friend in the past year.

As I concluded the business with the bank and walked out the doors, I thought of my brother as he had been at the train station in Beijing. I wondered what our relationship might have been without the traditions of China to separate us. And then my mind played for me a lovely glimpse of Kaihua and me, together, studying the teachings of Confucius. I could see Old Tutor and his patience in teaching us words of honor and of familial responsibility. I knew that he had been right. There is peace and happiness in caring for family.

I smiled as I remembered my childhood life. And I smiled as I looked forward to my new one.

North Borneo turned out to be a strange place. Some said that it had an intolerable tropical climate; others considered it a primitive but beautiful country. In 1959, North Borneo was a British Colony, which shared the world's third largest island with Brunei, a tiny but rich and independent country, and Indonesia. In 1963, after North Borneo merged with Malaya, becoming a part of Malaysia, it was renamed Sabah. My five years on the tip of that island saw the emergence of independence. Independence of a country. And independence of a woman.

I had passed that point in my life of attempting to define my expectations. I boarded the ship with the awareness that I had no idea what my life in North Borneo would hold. I was not intimidated by this awareness.

After two days on board the ship, I arrived in North Borneo and immediately embraced the richness of the tropical country, which was to become my home. North Borneo was lush, green, thick and moist. And so close to the sun. I could sense that it would be a lovely tropical cocoon, into which I could fold and begin the process of redefining my life, where I was to find peace, rest and solitude. Solitude can be soul nourishing for anyone, especially for a woman who had spent nearly thirty years raising children, running from wars and caring for an ill husband. Solitude had the feel of a delicious, indulgent extravagance. I savored my delicacy with a conscious passion.

At Jesselton, the capital of North Borneo, where I was warmly greeted by two government representatives — Thomas Jayasuriya, a tall, good-looking lawyer, and Dolly Xavier, a charming young woman from Hong Kong. Then they drove me to the Jesselton Hotel — the only Western hotel, where I would stay for a few days.

Jesselton Hotel was owned by a Chinese bank in Hong Kong and managed by a scholarly Chinese man named Lin. We quickly bonded in our heritage and the discovery that we had mutual friends. Mr Lin treated me as an old friend, giving me advice on the differences I would encounter in my new environment.

"Borneo is not Hong Kong, Zhaohua. The smallest gossip here becomes the headline of the day; it is best to put it in perspective — don't let yourself get caught up in it. Just enjoy it!" I can still see Mr Lin, as the locals would come in, excited, with their news of the day. He would remark with wonder at their news, ask questions of interest, and smile as they left. When I left Jesselton, after only four short days in the small town, I counted Mr Lin as my first new friend.

My position was in Tawau and I flew on a small British plane on which most passengers were government workers. Situated on the Kalimantan border, which divided the Indonesian area from British Borneo, Tawau was a rich province in North Borneo, while the Indonesian part of Borneo was underdeveloped and primitive. Many Indonesians crossed the border illegally in the hope of finding work on Tawau's numerous tobacco, cocoa, and rubber plantations. Of course the large plantations were owned by the British, who employed many local workmen, but filled all management positions with men from England. Compared to Hong Kong, Jesselton was a small town, and Tawau resembled a sleepy fishing village in China. There were a few shops — grocery stores, tea houses, one hotel and one cinema house — along the water, and owned mostly by Chinese. It was the antithesis of my Old Shanghai. Though it was small and isolated, the people were down-to-earth and friendly, and I felt comfortable almost immediately.

After a brief stay in a government guest house I was given a lovely and simply furnished wooden house. It was a bungalow, really, in a compound where the government officers lived. I commuted to work by bicycle, and my first position was that of personal assistant to Mr James Blow, the Resident of Tawau (head of the province). Mr Blow was soft spoken and prone to mumbling. I heard a rumor that he was planning to retire in Australia and buy a farm. After just a couple of weeks, I was tempted to ask exactly when the mumbling Mr Blow was planning to retire.

In my tranquil evenings, I would read for hours — books I had wanted to read for years. I wrote letters to my children, and of course, to Alice, and to other family members, getting regular replies from all but Judie. And I even resumed writing some poetry. I hadn't written poetry since I was a young girl at McTyeire — before Liankui — and I found again that special delight in practicing the art of words.

One evening I was sleeping and suddenly waking up with tears all over my face, thinking about the ineffaceable past. Also, I was inspired by the quiet surroundings of North Borneo:

To Think and To Forget

Vast is the land, green grass grows,
Virgin is the earth, the sunshine glows.
Bury sorrow, sow the seeds of joy.
Place to think; place to forget.

Friendliness and kindness here in plentitude.
Enjoying Nature, while in solitude.
Love given hy Him, that ever lasts.
Try to think, try to forget.

Coolness and tranquility are the night.
Shadow and reflection are my light.
In darkness, the good earth rests.
Time to think, time to forget.

Is this truly "The Land of Happiness?"
No rush, no worry, no sadness.
People are cheerful here, soft and content.
Learn to think; learn to forget.

Wake up in the dead of the night.
Filled with dreams and images of fright.
Finding tears flowing and the pillow wet.
How to think; how to forget.

Cock crows on the arrival of the dawn.
On the way, soon comes the morn.
Twittering and whispering are the birds.
What to think; what to forget.

To the earth, another day is coming.
Beyond the horizon, another world is being.
The spirit is willing, the flesh weakening.
Easy to think; difficult to forget.

I spent my weekends bicycling around the town, exploring and making friends with shopkeepers and local residents. It was on just such a bicycle outing I met Mrs Zhang — actually, she introduced herself to me.

"Hello, Ms Ching? Yes, it's a small town — everybody knows everybody here. I knew you had come from Hong Kong by the lovely *qipao* you wear. My name is Mrs Zhang, and I've been looking forward to making your acquaintance."

"Thank you, Mrs Zhang, it's a pleasure to meet you." I was aware that my words were genuine; I could feel instinctively that it was a pleasure to know this uniquely direct, but kind, woman.

"How do you like our little green oasis, Ms Ching? A little different from Hong Kong?"

"Indeed, and from Shanghai, where I was born. But different places have their own charm, don't they? I find it quite lovely."

"Yes, Ms Ching. There is a time for change. New places. And speaking of new, how would you like some new friends? I'm having a dinner party tomorrow evening — it's my husband's birthday, actually, he's the only doctor here, you know, and, well, I can tell right away that I should like to know you better, and you would most certainly enjoy the other guests — we're a friendly group. I know it's a short notice, but we'd love to have you join us."

"I'd love to come, Mrs Zhang. Thank you for including me."

"Our house is right on the corner; we live above my husband's office which is also the pharmacy. Seven? We're a casual group, Ms Ching."

"Please call me Zhaohua. And I shall see you at seven."

Mrs Zhang quickly resumed her errands, as though her actions — in a matter of minutes she had introduced herself to a stranger and invited me to an intimate dinner party — were routine and common in North Borneo.

Dr Zhang, as it turned out, was the youngest brother of the Iron General, Zhang Fakui, whom I had met at a party in the Autumn Garden in Shanghai so many years before — the same party where I had met my Colonel. I smiled as I relayed the acquaintance with Dr Zhang's brother, and thought of my Colonel, who had become a lovely memory.

I felt instantly at ease, and interested, in the other guests at the dinner party. Mr and Mrs William Thien were a most fascinating couple. Mr Thien was a man of diverse interests and having made no small fortune in his business ventures — cinemas, a travel agency, a hotel and cocoa plantations. He spoke fluent English and was active in local political affairs. His wife, Margaret, was most charming and spoke several languages. They lived on an estate about five miles from 'town' and invited me for a visit.

That was also when I met Mr and Mrs Noether, who lived in Taiwan, but had an Import/Export office in Jesselton. Mr Noether was German, and his wife was Chinese — she had, like myself, attended McTyeire in Shanghai. They were gracious people, and I could feel, intuitively, that they were to be part of my circle.

"A toast!" Dr Zhang raised his glass. "To our small world, which has seen fit to bring together this lovely collection of people, whose lives have so closely brushed in the past!"

"Hear, hear!"

"I think the world shall grow smaller, with time," William spoke thoughtfully. "The families of China have been uprooted and shall meet, I believe, in all corners of the world in the future. Even the residents here, the Hakka people, on this island, are descendants of China, you know. They are descendants of the soldiers of the Taiping Rebellion, which almost toppled the Qing dynasty. Chinese migrant workers, originally northern Chinese."

"Yes, I have always admired them," I spoke comfortably, drawn into the intimate conversation. "They were revolutionary and enterprising. We are not the first to be displaced by the wars of China — their ancestors moved from one place to another — in fact, their very name, Hakka, means guest people."

"You're quite knowledgeable in this subject, Zhaohua. How do you know of these people?"

"Oh, I've only read of them — now I have the opportunity to meet them!" We all laughed with ease. "After the failure of the Taiping Rebellion, the surviving rebels arrived here from China by fishing boats, floating at the whim of the winds. They were lucky, you know they didn't have to worry about passports or visas!" Again, we laughed.

As I engaged in the conversation and joined in the laughter at the dinner table, I had an image of Liankui, instructing me to smile, but not speak. I smiled. And I spoke.

"Were you here during the Japanese occupation?" I asked William and Margaret out of curiosity.

"Oh, yes." It was William who responded, his voice solemn. "It was … it was barbaric. My father, who worked for the British Colonial Government, was brutally murdered by the Japanese. I joined an anti-Japanese league. I'm lucky to be alive. The Japanese were brutal. Some sixteen per cent of the West Coast population was killed — murdered — many nearby islands were almost completely depopulated. It was genocide. They did spare some of the young Chinese girls, though. Of course, they needed prostitutes for their soldiers." We all knew that William Thien had seen so much more than he could say. And I knew that what he had seen resonated in him like cymbals at a concert, and that he, like so many Chinese, would not be able to forgive the Japanese for their atrocities.

We all sat for a while, silent, each allowing — for just a moment — our own ugly memories to surface in the safe presence of friends.

I spoke first, "May the heroic struggle, by these people — and others — against the brutality of the Japanese always be remembered," I raised my glass slowly.

Dr Zhang, the consummate host, joined the toast, "To the Allies! Toast! And to North Borneo! Bottoms up!" As we cheered and toasted and gladly tucked away our memories, the homemade birthday cake was served. All the guests joined in singing, "Happy Birthday, Dr Zhang."

Those beautiful friends helped to ease the loneliness, which inevitably crept into my days. It was a beautiful, tropical country. But I was born in Shanghai, in Old Shanghai, at a time when it was the most vital city in the world, and there were times when I found myself craving the energy of a city. I would lie awake in the quiet nights, and feel quite alone on this tropical island.

I had been unable to sleep that night. My bungalow was isolated and though it was not a cool evening, I had a chill in my spine. I fell asleep somewhere near dawn.

I awoke soon after to a strange noise. I could feel it. Danger. My eyes were instinctively drawn to the window on the opposite wall — there were eyes peering in at me. The man raised his face and his hand as though he were going to climb in through the window. I saw him clearly. My skin crawled. Frightened, I ran onto the balcony and screamed loudly for help. Immediately, a number of British officers came to my rescue. They found a long bamboo pole, which had been used as a ladder to climb to my window, and promptly removed it. The man disappeared and was never caught, but the fear remained.

There were many sleepless nights, and I could sense that he was close by. Eventually, I applied for a transfer back to Jesselton.

When I was transferred to Jesselton to work in the secretariat for British officers, it was only with a bit of sadness that I said goodbye to my new friends in Tawau, with whom I had often dined after that first special evening. Our friendships would continue. I had learned, most completely, that new places could be a very wonderful thing.

Jesselton, now known as Kota Kinabalu, had its own gifts of solitude and friendship. I was given a bungalow in Tanjong Aru — a small home, common to this isolated area. And it was such a humble place to live, so seemingly unaware that this was a private, tropical paradise by the ocean. The beaches were wide, and the sand was fine and light golden in color. There was always an ocean breeze — the wind seemed drawn to the tall, feathery casaurinas, which lined the beaches, giving that magical, tropical element. I spent many evenings walking the beaches, feeling that breeze, and watching it play with the layers of green. Sometimes, after it rained, a spectacular rainbow appeared. I marveled at the joys to be found in nature, and could not imagine having spent my entire life in Shanghai and missing such wonderful knowledge.

From Jesselton, I took the gift of my friendship with Joan Eager, a young English woman, who, like myself, had come from Hong Kong to work for the British government. Joan and I spent many evenings dining late on the porch of my bungalow, which she found charming in its simplicity, and we would swap stories of our lives, so very, very different — and yet so similar and familiar — in those ways in which women have always been alike. She would bring me cakes and fruits in the evenings while I crammed for examinations in the courses I continued there. It was in Jesselton that I earned my professional degree as Corporation Secretary from the Corporation of Secretaries in London, through the Education Department in North Borneo.

Again, I was to experience the richness to be found in the friendships between women. Joan and I would spend our weekends swimming or riding scooters around the city. We often attended tea and dance parties and dinners together. And we talked. About the past. About the future. Joan and I laughed so easily together.

We even took a short trip back to Hong Kong together. We shopped and dined, and explored the New Territories.

There were also others in Jesselton who contributed to those lovely days in my life. I think the warmth and relaxed atmosphere, which is unavoidable in the islands, enters the spirit. The English officers for whom I worked, and their families, seemed to take me in warmly as an equal. Though I was in a remote, tropical colony, my appetite for the international was met in their company. Trevor Jones, one of my first bosses in Jesselton, though quite young, had worked in a British colony in Africa before his arrival in North Borneo. His wife, Monica, who was most elegant, held a master's degree in English, and also spoke fluent French. I was often invited to their home and enjoyed family dinners with them and their young son, Hugh. Our friendship continued even after I was transferred to work with Mr John Macartney, who had earned his master's in political science at Cambridge University. The Macartneys also welcomed me into their lives, and it was through the Macartneys that I became acquainted with Mr Peng, and Mr Salleh, and their lovely families.

I was always invited to their lovely dinner and cocktail parties — I remember the first dinner at the Sallehs' home. It was an enchanting evening, I do love new experiences, and though I had been in North Borneo for years, it was my first time in the home of a native Malay. Mrs Salleh was an immensely rich and tropical woman, quiet in her elegance, always draped in a beautiful sarong. The balcony of their home seemed alive with her beautiful orchids and tropical flowers which were hanging in baskets and swinging in the breeze, as if in time with the wind chimes which played softly in the background. They were such gracious hosts, serving a large pot of curried chicken cooked with coconut milk, along with brown rice. There was a table full of nuts, dried fruits, and fresh fruits and vegetables. As usual, Mr Macartney was the life of the party as he fell into one of his humorous stories. They always started so casually, and before we knew it, we were all absorbed in one of his tales. On this particular evening, he was lighting one of his favorite cigars.

"There's a story about this brand of cigars, you know. Pay attention through the evening — the ashes last a very long time. One day, an Englishman was sitting in a first-class cabin on a train, smoking one of these cigars. An 'oh-so-sophisticated' woman boarded the train and was seated next to him. After the train had been moving for about twenty minutes, the woman suddenly jumped up and pulled the emergency cord. As the conductor rushed to the cabin, she — very loudly and most indignantly — began accusing the gentleman of making unwanted physical advances toward her.

"Now, being a man of excellent tastes and refinement, the gentleman did not for a moment lose his composure. When the woman calmed down and the conductor turned to him for an explanation, he simply pointed to his cigar. 'Do you see this cigar, conductor? Look at these ashes — it must be obvious that I have been sitting here smoking this cigar for quite some time; and even I could not assault this lovely woman without disturbing these ashes. I ask you, would it be possible? ...'"

We laughed as Mr Macartney switched from role to role in his story — the composed gentleman, the hysterical lady, and then the conductor.

I remember, it was soon after that dinner party that Joan remarked, with great insight, that we were witnessing — indeed we were part of — an historical evolution happening before our eyes.

In 1963 the Federation of Malaysia was suggested by the Prime Minister of Malaya. They were reluctant to accept Singapore, but did so at British insistence. The United Nations sent a delegation to Jesselton to poll the people about their wishes for the political destiny of their country. In fact, most native people were politically naive.

In September of 1963, North Borneo peacefully evolved from a British colony into part of an independent country, and was renamed Sabah. It was a part of the Federation of Malaysia, which consisted of Malaya, Sarawak, Sabah and Singapore.

Of course, the British government would stay for a certain period while helping to ease the transition, but our positions would finally be eliminated as this country defined herself. As Sabah wrote her definition, my friend Mr Peng, a Chinese businessman who was well educated in many areas, became the Minister of Education.

Mr Salleh, my jolly friend, went on to become Minister of Local Government and, after a few years, I learned that he was appointed Prime Minister of Sabah. As I read of his appointment, I recalled the lovely evenings spent in the home of Mr and Mrs Salleh. Those memories of Jesselton, North Borneo, are laced with warmth and layers of green, and the friendships were to be lifelong.

I felt the inherent rightness in the independence of that tiny country of which few in the world have even heard.

My five-year stay in North Borneo had given me peace, happiness and a broadened experience of working and living. I had witnessed the history of Malaysia in the making. I had discovered that a simple life was a delight in itself, with no need for fancy clothes and no worries about money. I had also made some true friends rare in our complex society. I said goodbye to all of them — Chinese, Malay, and English. Though I felt a deep sadness at leaving my friends, I, too, had reached a new state of independence. And I, now so nourished and defined, resolved to resume my own 'way.'

30

I left Sabah, now part of an independent Malaysia, and returned to Hong Kong, the closest place to home for myself and for so many Chinese. The city had been beautifully and aggressively rebuilt following the war and was readying itself to compete with Paris and New York. It was as though the energy of Shanghai, like so many of her people, had floated across the water and taken up residence in Hong Kong.

Without my children, Hong Kong felt alien to me. It bore no familiarity, nor comfort, nor association as home. Frank had gone to the United States soon after I had left for North Borneo, so now they were all there, with the exception of Judie. I did not quite know where she was. I had not heard from her.

I found a job with the Chinese Manufacturers Association, and a lovely apartment in a ladies' hostel on Robinson Road. I resolved to locate Judie, and to make plans to see my other children.

I wrote to the American Consulate for a visitor's visa to go to New York. The Consulate kept denying my request, stating that since my children now lived there, they did not believe I would return to Hong Kong where I no longer had any roots. They advised me to apply for an immigrant visa, but the waiting list for an immigrant visa was incredibly long because, by law, only 105 Chinese could be admitted each year.

I also wrote to Judie at the most recent address I had. It was Paris. Finally, I received a letter from her — it was Taiwan.

I did not immediately recognize the name over the return address: it was Sister Agnes Therese. But as soon as I saw the handwriting, I knew. My hands trembled and I sat down in my apartment, so thankful to be alone when I received her note. I closed my eyes for several moments and regained my composure before I read those lovely words, written by the beautiful and talented hands of my first child.

It was a simple note, but it brought my daughter back into my life. Judie said that she had been studying at the Ursuline House of Sisters in

Washington, DC, and her religious name was now Sister Agnes Therese. She was working, within her Order, toward a master's degree in English, and the Order had sent her to teach English at the Stella Maris Middle School for girls in Hualien, Taiwan. She said that perhaps I could visit her in Taiwan.

I had not seen my daughter in almost ten years. And a couple of tears made tiny ink puddles on the note.

But even though I knew that Judie was in Taiwan, I realized that it would not be easy for me to visit her. When Chiang Kai-shek retreated to Taiwan in 1949, his government closed off the island with an iron gate — fearful of Communist infiltration. It was very difficult for any Chinese to be granted a visa. But the friendships I had made in North Borneo helped me overcome this latest obstacle in my life.

I wrote to Mr and Mrs Noether, my friends from Jesselton, who owned an import and export business in Taiwan. I asked them to sponsor me for a Taiwan visa. The Noethers were wealthy and influential and helped me push through the paper work easily.

In April of 1964, I received my precious visa. I wrote to Judie immediately that I would be coming, and then to the Noethers with words of thanks. I also wrote to some first cousins who had fled to Taipei from the China mainland with the Nationalist government.

My two cousins, Helen Liu and her half-brother, Dr Chonghua Ching, who were children of my father's older brother, and whom I had not seen in many years, met me at the airport. They drove me to Helen's home and made me feel as comfortable and welcome as if we had never lost touch. Helen was elegant as ever, and I could see that she had fulfilled her role as a diplomat's wife most skillfully — her late husband was the consul in Saigon and the last consul general in Hanoi. We had a lovely lunch with Chonghua and his lovely wife; they made it feel like a grand reunion.

The Noethers invited me to dinner on the evening of my arrival and took me to dinner at the magnificent Grand Hotel, built beautifully into the side of a lush mountain with a breathtaking view of a deep rich valley. The restaurant was owned by Madame Soong May-ling, President Chiang's wife, and it most effectively relayed the exquisite taste of Madame Soong.

I was delighted to see my old friends, but I felt myself growing anxious over my meeting with Judie the following morning. We had corresponded regularly over the past few years, but her letters did not feel like letters from my daughter. She had embraced her role of sacrifice and a new life completely. It seemed to mean rejecting her earthly families. I had accepted her decision. But I missed my daughter.

Though exhausted from my trip and the reunion with family and friends, I barely slept that night. I woke early and was dressed when Helen walked into the kitchen. She had also dressed carefully, saying she had decided to accompany me to see Judie in Hualien as she was also anxious to see Judie. But I looked in her eyes and I knew that this woman — this dear cousin who shared my blood — was anxious about my reunion with my daughter. She did not want me to travel alone. And I accepted her company gratefully.

Hualien was a small, sleepy town southeast of Taipei, but across a deep range of mountains. Transportation was generally by bus — eight hours. Or a small plane, which took only 45 minutes if there was good weather. Typhoons were a constant threat on this side of the island and delayed flights, due to winds and rains, were a common occurrence. I had reserved a flight and written Judie of my planned arrival.

After a turbulent trip in a small plane, we approached Hualien. The semi-tropical mountains were breathtakingly majestic. We landed on an unpaved airfield and I looked around anxiously for Judie. We were approached by a young Chinese woman.

"Mrs Ching? Hello, I am Therese Jiao, a friend of your daughter's. I'm here to welcome you on her behalf. She is waiting for you at the gate of the school. Come, I have a car over here."

Helen held my hand as I swallowed my disappointment. I shrugged as we walked to the car and said that I had waited ten years for this day, another few minutes was nothing.

I noticed that the roads were rough and unpaved as we were driven through the terrain we had seen from the air. The varying layers of greenness were even more beautiful when seen from the ground. But it also became more remote and more isolated. I tried to soothe the uneasiness I felt at the thought of my daughter living in this thick and primitive region.

Upon arrival at the school, Helen and I were greeted most formally. The many teachers and the school's Chinese principal were gathered together for our arrival. And Judie was there, lined up with her 'Sisters.' She was wearing her white starched headpiece, her long robe and white cotton shoes.

Judie smiled and said hello with exactly the same impeccable manners as the other nuns. She did not approach me, or hold out her hands, and I could sense that I was not permitted to embrace my daughter. I tilted my face upward slightly, hoping my tears would not spill from my eyes. Helen looked on. I handed my daughter a few boxes of chocolates and a woolen jacket I had brought as gifts from Hong Kong. She thanked me politely.

The principal invited Helen and me to have lunch with the students — Judie was not allowed to have meals with outsiders, which included her own mother. Our lunch was meager and of poor quality. Helen and I ate quietly, taking in my daughter's chosen life. Stella Maris was a junior high school for about 200 girls, run by French nuns and tightly controlled and isolated from the outside world. The children played on the grounds, which were vibrant with poinsettia bushes and banana trees. But when I looked into the faces of the young girls, all I saw was Judie. And the Judie I saw, but could not even touch, did not resemble my child who had left me ten years ago as a determined young woman. She looked so thin and so pale — her skin had taken on a grayish tint. Her eyes bothered me most, I think. They were tired. I knew tired eyes well. I had seen the hollow exhaustion in my mother and in my own mirror. But to see them in my daughter was more than I could bear.

I could feel it. In my bones, I could feel that Judie was not well.

Before we left that evening, Helen and I were given a brief opportunity for an unsupervised walk with my daughter. I did not waste my few precious minutes with her.

"Are you happy here, Judie?" I looked intently into her eyes, trying to penetrate the emptiness I met.

Judie only nodded.

"Are there doctors? You are not well, Judie, I can feel it. When was the last time you saw a doctor? Answer me, Judie." I could not accept her silence.

"There is someone on staff with medical knowledge, but no doctors. There is aspirin if we have cold or fever. Don't worry, Mom. I am cared for."

"Health is not as simple as that, Judie. Something is wrong. I can feel it, Judie. You must see a doctor. You seem weak and your coloring ... if you have ... ," and I'm not sure where these words came from, at the time I thought them to be the words of a frustrated, desperate mother, "... if you have a lump on your body, Judie, or persistent pain, or ... oh, there are so many things, Judie, but if you are not well, you must report it to Mother Superior at once. Our bodies are a gift of God also; they require care and knowledge and to ignore things can mean life or death. I'm afraid for you, Judie. Please."

"I ... I might have an opportunity to go to Rome for tertianship,

Mother. Only four more years, here. It will be different. Don't worry, Mother." Judie handed me a farewell gift. An English book, *The Trapp Family of Singers*, about an Austrian family who had managed to escape the Nazis during the Second World War and now traveled the world performing together.

Then I left her there. My daughter Judie stood with that same group of women who were now her family, and waved goodbye to me from inside the school's iron gate. To me, the iron gate on that school looked like a prison.

Therese Jian, Helen and I were silent as we drove to the airfield. Before she left, Therese held my hands. "Mrs Ching, the Order … it is very strict. They demand absolute obedience to Mother Superior. And that each nun must sacrifice all for the sake of God. Like … like the Chinese Communists. Your daughter is … very loyal." Therese looked away from me. She just got into her car and left. We all knew there were no words.

As Helen and I climbed back into that tiny plane and fastened our safety belts for the bumpy ride back to Taipei, I shook with rage and emotion.

My mind questioned everything. How could the religion into which I had been baptized ask a vibrant, intelligent young woman to deny that she was human? To suppress her joy and her anger, her misery and her sorrow, and her love? These were natural feelings. How could it take my bright-eyed Judie and turn her into the shell I had spent the day with?

There was nothing I could do. Her obedience was to her Mother Superior, but Judie Ching was my daughter. And I prayed the prayers of a mother who has just glimpsed the slow death of her daughter.

Back in Hong Kong, I arrived at that universal realization of motherhood — the moment when we know that our children are no longer ours, when our hands are no longer able to help them to dry their tears or clean their scrapes. Something was wrong with Judie, I knew. More than her vacant look. I had raised my daughter to be a woman who made her own choices. And now both Judie and I must live with those choices.

When I left Hong Kong later that year, I left the East — the East in my bones and the East in my blood and the Eastern traditions that had so shaped my life — and stepped back into my dream, my passion, my own way. Of course, my way would never have been complete without the scars and joys of motherhood. And Liankui. And the wars. But, I knew, as I left Hong Kong, that those were rich elements which had contributed to my life, but they were not the sum, not the purpose. No, there was no immense sadness at leaving Hong Kong; there had been little left for me there.

Janet and James Woo had moved to Kowloon, but their children had gone to study in the United States. Margaret was in Hong Kong, but, of course, she was busy with her own family. Except for Judie, my other children were all in the United States, and though I was still unable to obtain a visa to even visit them, I was more determined than ever to get there myself.

During an interview at the US Consulate, I was told it could take years to be allowed to visit the United States. Immigration of Chinese was so tightly controlled. I decided to go to London instead. Immediately I applied for a Hong Kong British passport and a work permit, and got both without difficulty. With a passport, a work permit and my English business degree — Corporation Secretary — my immigration visa to England was granted.

When I arrived in London, this Western world city, I felt like I had found a lovely, comfortable old robe and slipped it on, and it fit just right.

London had that familiar energy of my Old Shanghai — that energy to be found only in international cities. But London was so Britishly Western. In this most delicious city I settled quickly, obtaining a job almost immediately on the basis of my previous government work experience. I secured a room in an international ladies' hostel, which served perfectly until I moved into a beautiful studio apartment near Belsize Park in North London, not far from Heath — of which I had read so much in the works of the British poets.

I had written a childhood friend, William Lee, of my arrival and, to my delight, he met me on my first day in London and took me under his wing during my stay. And a lovely wing it was! William was now the head in the London Office of an international shipping company; he and his charming wife, Joy, introduced me to some of the more obscure treasures to be found in London and included me in their busy and 'oh-so-London' social calendar from the first week on.

I reveled in the Western history. Of course, I had to take it all in — St Paul's Cathedral, Westminster Abbey and Buckingham Palace. I went to the British Museum and to Hampton Court, where King Henry VIII had lived with his many wives. I strolled Trafalgar Square where the statue of Lord Nelson stood atop a tall column, surrounded by a large gathering of tourists. Big Ben issued his warnings that time passed swiftly and would never return. When I visited the Tower of London, the old ghosts seemed to haunt me. I often smelled the aroma of scotch whenever I passed the pubs, which were full of people all the time. I was told that if the British stopped drinking, they would lose their sense of humor and inspiration. I looked up old friends, from both Hong Kong and North Borneo.

I settled into London life as though it were familiar. That happens, you know, when we pursue the path we are meant to take. Things fall into place, and our way is comfortable. In my studio apartment, without any family, in a new country, I felt completely at home, And I knew, intuitively, the time would come. I would see them — Frank, Priscilla, Anthony, and Alice. But my intuitions surrounding Judie were shrouded in dark shadows.

Judie's letters were sparse and dry; she suggested that I visit Paris while in London, which I did, making certain to see every site she recommended. Paris was so worldly and yet so soft. London was vital and majestic, but somewhat imposing compared to Paris. As for the people, the French were warm and friendly, the British reserved and helpful. I practiced my French and visited the historical sites. I stood in front of paintings and statues, and tried to imagine Judie, Anthony, Priscilla and Frank standing there in previous years.

I returned to London and decided my time in Europe would be a most wonderful place to tread water — lovely water. I toyed with the idea of settling permanently in London, but I knew that I could not feel settled until I had seen the lives of which my children had written — their completely Western lives. And I would be simply waiting, patiently and happily, but waiting nonetheless.

Unexpectedly, I received a notice from the American Embassy asking me to come for a physical examination, which I passed. President Johnson had changed the immigration law, substantially increasing the quota for Chinese.

On February 11, 1966, I left London by train for Southampton to catch the SS *Queen Mary* on her final voyage across the Atlantic.

The ship provided a luxurious class of travel, including exquisite sterling silver dinnerware, English china, and a live band. I had a beautiful cabin with a gorgeous bathroom. The voyage was a calm one and took about five days. Alone in my room, I wondered how my children had changed after living in the States. I pondered how I would adapt to the new environment. But I had already had the experience of living and working in London for a year, so it would probably not be too difficult. I had heard that America was the land of opportunity. Was it for everybody? Young and old? Male and female? Black and white? European and Asian? What kind of opportunities awaited me there?

On February 16, 1966, I stood with many other passengers on the deck of the huge steamer as it passed the Statue of Liberty, which looked so majestic, as the ship slowly entered New York harbor. My eyes filled with tears upon seeing the new world, and I said a small prayer of thanksgiving. For me it had been a long journey. I was fifty years old. And I felt like I had come home.